"This is one of the be: ⎪⎪⎪⎪⎪⎪⎪⎪⎪⎪⎪⎪⎪⎪⎪⎪⎪⎪⎪ ⏐.
Priests and laity alike w ⎪D0454467⎪ e
sacrament of penance, th

d

"In SHALOM: PEACE *The Sacrament of Reconciliation,* Father
Bernard Häring has written a pastoral, practical, provocative
yet understanding treatment of one of today's most critical
problems, the celebration of the Sacrament of Penance. The
book is a brief presentation of the theology of Penance and
then a discussion of contemporary considerations touching
the major areas of moral theology by a man who is at once
one of our foremost theologians and a deeply sensitive priest.
. . . Parish priests and people—be they old or new breed
clergy, backbone of the parish or marginal Catholic laity,
college students or their parents—will benefit immeasurably
from an honest, intelligent consideration of Father Häring's
suggestions concerning the sacrament which so intimately affects the basic concerns of the Christian, his relationships with
his fellow men and his relationship through Christ to his
Father."   *The Tablet*

"Here Catholic moral theology, set in the context of the life
and liturgy of the church, becomes understandable to the
non-Catholic. . . . By its honesty, its sharp probing of basic
issues and its humanity, Häring's book should help us all turn
to what he believes to be the goal of the sacrament of penance: the unity of the whole people of God."

Christian Century

"Fr. Häring highlights the sacrament of penance as the means
by which God brings peace to men, a peace that effects not
only the reconciliation of men with God but their reconciliation with one another. He looks upon penance as a sacrament of joy, abounding in hope and bringing the good tidings
of a peace that is lasting."   *America*

BERNARD HÄRING, C.Ss.R.

SHALOM: PEACE
THE SACRAMENT OF RECONCILIATION

Revised Edition

IMAGE BOOKS

A Division of Doubleday & Company, Inc.
Garden City, New York

Image Books edition 1969
by special arrangement with Farrar, Straus & Giroux, Inc.
Image Books edition published September 1969

CUM PERMISSU SUPERIORUM
P. Gerhard Mittermeier, C.Ss.R., Provinzial
Munich, 21 April 1967

NIHIL OBSTAT
Reverend Richard P. McBrien, S.T.D., Censor Delegatus

IMPRIMATUR
Most Reverend Henry J. O'Brien, D.D., Apostolic Administrator
December 20, 1968

The NIHIL OBSTAT and IMPRIMATUR are official declarations that a book is free from doctrinal or moral error. No implication is contained therein that those who have granted the NIHIL OBSTAT and IMPRIMATUR agree with the contents, opinions or statements expressed.

CONTENTS

INTRODUCTION

———

Priests, religious and laymen alike sense a lag in the celebration of the sacrament of penance, insofar as it often does not reflect the renewal begun by the Second Vatican Council. In no case, however, is the lag ascribed to ill-will. The task is a mammoth one. The author confesses frankly that he himself cannot foresee what the consequences of the biblical, liturgical, ecclesial and ecumenical renewal will finally mean for the sacrament of penance. This book is not prophetic in the sense of anticipating possible future changes. The goal is far more modest: to help priests, seminarians, those who instruct others and those who wish instruction themselves to make the best possible use of present opportunities. It would be pure conjecture on the author's part to anticipate any major changes, since they would go beyond his domain and belong to the competent authorities. However, *attitudes* can be modified, if not changed radically; and it is always possible to improve on what we are doing now. Thus this book seeks to provide the best possible service now, all the while preparing the soil for future developments.

The main objectives of the author may be summarized as giving fuller value to the kerygmatic aspect of the sacrament of messianic peace, and to the spirit of worship; and emphasizing and developing to a greater extent the role of the confessor as "brother among brethren," as messenger of joy and peace, as one who is seriously concerned with the formation of the conscience of mature Christians.

The book is addressed primarily, but not exclusively, to priests. The author will be happy if the work can serve ministers and laymen of denominations whose ecumenical interests lead them to seek information on the way their Catholic brethren understand the sacrament of reconciliation today. May the knowledge gained help one another in the Christian endeavor of a continuous conversion. Catholic laymen who wish to enter as mature "partners" in the celebration of the sacrament of penance may also be interested in reading these pages.

The seeds of the present volume were sown at the Pastoral Institute in Conception, Missouri, where the author conducted courses in 1964 and 1966, and at the University of San Francisco in 1966. The thought of writing a book on the sacrament of penance would not have occurred to him but for the encouraging response and cooperation of the numerous priests, young and old, on these occasions. On their own initiative, the hearers took upon themselves the task of transcribing the lectures from tapes. Mimeographed copies intended for the hearers began circulating among many other priests. Seminary professors used them as a basis for their courses on the sacrament of peace. All indicated to the author the great need of a publication on the subject. In the meantime, work was progressing on the manuscript.

The author is well aware that this effort does not represent the "last word" on the subject. Efforts will keep on going; others with more imagination will enter the field and propose new ideas.

If these pages happen to be in readable English, the author claims no credit. He expresses his most hearty thanks to Sister Gabrielle L. Jean of the Grey Nuns of the Cross (Chairman of the Psychology Department, Rhode Island College, Providence, Rhode Island), Mrs. Josephine MacDonald Ryan (Springfield, Massachusetts) and Reverend Patrick McGarrity, C.Ss.R. (Professor of English, St. Alphonsus College, Suffield, Connecticut) for their most valuable collaboration. The author's gratitude extends to his other confrères at St. Alphonsus College, namely, Reverend Joseph Krastel, Reverend John Hamrogue and Frater Miguel Mahford for their contributions and reactions.

B.H.

Yale Divinity School
New Haven, Connecticut
April, 1967

1. THE GOOD NEWS OF
MESSIANIC PEACE

For the Israelites, the word *shalom* or "peace" had messianic overtones. It connoted the peace of God, and the Chosen People were promised this peace through the Messiah, whenever He would come. The Jewish people continue to hold the word *shalom* in high esteem, even apart from its religious meaning. The word is still the central expression of all that can be hoped for and given.

I can recall several occasions when the greeting *Shalom alecham* transformed an otherwise difficult situation into one of friendship and mutual trust. These occasions usually involved my meeting with Jews. On introducing myself, I would notice the reaction caused by the name, Häring, disclosing as it does my old German lineage. But when I immediately followed up the introduction with "*Shalom alecham,*" the reaction was spontaneous—a warm handshake and the atmosphere of trust that is conducive to friendship.

In its true religious sense "Peace with you" suggests the great time, the Messianic time when God will bring His own peace to men. That peace will effect the reconciliation of men with God as well as with each other. God's promise of a Messiah to announce the good tidings of peace was fulfilled in the person of Jesus Christ who, shortly after His Resurrection, appeared to His disciples and made the long-awaited proclamation. St. John's version of the event follows:

> Late that Sunday evening [Easter Sunday], when the disciples were together behind locked doors for fear of the Jews, Jesus came and stood among them. "Peace be with you," He said. And then he showed them his hands and his side. So, when the disciples saw the Lord they were filled with joy. Jesus repeated, "Peace be with you." And then he said, "As the Father sent me so I send you." He then breathed on them saying, "Receive the Holy Spirit, if you forgive any man's sins, they stand forgiven; if you pronounce them unforgiven, unforgiven they remain.

John 20:19-23

The fact that Our Lord punctuated His proclamation of peace with a display of His wounded hands and side is significant. It indicates that while the Easter mystery is always the mystery of the Resurrection, that Resurrection inexorably refers to His sufferings and death. The total liturgy, then, is not simply the presence of Christ, but the powerful, acting presence of the Risen Christ revealing pierced hands and side, the signs of His sacrifice. In the Liturgy, Christ is still proclaiming the Gospel. (Cf. *Constitution on the Sacred Liturgy*, Art. 33.) In the Sacrament of Penance, it is He who proclaims His Messianic peace.

ENCOUNTER WITH THE LORD

The Sacrament of Penance is primarily the liturgical proclamation of the Easter mystery applied here and now to the faithful, both to those who proclaim it as well as to those who receive it. Through the confessor, Christ again announces the peace of God revealing, as He does so, the wounds that have won us this peace and reconciliation.

Once, at the great opportune moment (*kairos*) on Calvary, Christ defied the boundaries of time by gathering onto Himself the sins of all mankind: past, present and future. Today, in the Sacrament of Penance, He again transcends those boundaries by bringing the saving action of the Cross and Resurrection to the penitent.

When the disciples first encountered the Risen Christ, He proclaimed His peace to them, revealing simultaneously the wounds through which that peace flowed. This encounter freed the disciples from their crippling fear and filled them with joy. Since then, Christ comes to the penitent as the bearer of the same good tidings. His "I died for you" includes His triumph over death and fills the penitent with joy, for it marks the sinner's liberation.

However, the joy of the penitent depends to some extent on the confessor who represents Christ: does he proclaim the good tidings in the spirit of Christ or does he turn the sacrament into an inquisition? More will be said about this later. At this point, we wish to examine the confessor's role as illumined by the Gospel, and more importantly still, how the penitent encounters Christ.

THE POWER OF JOY

The interim between the Lord's burial and His resurrection found the Apostles very sad men, desperately aware of their own sin. Perhaps Peter was the most despondent of all. Had he not disowned his Master? "I don't know this man" were the words he had used. And the Gospel tells us that Peter wept in sorrow. But when the Lord appeared to Peter and the other Apostles shortly after His resurrection, He greeted them with "Peace be with you." Hearing these words and recognizing the Speaker, the Apostles "were filled with joy." For this salutation, this "shalom" was nothing short of a reconciliation. The Lord showed them that He forgave; He healed the sinner.

A good confessor is fundamentally a man who is grateful for his own experiences of reconciliation. He is a man who has deeply felt the Lord's "shalom" and has been filled with joy by it, just like the Apostles. For then can he understand why the Lord repeated a second time, "Peace be with you," adding "as the Father sent Me, so I send you." He can better appreciate his mandate to act in the name of Christ, proclaiming as Christ did, the good tidings of reconciliation. It is this understanding that urges a confessor to fulfill his mission in a Christlike way, bringing the good tidings to the sorrowful sinner, the desperate penitent, and filling him with joy.

MESSINGER OF CHRIST'S LOVE

It is important for a confessor to grasp the significance of Christ's words, "As the Father sent Me, so I send you." To limit the term to a matter of "jurisdiction" in comparison with Christ's power would be a mistake. "God so loved the world that He sent His only begotten Son" (John 3:16). Love, then, accounts for Christ's coming. His great mission was not to flex divine muscle but to make known the love of the heavenly Father. Christ Himself, as the image of the Father, is the visible expression of that love. Now Christ, in turn, commissions his Apostles, the priests of the world, to take His place in the proclamation of this peace which is nothing short of the love of the Son and the love of the heavenly Father for men.

In his *Praxis Confessarii*, St. Alphonsus explains that the quintessence of a confessor's obligations rests in conveying the image of the heavenly Father. And since the true image of the Father is found in the glorified Christ pronouncing the words of reconciliation, the confessor should imitate this loving manner of the Lord. The confessor's approach must be, not that of a judge, but of "a spiritual father," of a brother among brethren, so that penitents may experience through him the goodness of God. They should be led to say: "If God's ministers are so kind, so understanding, how compassionate God Himself must be! How good and holy and just is the Law of God!" A great command for all Christians is "be compassionate as your heavenly Father is compassionate" (Luke 6:36). It behooves the priest and confessor to fulfill this command in an outstanding measure.

On the other hand, God is not a doting grandfather nodding "Yes, yes" to every fault, fearful of assuming the posture a father must necessarily take at times: one of firmness. The confessor's role is that of a loving father. The sacramental mission assigned him is to make visible the heavenly Father's love by being assimilated to Christ, the true image of the Father, the real messenger of peace.

PEACEMAKER THROUGH THE HOLY SPIRIT

"And then He breathed on them saying, 'Receive the Holy Spirit! . . .'"

Through the power of the Holy Spirit, Christ's humanity basked fully in the light of His divinity. It was the Holy Spirit who anointed Christ for the double role of High Priest and Victim.

Ordinary men, also, have been anointed through the Holy Spirit to play the dual role of priest and victim. The 'anointed' receive the Holy Spirit abundantly, and in receiving Him, receive a special identity with other men. They are now victims sharing vicariously the sufferings and the sorrows of the sinner, united to all men in solidarity. Just as Christ anointed by the Spirit made Himself (St. Paul says *harmatia*) conjointly responsible with men for the burden of their sins, though He had committed no sin, so must the priest.

As spiritual men, priests are liberated by the Holy Spirit from what would otherwise become an external, mechanical sacramentalism. The Holy Spirit gives priests the power to suffer with the people, and to be joyful with those who have cause for rejoicing. For through the Holy Spirit, priests as spiritual men have become sharers in the life of Christ in a special way. Their mission, like that of Christ, is one of charity, of love. Because of His anointing, Christ was to make a Sacrifice of Himself, a gift; so should the priest.

"IF YOU FORGIVE ANY MAN'S SINS THEY STAND FORGIVEN."

This message of Christ to His priests is one of peace and of life. It has its counterpart in the Old Testament in the Book of Ezechiel, in a passage that applies to the Sacrament of Penance in a very special way:

> The Lord's power let hold of me and by the spirit of the Lord I was carried away and set down in the midst of a plain which was covered with bones. And all of them parched quite dry. "Son of man," He said, "can life return to these dead bones?" "Lord," I said, "Thou knowest." Then He made me utter a prophecy over the bones. "Listen dry bones to the word of the Lord. Listen to the word of the Lord. A message to these bones from the Lord. I mean to send my spirit into you and restore you to life. Sinews shall be given to you, flesh shall grow on you, and skin shall cover you, and I will give you breath to bring you to life again. Do you doubt, then, the Lord's power?" And so I prophesied: "Come, breath of life, from the four winds and breathe on these slain men to make them live." And so I prophesied as He had bidden me, and the breath of life came into them so that they lived again and all rose to their feet, host upon host of them.
>
> *Ez.* 37:1-10

What is striking in this text is that *ruah*, the spirit of God, fulfills the work of raising dead men to life. It is the spirit that restores to life. The New Testament text on the forgiveness of sins should be read in the light of this text from the Old Testament. The great prophecies from the Old Testament are fulfilled in the Son of Man who is able to restore life and forgive sins. From Ezechiel, we see that He would do this through the Spirit. In the New Testament, Jesus Christ proves that He can forgive sins by the very fact that He has power to restore life. "The Spirit of the Lord is upon me. He has anointed me. He has sent me to announce good news to the poor, to proclaim release to the prisoners" (Luke 4:18).

Jesus Christ sacrificed His life in the Spirit. His heavenly Father, to show that He accepted this gift of His own Son, raised Jesus back to life through the Spirit. The place of the Holy Spirit in Christ's mission is central.

The priest has also received the Spirit in a special way, enabling him to prophesy and to proclaim like Ezechiel, knowing that it is the Lord who acts through his words. For the words of the priest administering absolution are more than a mere sign. They are a *signum efficax*, a word and sign of God's mighty action.

Though it is essentially through Baptism that those who are 'dead bones' receive the Spirit and are raised to life with Christ, nonetheless, the prophecy applies also to the Sacrament of Penance. The essential work of the Sacrament of Penance is to achieve a conversion from weakness to strength, from sickness to full health. For some, it means a conversion from death to life. Penance is a great prophecy through the Spirit both for those who are in mortal sin as well as for those in venial sin. For all sinners of good will, the Sacrament of Penance means good tidings. It is a proclamation of the Easter mystery, a proclamation which is applied here and now to them: they are dying to their sins and are being raised to a new life.

LITURGY OF THE MESSIANIC PEACE

Confessors and penitents ought to be fully aware that the Sacrament of Penance is liturgy. It is the efficacious proclamation of the word of God. Therefore, we have to celebrate the sacrament in a way that focuses attention, not on the sins of the penitent, but totally on the Lord who is proclaiming the good tidings, giving the active word of His peace in loving attention to the penitent. Many Christians fail to attend first to the Lord's message, but become engrossed in their own part in the reception of the sacrament. Let me explain.

For several years I preached missions. At times, this brought me into predominantly Protestant areas where Catholics did not always have easy access to the sacraments. In catechizing these people, I used to make it a point to ask about the Sacrament of Penance. "What is the most essential element, the greatest aspect of the Sacrament of Penance?" Time and again the answer would come back: "My sorrow." When I replied that something else was still greater than contrition, a volley of responses would follow: "Good purpose," "Firm resolution," "Examination of conscience," "That we accuse ourselves thoroughly with material integrity," "Fulfill our penance." These replies came from child and adult alike, even from the most intelligent among them. And I still remember how happy I was when finally, after all the imperfect answers, a little boy said: "I know. The greatest thing is what Jesus does. He forgives my sins. He cleans my soul." That boy had been prepared by his mother for his first confession. She had certainly done a wonderful job in making the child aware of the meaning of the Sacrament of Penance.

When we celebrate the Sacrament of Penance, then, both confessor and penitent are giving praise to the Lord. It is cult, adoration, glory to God, "whose law is just, holy and good." It is especially praise to the merciful Lord. And still, the Sacrament goes further. For in and through this Sacrament, Christ proclaims His own life-giving power to the penitent. He Himself brings peace; He Himself glorifies His name as Redeemer and thus glorifies the name of the heavenly Father. He hallows the name of the Father, and because He does so, we too can hallow the name of the Father who is merciful. We join Christ and through this active Word of God, by praising Him, we are liberated from our anthropocentric concerns and from our self-centeredness.

HERALDS OF THE WORD OF GOD

Priests, to whom the Lord has given the great power to utter the prophecy of good tidings in His name and through whom the Lord is acting, are servants of the people. They are not primarily judges but rather ministers, servants in a holy ministry.

The Sacrament of Penance is the liturgical proclamation of the word of God, of the good tidings, the *kerygma sacramentale*. As priests, we are totally directed towards the work of redemption, towards the Easter mystery, towards Christ's own acting word. The brief exchange between penitent and priest in the confessional is directed towards the words: "I absolve you from your sins, in the name of the Father, and of the Son, and of the Holy Spirit. Amen." This is an efficacious proclamation and, we are happy to say, it is finally rendered in the vernacular for the penitent to understand.

I cannot help but recall the stir in some quarters caused by the talk of a possible vernacular absolution. I remember one rather amusing incident that my friend, Father Löw, experienced in this regard. It took place about seventeen years ago. Father Löw, who was then the *Relator Generalis* for the Sacred Congregation of Rites, had a new French ritual submitted to a general session of the Congregation. Most of the texts in the ritual were in French, but Father Löw still pleaded for approval of it. After the session, a monsignor who had heard about the approval met Father Löw; he was unaware of the priest's identity at the time. The monsignor began to revile the actions of this Father Löw who, he thought, was destroying the Church. In fact, the monsignor felt that Father Löw even showed heretical tendencies. He did not doubt that if the French asked Father Löw for permission to have the sacramental form of penance in the vernacular, Father Löw would accede to the request. Father Löw, I assure you, was a very gentle man, even rather shy. But there are moments when gentle and shy men get excited. "Do you think, monsignor," Father Löw said, restraining himself, "that it would be the greatest evil in the Church if the poor sinner were to understand the words of reconciliation?"

Thanks to the Second Vatican Council, the penitent now does hear the words of absolution in a language he understands. However, the priest is faced with a more difficult translation than simple language. He must translate the meaning of the words of absolution into the penitent's life. He must receive this man, this woman, this adolescent, just as they come to him. He must take onto himself the burden of the penitent, and be in deep sympathy with him. Only then can he hope to indicate to the penitent the profound and joyful meaning of the words which he, as an instrument of

Christ, utters: "Peace be with you! Your sins are forgiven. The Lord has paved for you the way of a new life." This translation of the message of peace into the life situation of the penitent is the primary duty of the confessor.

All that will be said in the following pages must be understood in relation to this central action of the Sacrament of Peace. It is this action that urges the priest to be a humble instrument of Christ who "shows His hands and His side," who gives proof of His divine love, of the power of the resurrection. He is telling us, and through us the penitent, "Shalom, Peace be with you."

The role of the priest, though humble, is wonderful. It is neither the role of the dead instrument nor of the inflexible inquisitor. It is the role and function of a prophet. For just as God spoke through the prophet in earlier days, so now He speaks through the priest. Christ is still proclaiming His Gospel; it is Christ Himself who continues to preach the good tidings of peace and forgiveness. (Cf. *Constitution on the Sacred Liturgy*, Art. 33.)

THE HOUR OF GRACE

Our approach to a *praxis confessarii* is rooted in chapter twenty of the Gospel of St. John, as pointed out earlier. We can elaborate on this approach by glancing at St. Mark (1:14-15). There we find a summary of the manner and matter, in short, the essential structuring of Christ's preaching: "Christ at the time began to proclaim joyfully the good tidings coming from God. 'The favorable time has come' (*ho kairos pepleromenos*), the kingdom of God is upon you (*metanoeite*), be converted, be renewed in the spirit and believe the Gospel." In the preaching of the Church, these words are brought into effect. They are realized in their fullest sense in the Sacrament of the Eucharist, and in a very special way in the Sacrament of Penance. For in each of the Sacraments, Christ Himself proclaims the good tidings coming from the heavenly Father. Each of the two Sacraments occasions the *kairos*, the great moment prepared by God.

A POSITIVE JOYOUS RESPONSE

"The Kingdom of God is upon you." With these words, Christ indicated His desire to rule us through His mercy and His goodness. His compassionate love urges us to repent for our sins, whereas by ruling us through His goodness, He rules us also in justice and holiness, *i.e.*, toward a life which responds to Him through goodness to our brothers.

The proclamation of the dynamic presence of the Kingdom of Heaven is also an urgent appeal: *metanoeite*. The Vulgate translation of this word is: *poenitemini* (Mt. 4:17 *poenitentiam agite*) meaning: "Do penance." There is no doubt that the word *metanoeite* denotes also repentance and penance, but it suggests more than that. It is a good tiding of the messianic time in which God fulfills His word: "A new heart I will give you, and a new spirit I will put within you . . . I will put my spirit within you" (Ez. 36:26-27). The appeal, "Be renewed in your spirit," is a part of the good tidings. Since the Lord now brings back His own people to His land, that is, to His own heart, the life-giving appeal sounds: "Return to the Lord."

In the Sacrament of Peace, God Himself gathers His people and renews men's hearts, and so His kingdom is truly upon us. But the act of reconciliation brings also the exhortation and promise: "If by the Spirit you put to death all the pursuits of the selfish nature, then you will live" (Rom. 8:13).

"BELIEVE THE GOSPEL"

The Sacrament of Peace is "a sacrament of faith." The grateful reception of the good news, "Peace with you," can change our life. We are only converted to the extent that we embrace the Gospel of the messianic peace.

If priests hope to convince people of the nature of this sacrament, to obliterate the idea that penance is some sort of magic washing, then there are some practical problems to solve. For instance, in the event of an insufficient number of confessors, should we continue to lead all of our grammar and high school students to church each month where we condition them to rapid confessions? Must not better forms of communal celebration be found? Would it not be better, even at the risk of some children not using their personal initiative to confess for two or three months, to introduce a system of rotation whereby only a certain number of the children would be invited to confession monthly, giving the confessor more time for counseling? Should we reduce the sacramental celebration to the mere giving of absolution? Or should we not rather build up our *praxis confessarii* in such a way as to leave no doubt that penance is "a sacrament of faith"? A communal celebration about which we shall speak later on should help to deepen the faith and to awaken the innermost powers of a Christian conscience.

The celebration of the Sacrament of Penance must reproduce the structure of the action of Christ appearing to His desperate Apostles. The celebration must be an obvious proclamation that now is a great opportunity, a time of grace and renewal.

The penitents can be renewed only if they joyfully believe the Gospel message of the Risen Christ. Then will they be "filled with joy" as the apostles were on that first Easter morning. The more personal joy the penitent experiences, the greater hope there is of his persevering conversion. For ultimately, the perseverance of the penitent's conversion rests not on the inquisition for material integrity or on isolated threats of the sulfur and fire of hell, but on the joy received from the Sacrament.

After the retreat which I preached in the Vatican, I was amazed by an old missionary who asked me severely, "Were you faithful to St. Alphonsus? Did you preach the Eternal Truths?"—"Surely, Father," I said, "I preached the eternal truths. But may I ask what you mean by the eternal truths?" —"Oh, everyone knows what the eternal truths are—hell, fire, and damnation," he replied. I found this reply a rather strange limitation of the eternal truths, as though Christ's mission consisted in preaching an impending disaster rather than salvation. How could we account, then, for Christ's mandate, "Preach the Gospel," the good news?

At the heart of our preaching should be the truth that God from all eternity is the Triune Love and that from all eternity His intention was to send His Son. Our Gospel is the good news of the Lord's death-and-resurrection which guarantees that our own death will be the fulfillment of our life. Hell is a place only for those who refuse to accept the Gospel, who refuse the opportunity for renewal.

The pulpit is not the only place for the proclamation of the eternal truth of Christ's death and resurrection. The priest must take the joy of the Gospel into the confessional with him and there dispense, not a message filled with threats, but the message of Christ's peace to the penitent.

In the Book of Nehemiah we have a prototype of this approach. After the Jews returned from exile, they found themselves harassed, on the one hand, by many enemies, and on the other, by the challenge of raising a protective wall about their city while fighting off these enemies. In the course of this distressing situation, the priest Ezra gathered the people together in the street and began to read, explaining to them the Book of the Covenant. As the people listened, many were deeply moved and began to weep. But the priest Ezra told them, "Come now, let us celebrate a feast, and bring a portion to all those who cannot come. . . . Be not depressed. The joy of the Lord is our strength. . . . So all the people went to eat and drink, and to send portions to those who could not come, and to make great mirth, because they understood the words that were taught them" (Nehemiah 8:10-12).

This passage from the Book of Nehemiah suggests to us the true approach that we should use both in our role as confessors and as penitents. It is a key to a *Praxis Confessarii*.

Nothing is so important as that of bringing the joy of the Lord to the people. Those who listened to the priest Ezra reading to them from the Book of the Covenant believe that this message came to them from God. Ultimately, it was their faith in this Gospel and in the interpretation given by their priests that led to a period of rejoicing and conversion.

Today, Christ Himself preaches the good news to His people. Our faith assures us of this. And our faith likewise assures us that we, as priests, have received the Holy Spirit, have been anointed in a way similar to Christ, and like Christ, we are to bear the burden of the sins of others and rejoice with them on occasion. United with Christ and so uniting ourselves in deepest sympathy with the penitent, we can proclaim, as His living instruments and with a feeling heart, the peace of Christ.

In the Sacrament of Penance, our most noble task is to proclaim the joy of the Lord to the penitent.

2. PERSONAL ENCOUNTER
WITH THE LORD IN THE CHURCH

After breakfast, Jesus said to Simon Peter, "Simon, son of John, do you love me more than these?" "Yes, Lord," he said, "you know that I love you." He told him, "Feed my lambs." A second time he repeated his question, "Simon, son of John, do you love me?" "Yes, Lord, you know that I love you." He told him, "Tend my little sheep." A third time he asked him, "Simon, son of John, do you love me?" Peter was hurt because he had asked a third time, "Do you love me?" So he said to him, "Lord, you know all things; you know well that I love you." Jesus told him, "Feed my sheep."

"Truly I assure you, when you were a young man, you used to fasten your own belt and go wherever you asked. But when you grow old, you will stretch out your hands, and another will fasten a belt around you and take you where you do not wish to go."

[What he said indicated, in fact, the sort of death by which Peter was to glorify God.] And having spoken thus, He said to him, "Follow me."

John 21:15-19

In this Gospel, Our Lord insistently asked Peter three times whether or not he loved Him, whether Peter was still His friend or not. There is no doubt that the triple inquiry pertained to the previous triple denial of Peter. For on three occasions during Our Lord's trial, Peter swore to the Lord's enemies: "I do not know the man." Now Peter confesses his sin to the Lord, not simply by acknowledging that he knows Him, but by professing his love for Him in a more humble way.

The scene described here involves a very personal encounter between Christ and Peter, one that differed from their first encounter in the Cenacle Easter evening when Peter stood with the other ten. Is it too daring to compare these two events with the communal celebration of the Sacrament of Penance (Cenacle) and the individual confession (Sea of Tiberias)? By this personal encounter, Our Lord taught Peter, and through him all future priests, the full import of his pastoral task. Peter had disowned the Lord, but the Risen Christ personally approaches Peter and gives him the opportunity to confess his sin, humbling him, no doubt, but at the same time exalting him, purifying him and liberating him from sin. And Peter, though saddened by this need for self-avowal, responded to the opportunity with deep humility. In confessing his past sin of denial, he included a profession of faith in Christ and an assurance of renewed fidelity.

St. Peter, in this threefold confession, is a prototype of the priest who confesses and hears confessions. Peter experienced the redeeming love of the Savior, the Risen Lord. Through his penance and humble confession, he became worthy of the office of good shepherd. And an essential task of the good shepherd is the preaching of the Gospel which includes administering and celebrating the Sacrament of Penance.

It is of utmost importance for priests to understand and learn from Peter's example. For the priest himself is a sinner called to sanctity. He will solace other sinners only to the extent that he himself has crossed the Red Sea of sorrow, contrition and humility. Only then can he empathize with the penitent, awakening in him a deep sorrow as well as deep adoration of the justice and mercy of God. For only the priest who is assimilated to the Church in St. Peter, who humbles himself, who is aware of his own personal weakness—only the priest who, having been given a mission similar to Peter's, has taken onto himself the burden of the sins of others and is grateful for his own conversion to God can be a good messenger of salvation.

The confessor who thinks of penitents only in terms of "you sinners" cannot be a good confessor. The good confessor is one who, with clear recognition of what he is saying, prays with the whole Church: "Forgive *us our* sins as *we* forgive those who trespass against *us*." Peter, who confessed his sin, received the promise of the Lord: "Simon, I have prayed for you that your faith may not fail, and when you have come to yourself you must lend strength to your brothers" (Lk. 22:31-34). With this promise, Peter received the power to strengthen the faith of the people of God by proclaiming God's mercy to them.

SHARED BURDENS

The priest must be a man of penance, practicing the virtue at an ever higher degree. If he is to be a good shepherd and take onto himself the sins of all men, particularly those of his penitents, he must respond to the Lord's call on the anointed and fulfill in his own body that which is still lacking in the body of Christ. Like Christ, he is designated as a martyr to suffer and die for others, which can only be achieved through his intimate union with Christ who suffered for all mankind. His encounter with Christ, the Judge, obliges him to fulfill the demands of justice, thus claiming mercy for all those who recognize in adoring humility that God's law is just, holy and good.

SHARED SORROW AND JOY

The solidarity that exists between the priest and the penitent in the Sacrament of Penance was well expressed through the matter-and-form nomenclature of scholastic philosophy, the terminology adopted by the Council of Trent. The priest's absolution, Trent tells us, the proclamation of the peace of the Lord, is the form (*forma*) of the Sacrament, while the humble confession of the penitent is the *quasi-materia*. Penance and Matrimony are unique in this respect. The matter and form of the other Sacraments are administered by the same person. For example, in Baptism, the priest, while pouring the water (the matter), proclaims the good tidings: "I baptize you . . ." (the form). In the Sacrament of Penance, the priest and penitent are destined to concelebrate the sacrament by mutual cooperation. This word "cooperation" is not exhausted by the fact that there is a physical, local encounter between priest and penitent, as the Church demands. (Let me interject here that I personally believe that the Church could, without difficulty, allow absolution to be given over the telephone. For, a telephone conversation does bring about a real presence or personal encounter between the two parties.) Cooperation signifies far more in this case; it calls for a unity between confessor and penitent based on sympathy and understanding, a unity in penance and in the praise of our merciful and just God.

The main effort of the priest is aimed at preparing the penitent for the message of peace. But if the confessor is a man deeply penetrated with the spirit of penance through meditation and through his own penitential experience, he will be in a better position to help the penitent grasp more perfectly the justice and goodness of God's law, and he will the more readily unite himself to the penitent in the praise of that law.

SIN: AN ATTACK ON GOD AND THE CHURCH

The priest must disclose to the penitent the effects of sin in relation to God and the Church. Strange as it may sound, sin is an encounter with God. It is a deliberate "no" to God's invitation to grace. When a man is called in any way by God, he sins by rejecting that call, whether it be by a direct refusal or simply by running away from doing what he knows he should do. Sin is a deliberate "no" to the redeeming love of Christ, and this rejection hurts Christ. It hurt Him on the cross; it hurts Him today through His Church. But every sin, besides striking out at Christ, likewise attains the family of God. The one who says "no" to God says it within the realm of the people of God, by disassociating himself, by distorting the harmony of the family of God. He destroys the intended order of love within creation.

The Church suffers a deep loss especially through those sins involving a direct refusal of the invitation of grace. Each individual member of the Church, realizing the wealth of which he has deprived the Church, should do penance, seeking the forgiveness of the whole Church for what he has done to her. To some extent, every sin means persecuting Christ in the Church. Even today, Christ continues to suffer, not personally as a victim on the cross, but through the Church, His body. This is actual suffering because it involves actual loss. That is why the personal call of each one of us to membership in Christ's Church enjoins one to give fully of himself to the Church if he is to find his true identity. By sinning, a man not only loses his true self, the personal perfection expected of him, but he also hurts the Church.

Serious sin entails a division, a separation, not simply between man and God, but between man and the Church of Christ. The immediate significance and the principal grace of the Sacrament of Penance is to restore us to the unity of the people of God, and in so doing, to unite us with God. The deeper our unity with the people of God, the deeper will be our unity with God Himself. One need only ponder the fact that the Church assumes the sacramental function of effecting unity between God and man because it is she who preaches the Gospel of reconciliation and explains the divine law. It is the Church who, with an eye to divine law, decides whether one is worthy to receive the Eucharist. She tells us that if one has sinned gravely, with full freedom, with full deliberation, distorting the order of charity, he is not worthy to receive Holy Communion, the highest sign of the unity of the people of God.

The Scholastic theologians of the middle ages concurred that every mortal sin was, in a sense, an *excommunicatio*. They did not mean by this that every mortal sin brought with it a juridical sanction. They were pointing rather to the

tragic effect of serious sin whereby the sinner is cut off from
the sacrament drawing all Catholics in union with God, and
through Christ, with all the Church. The sinner must first
confess to the Church before he becomes worthy once more
of receiving the greatest sign of unity, union with Christ and
union with the Church. Inasmuch as mortal sin damages the
sinner's union with both God and with the Church, he must
receive reconciliation with God through reconciliation with
the Church.

Even recent editions of the *Pontificale Romanum* (cf. the
liturgy of Penance for Ash Wednesday and Holy Thursday)
stress the aspect of the sinner's reconciliation with God
through a reconciliation with the Church. In the bishop's
prayers and exhortations, the penitents are made aware of the
great harm they have caused, how they have actually tainted
the Church by their sins. Then, on Holy Thursday, the day
we commemorate the institution of the Holy Eucharist, the
bishop supposedly receives the penitents, taking one of them
by the hand, and this penitent in turn taking another by the
hand and so on, until all are physically united. The penitents
are then led to the altar whereupon the Sacrament of Unity is
celebrated. The symbolism is great: the bishop is a servant
of this unity.

PERSONAL AND COMMUNAL RECONCILIATION

One of the most important aspects of Christian morality is
reflected in the synthesis of the communal and the indivdual.
Each one of us, by sinning, refuses an individual gift of God,
an individual call of Providence, an individual grace. In this
sense, the refusal is personal, but not private. For all these
gifts, all these graces were offered to that individual in order
to build up the Church of Christ. Though we must confess
our individual sins, we must never stop seeing them in the
perspective of the entire Church. This view will serve both
the penitent and the confessor in good stead. A realization of
the communal as well as the personal effects of sin encourages us, not simply to avoid sin, but to be a source of light

to others. Through sin, the entire Church suffers, losing something that is infinitely great. Sin is a refusal of God's invitation to grace.

The grace of God urges us to love His will and gently reproves us for transgressing His law. While delimiting arbitrariness, the law of God calls us to keep, to serve and to live according to this love because it guarantees our own personal fulfillment in true love and, through us, the fulfillment of the Church.

The Redeeming Christ came to reinstate us into the unity of God's triune love, a unity we had lost through sin. But at the same time, He came to lead all men into the unity of His own Body, of His family, the family of God, the people of the Redeemed. The Sacrament of Penance is a means of sustaining and, if need be, of restoring family structure. The good penitent is aware that this Sacrament brings him face to face with Christ Jesus, through the grace of the Holy Spirit. The sin that he confesses has disrupted, in some way, the harmony of God's people; he had sinned against the Body of Christ. Justice demands that he make reparation for the damage. Since no one can claim loving an Invisible God if he does not love his brother whom he sees, there is no way for the sinner to return to God if he does not return through Christ's Church to a greater oneness with his brothers.

The Sacrament of Penance awakens us to the fact that Christ took upon Himself the burden of everyone's sins. He did this with a view toward building up His Church, and so it is with the celebration of the Sacrament of Penance; it is imperative to build up the Church. The whole Church suffers from the sins of its members, especially from indurate hearts. "If one organ suffers, they all suffer together. If one flourishes, they all rejoice together" (I Cor. 12:26).

THE PILGRIM CHURCH

With St. Peter, everyone of God's people is asked by the Lord: "Do you love me?" And just as the Lord's friend asked for forgiveness through his profession of love, so the Church,

Spouse of Christ, daily seeks forgiveness from the Risen Lord. St. Augustine repeatedly says that the whole Church praying the words, "forgive us our trespasses as we forgive those who trespass against us" is confessing the sins of sinners. By doing so she does not divide the people of God into two groups: sheep and goats, saints and sinners. The Church is holy, but by vocation. She still has many sinners in her midst, and all her true sons and daughters, really close to God, admit readily to their need for greater conformity to His will. They acknowledge their status of sinners each time they confess or utter the words: "Forgive us our trespasses."

Through an encounter with Christ, our Judge and Redeemer, the Sacrament of Penance also provides an encounter with the Church who places herself under the saving judgment of Christ. Therefore the priest is asked to represent this humble Church in the full consciousness that she is submitted to the final judgment of Christ. Through a humble confessor, the penitent grasps the succoring hand of the pilgrim Church. The confessional becomes the meetingplace of God's mercy and man's constant need for reform and conversion; we rediscover our brotherhood in the sacrament of peace.

A communal celebration of the Sacrament of Penance may serve to highlight the significance of the "Communion of Saints" as pilgrimage and conversion: through self-denial and penance, all sons and daughters of the Church preparing themselves to sustain the burden of the sins and the effort of conversion of all the others. The saints typified this spirit by doing penance not simply as atonement for their sins but also for the sins of all men. The proclamation of God's healing judgment must therefore always extend to the whole body of Christ. The priest's mandate received for Christ through the Church is to seek the reconciliation of his brethren to God and to lead them in following Christ. "Christ was innocent of sin, and yet for our sake, God made him one with the sinfulness of men, so that in him we might be made one with the goodness of God himself" (II Cor. 5:21). Participating in God's economy of redemption, the priest appeals to the penitent for response to God's favor through penance, self-denial, humility, all in view of strengthening the mystical body of Christ.

Peter's reinstatement in the Lord's grace implied more than mere forgiveness; he was expected to exercise his authority by strengthening his brothers; "when you have come to yourself, you must lend strength to your brothers" (Lk. 22:32); similarly, each Christian receiving forgiveness is urged to fulfill his role in the common effort for Church renewal.

COMMUNAL CELEBRATION OF THE SACRAMENT OF PENANCE

Every sin is a free "no" to God, a "no" that enslaves men to a frustrating monologue. The sinner is not without realizing that in one way or another he was called by God to gain light and to bring light to the world around him. With every serious sin, a person turns his back on God instead of heading toward Him. At the same time, he afflicts the Church. He who says "no" to God says it within the framework of the people of God, indeed, in the framework of the whole of God's creative plan. He contributes to the partial destruction of the order of redeemed creation. He disturbs and upsets the members of the family of God. The liturgical celebration of the sacrament of peace should make us ever more conscious of these social dimensions of sin and the personal and communal character of conversion.

The liturgical renewal is very much concerned with this social dimension, especially since the end of the Ecumenical Council. Until now, experimentation has lawfully remained within the limits of a kind of Bible Vigil for the preparation of individual confession and thanksgiving for absolution. Others speak of penitential rites (paraliturgical) where God's mercy is proclaimed in view of all the signs of his justice and forgiveness. Often, some or all the members of a community which celebrates a communal liturgy go individually to confession; then at the end all the priests proclaim together the absolution of the sins whereby it is left open as a question whether this absolution applies "sacramentally" only to those who have here and now confessed individually or to all who, with a contrite heart, have participated only in the communal celebration.

The communal celebration is especially meaningful in communities of religious, in seminaries and during retreats of groups working or living close together. It could replace, at least from time to time, the monthly individual confessions of whole classes of school children who desire this. France's hierarchy has given some guidelines (emphasizing, however, that they were not permitting group absolution or doing away with the necessity of personal confession of sins):

> These celebrations permit the sacrament to be related once again to the word of God, which is at the very source of the Liturgy. They permit the celebration of the word where it is now lacking. They thereby permit the faithful to see that this sacrament is, like all others, a sign of faith, for faith comes from the word heard. And they emphasize to the conscience that repentance takes its origin from the appeal to conversion.
>
> They constitute, too, one of the "common celebrations" to which the Council constitution on the Liturgy gives preference whenever they conform to the proper nature of the various rites. For, if the sacrament of penance is administered privately, it manifests less meaning than the sacrament really bears. For the sacrament is communitarian, bringing about reconciliation with God in and through the Church. Therefore, these celebrations permit the identification of the role of the Church in penitential action as well as the prayer of the Church for sinners.
>
> They furnish an excellent opportunity to teach the faithful to better make their examination of conscience, to establish a hierarchy of faults, and to revive their sense of sin.
>
> These celebrations are especially opportune during Lent, during a retreat or a parish mission, on the occasion of a pilgrimage, and so on. They should not be presented as some new institution, destined to replace the old. They should not be the occasion for the faithful to confess less frequently, but to confess better.

In large parishes with only one or a few priests, there is probably no other way of restoring a normal eucharistic life without an official introduction of the communal celebration of the Sacrament of Penance and General Absolution. It would have to be done in a way to assure all of the forgiveness of their sins to the extent of their good will. In fullest continuity with the Council of Trent, there could be laid down the one condition: that those who have a clear conscience of having committed a mortal sin would be absolved without previous individual confession and could go to Communion, but would be obliged—as far as possible—to confess the mortal sins at least within the next paschal time.

The individual confession is still very meaningful after the communal celebration and absolution. Did not St. Peter on the very day of the Resurrection receive the message of peace together with the other Apostles? Yet later, he was invited by the Lord to a more individual confession of his sin and profession of faith and love.

Note: An order for a communal celebration of the Sacrament of Peace can be found in the Appendix, page 345.

3. THE DIFFERENT ROLES
OF THE CONFESSOR

Christ's action in the Sacrament of Penance should serve as a beacon light when viewing the role of the confessor. Obvious as the statement may seem, it is needed as a warning against a too rigid moralism or an overindulgent psychology.

I have no propensity for discussion bearing on such questions as: which is the primary role of the confessor, to heal the penitent or to forgive his sins? The reason is simply that I view the Sacrament holistically, as an integration of both roles. Nevertheless, I deem it necessary to comment briefly on each of these roles.

There are some confessors, especially older priests whose seminary training offered little in the way of sociology and psychology, who judge all cases from the viewpoint of juridical morality alone. Whenever a penitent presents himself to one of them, this confessor has an eye only for the human responsibility and human guilt in view of a law. Such a confessor concerns himself only with objective principles: "What is the measure and extent of the guilt of this man? My duty is to forgive him to the extent that he recognizes his guilt as transgression of a law." In short, these confessors focus only on law and sin against law. This is my referent when speaking of a too rigid moralism.

I recall the case of a man given to masturbation. Beset by the problem for almost thirty years, he had, during that time, dealt with confessors preoccupied solely with information regarding the exact number of mortal sins, who lectured him on the gravity of his offense. In time, the man became convinced of his incorrigibility. He had prayed hard, but his prayers seemed to go unheard. Guilt coupled with shame gnawed at him night and day. He was ashamed to face God and even felt ashamed to face his friends. Finally, his feelings of worthlessness led him seriously to contemplate suicide.

When he first came to me, he was already a desperate man. I counselled him to accept his habit of masturbation as a trial. I assured him that even though he had not yet succeeded in overcoming his habit, that surely all his efforts and prayers indicated that his failures stemmed more from psychological difficulties than from intention. Finally, I assured him that he might accept this affliction as suffering and that this cross might even help him to come closer to Christ, our Redeemer.

I met the man several years later when he rushed up to me on the street and said, "Father, I can never express how grateful I am to you." He identified himself and concluded his story in a way that not only humbled me but warmed my heart. "When you told me that I might accept my trouble as suffering," he said, "I felt for the first time that I could even overcome it."

The fault committed by the moral legalist against his penitents is one of not knowing when the restoring action should be used to counterbalance the moral principles. But whatever is thought, said and done must be viewed in the redeeming action and love of Christ.

On the other hand, there are confessors who focus exclusively on the misery of the penitent. They go to the other extreme. This is a newer tendency fathered by modern clinical psychology or psychotherapy. In fact, in many instances, psychiatrists and depth psychologists have persuaded people to ignore guilt feelings entirely, alleging that they are merely neurotic hangovers of repressed childhood fears.

Once, on a train, I was approached by a student who told me that she had gained a new outlook on life, one that was no longer cluttered with fears.

She continued by saying that life had become more or less beautiful for her now. To her surprise, I asked her how long she had undergone psychotherapy. She gave me an honest answer; she had paid for 110 hours of treatment. She had been undergoing therapy that differed in no way from the services of quack psychologists whose main concern is denial of the reality of guilt. "It is just misery," they say. "And the greatest misery of all is to mistake misery for guilt."

Understand me well: in no way am I claiming that a sinner may not feel wretched; nor am I saying that misery cannot at times be confused with guilt. In fact, I can illustrate this latter point with a case. I received a letter from a very intelligent young woman who told me that she felt such misery after committing any fault that she wondered if her faults were not all sins against the Holy Spirit. She was definitely confusing her misery with her guilt, and in my opinion, she was in need of some psychological help. My objection is not psychotherapy as such, but to a psychotherapy that denies all guilt whatsoever.

The Sacrament of Penance is supposed to inspire us with a deeper knowledge and desire for the accomplishment of the law of God; to heal us from the misery of sin; to judge us in order that we may avoid eternal damnation at the last judgment. Finally, the Sacrament of Penance has a liturgical aspect, namely, the cult of Almighty God, an expression of trust and love toward the heavenly Father. In order better to understand these various aspects of confession, we have to make a careful study of the different roles that Christ performs in the Sacrament: the role of Teacher, of Physician, of Judge and of High Priest.

CHRIST AS TEACHER

In the Sacrament of Penance, Christ is the teacher of the internal law of grace. His teaching strategy hinges on the action of the Holy Spirit who purifies our hearts and proclaims Christ's mercy through the ministry of the Church. Through this purification and proclamation, the penitent becomes aware of his obligation to live according to a renewed spirit. In the words of Jeremiah: "On that day I will grant them a new covenant, and I will write my law upon their hearts and in their minds. So that all can know me, all will be taught by God" (31, 31). Ezechiel adds: "I will put a new spirit in their bowels" (11:19; cf. 18:31, 36:26) and "I will give you my spirit" (27:6).

Christ is the teacher of the law in a unique way. He causes the penitent to share in His own life and so in the law of the New Testament. "I will put my laws into their mind, and upon their hearts I will write them, and I will be their God, and they shall be my people" (Heb. 8:10). In short, this law is the Law of Love: love God and love your neighbor.

For those who approach the Sacrament of Penance with mortal sin, Christ is quite eminently the Teacher of the New Law, for a man in mortal sin is not yet *truly within the law of Christ.* He is not under the law of grace. Rather, he is under a threatening law, one that promises death and destruction. Therefore, when such a penitent is reconciled to Christ through the grace of the Holy Spirit, the presence of Christ regenerates the power of the New Law even as it redeems the "new man." The penitent again dwells in Christ and Christ dwells in him. St. Paul states it thus: "For the law of the Spirit of the life in Christ Jesus has delivered me from the law of sin and death" (Rom. 8:2). And: ". . . if you are led by the Spirit you are not under the law. . . . But the fruit of the Spirit is charity, joy, peace, patience, kindness, goodness, faith, modesty, continency. Against such things there is no law. And they who belong to it have crucified their self-centered nature with its passions and desires. If we live by the Spirit, by the Spirit let us also walk" (Gal. 5:19, 22-25).

On the other hand, if the penitent coming to the Sacrament of Penance is in the state of grace, it is inaccurate to say that Christ gives him a new participation in the law of grace. More precisely, He teaches the penitent, through the purifying, redeeming action of the Holy Spirit, how to progress in continuous conversion in gratitude toward God and in compassionate love toward neighbor. For the average good Christian, the Sacrament of Penance is intended not so much for conversion from death to life as for continuous growth of life. And so we come to the role of the priest as a sharer in the teaching power of Christ.

The priest in preparing others to receive the Sacrament of Penance, and the confessor actually celebrating the Sacrament are expected to teach Christians what the Apostles first taught their penitents, namely, what being a Christian means, what they are to become:

> Were you not raised to life with Christ? Then aspire to the realm above where Christ is seated at the right hand of God. And let your thoughts dwell in that higher realm, not on the earthly life of the selfish nature . . . I repeat, you died. Then put to death those parts of you which belong to the selfish nature. As God's chosen people, His own, His beloved, put on the garment that suits you: compassion, kindness, humility, gentleness, patience . . . Let the message of Christ dwell in you in all its richness.
>
> Col. 3:1-16

As the represenative of Christ, the confessor should direct the penitent's attention inwardly to the action and the demands of grace. The priest would do well to remind the penitent of his having been raised to life in Baptism and of his obligation then of dying to sin. Now, in the Sacrament of Penance, he must desire and be ready to realize this death to sin more and more in his daily living.

There is no denying the need, at times, for moral exhortation. I purport to clarify the relative importance of such exhortation: it should never supersede the instruction of the penitent on the internal aspects of the Sacrament. Attention to Christ's teaching role in the Sacrament will help keep the priest's admonition from being pure moralism and will likewise help the penitent consider more seriously the implications of having this Christ-life within him.

The confessional was never meant to be used as an unlighted courtroom of sheer legalism. Neither was it to be the uncomfortable counterpart to a psychoanalyst's couch. For, within its confines, the redeeming action of God takes place.

Moral teaching and psychology have their place in the confessional, but as complements to God's action for growth in faith, hope and love, in short, as adjuncts to the life of grace within the heart of the penitent. To divorce the external law, namely, what is of moral obligation, from the teaching of the internal law, *i.e.*, what Christ Himself teaches through the grace of the Holy Spirit, through His purifying action, is to leave a serious gap in the penitent's formation. In such a situation, the confessor would fall short of Christ's expectations relative to the role of His representative. It is in an effort to emphasize this point that I deliberately returned again and again to the primacy of the internal law, the primacy of the gracious action of Almighty God.

CHRIST: PHYSICIAN AND JUDGE

From the earliest times, the Fathers of the Church have called Christ "the Divine Physician," "the Divine Healer," "the Redeemer." There is a commonality in all these titles that makes them interchangeable—each connotes the idea of saving. Christ is the Physician, the Healer, the Redeemer because He saved us from our misery. Through Christ we are restored to life and to health.

Christ's role as Divine Physician is intimately linked with His role as Teacher of the New Law. As Teacher, He revealed to us the inadequacy of the Old Law. St. Paul says that He set us free from that law and from our slavery to sin under it (Rom. 8:2). However, Christ taught us a New Law, a law of love, which by its very nature, has healing and redeeming power. He taught us that this law is not one imposed from without, impinging upon the freedom of man. Rather, it is an internal law which He Himself imparts to the heart of man by making man a sharer in His life. The sharing is what brings us into contact with Christ's law marking the beginning of the saving action of love and grace in our hearts. The overlapping of roles of Teacher-Physician is obvious here.

But Christ is also our Judge, a role which can be understood only when viewed in conjunction with His role as Physician. In order to save the world, in order to function as Physician, He had first to take upon Himself the judgment due to our sins. And so He, the wholly innocent Lamb of God, consented to be judged and sentenced in our place. In so doing, He saved and healed us from the final judgment of condemnation. This is why the faithful can look forward with joy to the Second Coming of Christ, because He who will come as Judge is likewise their Redeemer.

In the Sacrament of Penance Christ heals us through the saving judgment of the cross. It is on the cross that He accepted the burden of our sins, and so to the cross we submit our sins for merciful judgment. Christ, our true Judge in the Sacrament of Penance, is the One who liberates us from our sins.

The confessor likewise participates in Christ's role as Judge. His judgment will depend on whether or not the penitent desires to be healed; at times, he will be unable to arrive at a clear decision on the case. He will then proclaim absolution and peace conditionally. In the majority of cases, however, his concern as judge will revolve around the penitent's sorrow. In order to make his judgment a worthy instrument of divine healing, he should try to explain the motives for a deeper sorrow. An effective way of arousing sorrow for sin is to direct the penitent's attention to the cross of Christ where the horror of sin is manifest. For the terrible judgment leveled at Christ and leading to His crucifixion was the result of Christ's taking our sins upon Himself. God's judgment on Christ for being found with these sins was so severe that Christ, the God-Man, cried out in fear: "My God! My God! Why have you forsaken Me?" Christ Himself, in His humanity, only discovered the full horror of sin on the cross. So might the penitent when confronted by the cross learn not only to hate sin, but to love the mercy and kindness of the crucified Redeemer. It may be that a fuller appreciation of the justice and holiness of God's law will ensue. Perhaps he will be ready to embrace more thoroughly that law in its fullness: "Love one another as I have loved you."

CHRIST THE HIGH PRIEST

We cannot gloss over the role of Christ as High Priest in the Sacrament of Penance. Christ redeems us by making Himself a victim for us, offering Himself in sacrifice to the Father. Thus he paved a new way of life in the hope of directing all our desires toward that one great demand: "hallowed be thy Name." Christ, bearing the burden of men's sins, gave glory to the Father in the name of mankind. He offered Himself as sacrifice for the glory of His Father and for our redemption.

Giving glory to God is the antithesis of sin. Sin consists in self-centeredness; conversion consists in the grateful acknowledgment that we all belong to the kingdom of priests; that our highest function is to glorify God in all things through Christ's priesthood. But in the priesthood of Christ an adoring love of God is impossible unless we offer God signs of sincere contrition and satisfaction, just as Christ once offered Himself.

In exercising his priesthood in the confessional, the confessor should adopt the attitude of adoration. This is hardly the attitude of the priest rushing an absolution so that he might get back to his breviary. Let the priest so conduct himself in the confessional as to make the penitent more aware of the fact that the celebration of this Sacrament is one of the most wonderful ways of praising God, one of the most wonderful forms of liturgical prayer.

In this Sacrament, the confessor and penitent have the opportunity of uniting in a common effort to proclaim the glory of God, the glory of His merciful and just love.

THE CONFESSOR: ALTER CHRISTUS

I introduced the chapter by stating that the role of the confessor is a blend between forgiving sins and healing souls. Having discussed the facets of Christ's role in the Sacrament:

Teacher, Physician, Judge, and Priest, I would like to return to a fuller treatment of the action of the priest.

The priest in the confessional should be ever mindful that he is performing an act of liturgy. He has the privilege of proclaiming, in the name of the Church, the wonders of God's mercy: "Give thanks to the Lord for He is good, for His mercy endures forever" (Ps. 117). As the instrument of God, He pronounces words that bring peace and renewal to the heart of the penitent. With his zeal prompting him to do all in his power to enlighten the penitent regarding Christ's action as the Prince of Peace, he will so dispose the penitent that the latter will leave eager to propagate that peace among others.

The last century found itself dominated by a legalistic spirit regarding the Sacrament of Penance. Many priests were given to believe that they were to act chiefly as judges in the confessional. As a result, confession became a sort of inquisition. It left a bitter taste for confession in the penitent's mouth. If these Catholics did not completely resent the Sacrament, many of them came to fear it and passed on this fear to their progeny. Oftentimes, the priests themselves were upset by the approach they felt compelled to adopt in the confessional. They were ashamed of the inquisitional manner and the mechanical method of judging solely on the basis of numbers. I recall an old priest telling me at one time that the feature of Heaven he would relish most would be the fact there would be no confessions to be heard. Shortly after this, to his surprise, his superiors, in consideration of his age, dispensed him from the obligation of "going into the box." When he saw me again, he expressed his delight. Congratulating him, I told him that I could surmise why he felt so good about it. I told him that he was a very kind man and that it was likely that more often than not, in the confessional, his heart engaged in a tug-of-war, finding itself torn between his natural kindness and the legalistic theology he had been taught. After recovering from the surprise, he slowly admitted that this was precisely the case.

In the past, a similar cross was borne by many priests going into the confessional because they felt intuitively that this cold impersonalism, this harping on exact numbers and details violated all the rules of reasonable psychology. Famous is the case of the great moralist August Lehmkuhl who, after having written volumes of cases, never sat in a confessional himself and even refused to hear confessions when ordered by his superior; he was too frightened.

The priest should see himself in a positive light in the confessional; he is a representative of Christ who teaches the wonders of His law through the purifying action of the Holy Spirit. Uniting himself with Christ, the priest is able to teach the wonderful paths He opens for growth in Christian life and Christian joy. Through the priest, the penitent is permitted to experience Christ as the Prince of Peace, the Divine Physician.

It might be well for each priest to meditate often on the fact that in the confessional he is to represent the Redeeming Judge. Christ's judgment of us was made as He hung dying on the cross. It was a judgment made through His love for us. Such meditations will stimulate our desire to enter the confessional to dispense Christ's merciful judgment. I can honestly say that I feel it to be a great lack in my life that in the last few years, because of my work, I have been kept from spending the hours in the confessional which I previously spent.

Dispensing the Sacrament of Penance is one of the highest functions of the priesthood: "How blessed are those who are peacemakers." In the confessional, the priest is given the opportunity to proclaim the peace of the Lord. His action as judge must be totally integrated with the action of declaring God's peace. He serves the people by teaching them the law of life, the law of the Spirit, by directing them and helping them direct themselves toward the wonderful actions of Christ.

Hugo of St. Victor says that Christ, while freeing us in the Sacrament of Penance from the knots of sin, ties us with the sweetest bonds of gratitude. That statement can only be understood if the priest sees his role as that of another Christ, another image of the heavenly Father. He is to represent Christ the great Peacemaker, the Prince of Peace, the Healer, the Redeemer who in adoring love, sacrificed Himself and redeemed us.

The priest-confessor should remain constantly aware of the fact that in the confessional he offers the penitent the opportunity to encounter the Prince of Peace.

4. THE DISPOSITION OF
THE PENITENT

Briefly stated, this chapter and the following comprise a treatise on the disposition of the penitent as a condition for absolution.

As a Sacrament, Penance serves to restore or to increase the harmony between God and man. This means that the penitent encounters Divine Truth through the message of messianic peace. It would be an abuse of the Sacrament to offer that message to men who have determinedly turned their backs on truth but who feel they can still receive the sacrament in spite of their reservations. Obviously when such persons enter the confessional, they are not aware of the fact that for the efficacious reception of this Sacrament, they have to be willing to alter their lives in accordance with God's truth. The confessor should make every effort to bring the sinner face to face with Almighty God, but in some few instances, the sinner makes any proclamation of the peace of God impossible.

It might be well at times to instruct a penitent that the most essential disposition, and the finest, is found in the words of the first beatitude: "Blessed are they who, deep in their hearts, know they are poor, because the Kingdom of

God is upon them." In brief, it defines humility. Humility impels the penitent to open his heart to the word of God and inspires him with a sense of gratitude for the gifts of the sacrament. God rewards the humble penitent in proportion to his readiness to receive the gifts of peace and joy.

Naturally, not every imperfection regarding the penitent's disposition justifies withholding the word of peace. A fundamentally good disposition may be marred to some degree by invincible ignorance, by imperfect contrition, or by a weak purpose of amendment. Such deficiencies need not disturb the confessor since one's willingness to accept God's gifts as the rule of life is subject to the law of growth. I will have more to say about these imperfections as the book progresses. One thing is certain. The presence of the confessional box in our churches is indicative of our status as pilgrims still striving toward perfection. When the priest enters the box, he does so in view of encouraging some to continue valiantly, of comforting and reviving others who have fallen by the wayside. Obvious as it may seem, braggadocios do not cluster around confessionals. No one who comes to confession should be expected to have attained the goal of perfection.

"BLESSED ARE THEY WHO . . . KNOW THEY ARE POOR"

The first beatitude furnishes us with a key to the proper understanding of the Sacrament of Penance. The Kingdom of God belongs to those who realize they are poor in spirit. A consequent obligation befalling the confessor would be to indicate to the penitent not only the direction to travel on the road to sanctity but also the distance to be covered.

The greatest obstacle to a sinner's absolution, the worst disposition he can have, is one of self-satisfaction. The self-complacent individual gravitates around the perpendicular pronoun "I" and the twofold love of God and neighbor is seen from a deflected angle. Self-satisfaction precludes humility, a realistic appraisal of self in relation to God and fellowman. As an illustration of this fact, we have only to contrast our Lord's treatment of the poor and ignorant sinner with his treatment of the Pharisees who boasted of their knowledge of the law and condemned others for not keeping it as they did. These Pharisees received only the scorn of Christ. The sinners who acknowledged in their hearts how truly poor and in need of redemption they were met with His graciousness and infinite mercy.

No virtue is so necessary for the penitent in the Sacrament of Penance as the virtue of humility. Humility gives a man a healthy and deep consciousness of his sins. The concern of every priest, then, should be to so preach, catechize and celebrate the Sacrament of Penance, to so dialogue with the penitent as to lead him to a fuller comprehension of the first beatitude. This task can be accomplished only by patient guidance and instruction. Insofar as a man recognizes his poverty in spirit, he will recognize what sin really is. Then his concern about sin will hinge not so much on material integrity and enumeration of sins, but rather on the great injustice and misery caused by offending God. Humility will enkindle his desire to draw closer to, in fact, to meet his Healer, his Redeemer. My mission life has provided me with many enriching experiences to prove this. I would like to share one with you.

Shortly after World War II, I was assigned to preach missions to certain refugees from East Germany and Rumania and other such countries. Many of these poor people had lived in areas where access to the Sacraments had been difficult, if not impossible. But now, hearing again the words of Christ's Gospel, they longed to return to Him. Some had not experienced the peace of the Sacrament of Penance for ten, twenty, and even forty or fifty years. I had not the slightest doubt that the subjective guilt of these people was greatly diminished due to their ignorance of the nature of sin. I was edified by their humility, by their recognition of the fact that they were truly "poor in spirit." At no time did I expect such basic humility to lend them an instantaneous knowledge regarding the confession of their sins. These people had not discovered or did not remember the details of the moral law. They had only discovered that their separation from Christ caused a terrible lack in their lives. Many would confess in this fashion: "Father, I have not killed anyone. I didn't steal. I was an honest man, or at least I haven't stolen property from any poor people. I have sinned against charity, but I was not so very bad." But I knew that a recognition of all the things that were not right in their lives would only come gradually; that their humility which had just taken root was subject to the law of growth. For the next few years I returned to these people to teach them and to hear their confessions, and on each visit, I marked their gradual progress regarding what is right and what is wrong. I particularly noticed their deepening realization of how sad it is to remain away from the Lord for any length of time. In fact, many of them had several times travelled great distances to go to Mass and receive the Sacraments.

Perhaps the finest example of how the first beatitude functions in our lives can be drawn from what we know about the confessions of the saints. Oftentimes, these saints were steeped in sorrow about things that many of us do not even consider wrong. But their humility had given them a delicate awareness of what it meant not to follow the path to the Kingdom of God wholeheartedly. When a penitent realizes how poor in spirit he is, the confessor has a good sign that the kingdom of God is already upon that man. Such a man will feel the need to strive harder, to encounter still more perfectly the Divine Physician.

It belongs to the confessor to awaken this humility in the heart of the penitent. The confessor should instruct him to an awareness of the progress that is still to be made; inform him that the Kingdom of God means using the present opportunity to the fullest, that every gift of God, natural and supernatural, is a call from the Kingdom.

THE LAW OF GROWTH

The kingdom of heaven is like a grain of mustard seed, which . . . is the smallest of all the seeds; but when it grows up it is larger than any herb and becomes a tree. . . .

Mt. 13:31-32

It is really our view of the Kingdom of God that is subject to the law of growth. Many of the Gospel parables attest to the fact that growth is a necessary phenomenon in man's acceptance of that Kingdom. This maturation, though in some respects like the growth of plants, is much more than what a horticultural analogy can suggest. It is not just a vitalism taking place without our free will. The Kingdom of God itself appeals to us to grow in liberty, in freedom and in responsibility. But each can grow only according to the measure of grace which God bestows on him, in accordance with the present opportunity. The parable of the talents illustrates this truth: each man was expected to use well whatever he had received; one had received five talents, another two, and still another only one. Each must be ready to take the modest step that the present opportunity permits him. Only then will a man open up new horizons for himself.

Christianity is life and where life is there is a need for growth: growth in overcoming obstacles, growth in the struggle against the base impulses of lower nature, growth away from self-centeredness. We must accept and respect this law of growth within us. We have to accept joyfully the present opportunity offered to us and use it to the fullest.

As a confessor, the priest must educate the faithful to sanctity. This education will involve urging the penitent to make the most of the present opportunity that God offers him. It will mean restraining him from outlandish goals proscribed by his present condition, and helping him capitalize on God's present gift of grace. As always, Our Lord serves as Exemplar to confessors as he accommodates his teaching to the readiness and to the pace of the penitents. In the Gospel, by His many miracles and signs, Our Lord prepared His disciples for that day when He would ask them: "Who do you say the Son of Man is?" And it was only when they knew that He was the Messiah, the Anointed One, that He began to teach them the great mystery of His death and resurrection. This last lesson called for the greatest patience on the part of Our Lord. But even after He had fully instructed them and was celebrating the great sign of the New Covenant with them, He still said: "I have much to tell you yet, but the

burden would be too heavy for you just now." In so speaking,
Our Lord made the Apostles attentive, urging them to even
greater docility, assuring them that they would receive the
Holy Spirit in an abundant manner.

In the manner of Christ, the confessor must exhort his
penitents to watchfulness. Having ascertained their readiness,
he must help them find the next step, the step that is possible
here and now. He must not impose upon them ideals that
go beyond their stage of development, nor should he discourage them from taking courageous and heroic steps when
he is convinced that they are called to these by God. As confessor, a priest can likewise fail by demanding too little of
the penitent. I have in mind the confessor who deters a
penitent already acquainted with a religious experience, who
feels that God is urging him on to greater generosity. The
confessor of such a penitent would be ill-advised to persuade
him that he has no legal obligation to go further, that all is
right because no law requires more of him. The confessor
should encourage his penitent along the road of generosity.
In fact, he might even encourage some penitents to do penance for their former lack of generosity and lack of vigilance.
Being a confessor demands far more than a legalistic approach
to moral theology. Legalism caters to routine and conformity,
not to the individual.

A PATRON OF CONFORMITY

In Greek mythology, there is a famous legendary figure by
the name of Procrustes. I like to refer to him as a Patron of
Conformity. Procrustes was an innkeeper who loved to lure
guests to his establishment. Once there, the guests fell victim
to Procrustes' greatest eccentricity: his compulsive need for
absolute order. This compulsiveness extended even to a regulation regarding sleeping facilities. Each guest had to fill to
capacity the bed in which he slept. The small guests had to
be stretched to meet the size of the bed. The tall guests'
fate was even worse; Procrustes would hack off the head, and

if need be, cut off feet and legs to adapt the guest to the length of the iron bed.

The Procrustean myth is very old, but the story is not as "unreal" as one would believe. Unhappily, we sometimes find a present-day Procrustes in our confessionals. He is the legalist who offers a rigid bed of static juridical morality. He stretches the limbs of those penitents who are still too tiny and small with the stock imperative: "You have to keep the rules I have learned in moral theology. If you don't, I cannot give you absolution." Those who have outgrown the confines of such a static theology, those who have received and are now trying to double a gift of five talents, he advises to slow down, or at least to ignore feelings of culpability with regard to higher goals: "You need not strive so hard." Or, "You need not strive any longer; maintain what you have." In so speaking, he pares down their aspirations and leaves their dynamism to die out.

The Procrustean confessor is a staunch proponent of external, static law. He fails to interpet the law of life, the law of the Spirit who gives life in Christ Jesus. He is impatient with those who do not measure up to his static law; he is overbearing with those who have attained or outgrown the stature of his juridicism.

What I am saying in no way denies the need for guidelines in morality. It is not Procrustean to demand limits or boundaries, but we must know that these limits are not the whole of life, that they are only one aspect of the Law of God. My objection is to the confessor who concentrates solely on these limits or laws. Rather, the confessor's preoccupation should be to orient the penitent away from the limits, helping him learn to fly so that he may someday soar. This orientation is a gradual process that comes about by demanding from the penitent only what is possible for him now. Every confessor is duty-bound to recognize and respect this law of growth. The question that would follow logically then, would be: "Is this penitent striving? Is he seeking a better life and a deeper knowledge of the Lord?"

INVINCIBLE IGNORANCE

Our Lord exercised the greatest patience with His apostles.
He did not impose on them from the very beginning an elaborate code demanding, "Now swear allegiance to every single
point." Instead, He prepared them step by step even in such
fundamental matters as questions of faith. The Church herself is continually proposing to us Christ's example of patience, of painful step-by-step progress. For instance, today she
continues to define dogmas that were not known explicitly in
her early history. Yet, the Church is as orthodox today as
she was then, and was as orthodox then as she is today.

As priests and confessors, we must imitate the approach
of Christ and His Church. Penitents who come to us from
an unhealthy, contaminated environment cannot be expected
to abolish a heritage of traits and disorders instantaneously.

At this point, I would like to broach the subject of invincible ignorance as an instance where we must gradually lead
the penitent on to perfection. Here I lean very heavily on
the tradition of St. Alphonsus who has been declared the
Patron of Confessors. One of Alphonsus' chief interests as
a moral theologian was the question of invincible ignorance
(for example, see *Praxis Confessarii*, n. 8).

St. Alphonsus maintained that cases of invincible ignorance
were not uncommon. He found such ignorance even with
regard to the general expression of God's law. When he began
preaching missions to the abandoned and ignorant shepherds
of Naples, he became more deeply concerned with the problem. He came in contact with penitents who were filled with
good will and longed for God's merciful justice. But many of
them could not yet have borne the instant and full burden
of the law, both natural and positive. They were willing to
learn, but even after some instruction, they did not understand all the exigencies of the Gospel. If St. Alphonsus had
judged these people strictly, according to the moralists of his
time, who were generally rigorists, he would have had to
refuse many of these poor people absolution. For the leading

theology was probabiliorism (different from today's) and, after the suppression of the Society of Jesus, this had become particularly rigoristic. In St. Alphonsus' day, the probabiliorists judged any doubt, whether of natural or positive law, big or small, in favor of the law. They did not question the existence or out-datedness of the law. Everything fell in the law's favor and the people were strictly judged and counselled accordingly. St. Alphonsus opposed this rigorism and held to a mitigated and moderate stand called equiprobabilism,[1] in spite of the trend of the time in Italy and in a great part of Europe. Emphasizing that allowance must be made for penitents laboring under invincible ignorance, Alphonsus appealed to his own confrères to help him search out arguments from authority to support his views. And although St. Alphonsus himself stated good reasons for his views, and found a sufficient tradition behind him, many, even among his confrères, considered him a revolutionary. Father DeMeo, a confrère and one of the most learned men of his time, wrote him a letter now found in the Redemptorist archives, in which he says that should Alphonsus continue to maintain that there can still be invincible ignorance among people who have already been taught, he would run the risk of having the Redemptorist Congregation suppressed. He told St. Alphonsus that many considered him suspect. But Alphonsus wrote back: "I prefer rather the suppression of my beloved Congregation for which I am ready to die than the imposition on souls of a burden they cannot carry. I have a

[1] Stated as concisely as possible, St. Alphonsus' system of equiprobabilism is concerned with two kinds of doubt: the doubt of law and the doubt of fact. In a doubt of law, the position to be followed is either one of liberty or of obligation depending on which has the stronger claim. If there is a strict doubt regarding the existence or the promulgation of a law, then liberty holds the stronger title. However, if the strict doubt concerns whether or not the law has ceased, then the law obliges. The doubt of fact has two aspects to it: (1) whether it concerns a principal fact, e.g., whether I made a vow or did not make a vow; (2) or an accessory fact, e.g., did I use full deliberation when I made the vow. In the former case, you apply the principles of a doubt of law. In the latter case, the principle is that when there is a strict doubt, an accessory fact is presumed to have been correctly performed.

responsibility for the Church, for souls." When we recall that there was no such science as psychology or sociology in Alphonsus' day, that he could refer to no scientific study revealing how much a man's judgment is influenced by his environment, we get a clearer notion of the greatness of this man. Cardinal Newman's distinctions regarding abstract knowledge, which is taught, and the concrete realization of this knowledge were yet to come.

St. Alphonsus' opinion was suspect in his own day. To some, it seemed that he was giving the penitent permission to continue sinning. However, the truth was that Alphonsus recognized that certain penitents, wishing to return to God, cannot be expected to run before they can walk. And so, in the interest of restoring these penitents to the order of God, Alphonsus chose silence on issues that the penitent could not hope to resolve at this particular point in his progress. It was not a matter of asserting that the wrong was right. It was simply a judgment that, though there was much to tell this penitent, the latter could not bear it just yet.

A confessor, then, who tries to prepare the penitent by educating him toward a deeper spiritual life is not a laxist because he does not demand full knowledge from the outset. At times, recognizing the penitent's invincible ignorance, he will be silent on some particular matter or matters. He makes the penitent aware that, in general, several things are lacking to him which he will come to know and understand later. He does not tell him: "It's all right. You continue acting that way." Rather, he indicates certain directions in which the penitent can make progress. This is what is meant by seizing the present opportunity.

Spiritual life has sometimes been compared to a warfare. I am not particularly fond of the analogy, but it may prove useful here where we are considering the confessor's approach to the penitent who cannot yet bear the full burden of the law. Directly to storm an enemy is not always the wisest way to win a battle. In World War I, the Germans attacked Verdun, but the French bravely defended it. Close to a million lives were lost in the battle, and neither side claimed a victory. By World War II, the lesson had seeped in. The German army did not attempt to seize Verdun by a direct take-over. Instead, it skirted the well-fortified city, keeping to the right and left of it, rendering all its strong weapons useless. Shortly afterwards, finding itself behind the German front line, Verdun surrendered. So too, if the confessor instructs the invincibly ignorant penitent in the joy of the faith with regard to points that the present opportunity makes assailable, he will find that the day will soon come when this penitent can absorb the clear teaching against a well-entrenched problem, teaching which he would have rejected earlier.

The approach I have suggested here is neither rigoristic nor lax. It avoids a static moralism in favor of the dynamic. It recognizes the law of growth as well as the present opportunity. However, the approach makes strong demands on the confessor who needs to establish a deep sympathy and solidarity with his penitent. He is no longer simply a measuring rod determining the inches and millimeters of guilt and sin. His experience will help him determine how far he can lead a penitent to a stronger spirituality, when he can teach him effectively, and when it is time to change tactics or rechannel energies. This method is quite different from situational ethics. Because of its prevalence in America, I have deemed it useful to state my position in relation to it and am therefore devoting the following sub-section to its development. I will then relate the situation ethics to the topic under consideration, namely, invincible ignorance.

SITUATION ETHICS

Dangerous forms of so-called Situation Ethics are current in our time. Roughly, there are two kinds of erroneous situation ethics. The more modern form is expressed by Joseph Fletcher in his book, *Situation Ethics, the New Morality.* Fletcher does not deny the existence of moral laws; in fact, he advises Christians to consider these norms carefully before acting. However, he goes on to say that since no moral law has any absolute value, a Christian, for the sake of love, can seek his self-fulfillment and true expression of love for neighbor in a way opposed to the general moral principles. Fletcher stresses the point that such a Christian must simply be careful that he does this out of true love, a love which is sometimes called "agapeic" or unselfish love, but generally explained as a form of pragmatism or utilitarianism. Fletcher goes so far as to say that a person, in certain circumstances, may even commit adultery or rape, moderately practice promiscuity, publicly disown God and the Church, so long as he has the right intention. The law of love, in Fletcher's opinion, might even justify dropping an atomic bomb on an open town. But I answer that Fletcher's concept of love is structureless. The fundamental principle of Christian ethics is not simply love in this pragmatic or utilitarian sense. The fundamental principle of Christian ethics is "to do in love what *truth* demands."

The older form of situation ethics erects its altars to human precepts and human traditions with a total carelessness with regard to fundamental divine commandments and a blindness to the exigencies of the natural law and of present opportunities conforming to "what truth demands." As a result, obedience to a "legal situation," a slavish application of human laws, is thought to justify the transgression of the law of God which is written into the heart and mind of man. This age-old form of ethics of situation does not distinguish between the letter and the spirit of the laws of the Church. It opposes the principles of *epikeia* which would provide a fulfillment of the absolute laws of God and of changeable human laws in view of the spirit of the Gospel. It opposes the natural law insofar as it would show no regard for the exigency of the true nature of the person and the community. In short, this form of situation ethics interests itself solely with the mechanical application of human laws. It was this very thing that Christ condemned in the Pharisees: "Then the Scribes and Pharisees from Jerusalem came to Him saying, 'Why do your disciples break the old, established tradition?' . . . But He answered, 'And why do you transgress the commandment of God because of your tradition?'" (Mt. 15:2-3). Or again, ". . . in vain do they worship me, teaching as doctrine the precepts of men" (Mt. 15:9). Finally, Christ said to His Apostles, "Why do you not understand that it was not of bread I said, 'Beware of the leaven of Pharisees and Sadducees?' Then they understood that he bade them beware not of the leaven of bread, but of the teaching of the Pharisees and Sadducees" (Mt. 16:11-12).

Modern situation ethics is a reaction against the older, legalistic form of situation ethics. Both forms, however, are insensitive to distinctions. Where the legalistic situation ethics makes man-made laws (positive human laws) immobile by refusing to recognize (1) the distinction between Eternal Law in God's Wisdom and the ever inadequate expression of that law in human terms and (2) the distinction between positive human laws and those moral exigencies which express the very calling of the human person, the modern situation ethics confuses the flexible character of positive laws with a structureless concept of love in which no principle is considered absolutely true and always valid.

Situation ethics, then, in its pejorative sense, refers to a standard of conduct which permits a person who has or could have full knowledge, as opposed to one in invincible ignorance, to seek his happiness and salvation outside the golden circle of Divine Law. It is as "static" and "minimum-oriented" as the legalistic morality.

The approach advocated in this chapter, however, is a "dynamic" one, moving the person ever onward toward a fuller realization of Christian life. In our case, it involves penitents who are striving to find their place within the order of God, but who, because of environment or some other extenuating circumstance, are incapable at present of leaping into the center of that circle. Confessors, aware of a person's invincible ignorance, should strive to motivate the penitent to a deeper faith, a greater hope, with the energies of the Gospel of joy and love. They should help him establish a personal relationship with God, a more personal prayer life, and encourage him to exercise fraternal charity.

CONQUERING IGNORANCE

What I have said above should not preclude shaking up or shocking a man who is simply ignorant of the extent of Divine Law. A confessor should be particularly persistent when he is dealing with a penitent who has received five talents. Such penitents might be priests or sisters who may be lax in fraternal charity, in pastoral patience or in the fundamental pastoral approach of watchfulness. The confessor must sometimes shock them into a realization of what their life demands even at the risk of their friendship. But his motive must be one of charity, always taking care to act at the most opportune moment and in the most humble solidarity with his penitent.

In cases where the penitent's ignorance is a great danger to others, where perhaps his example will contaminate others, the confessor would be obliged to take a still greater risk in shocking him by laying the truth before him. In this instance, the confessor looks to the good of the whole Church.

PSYCHOLOGY OF LEARNING

There is a definite need for the priest to study psychology and sociology if he is to be an effective guide in the direction of penitents. Psychology will make him aware of the frustrations, conflicts and maladjustments prevalent in this day and age. Sociology will reveal the impact of the environment on the people. Both will serve to bridle his impulse at times to say: "You have to do this and if you don't obey, you're showing your bad will."

Finally, there seems to be a need for some sort of common pastoral planning which, perhaps, could be achieved through Episcopal Conferences. One of the aims of the Conferences could be to try to reduce the inconsistencies of practice that people meet within the confessional. It is not uncommon to hear the people themselves complaining that Father So-

and-So says that this is perfectly all right whereas Father Such-and-Such finds it objectionable and wrong. Inconsistencies of this nature tend to make people suspect that perhaps the priest in the confessional does not represent the Church. These people do not understand that there are areas in theology that are open to different opinions. However, each priest should seek to explain as clearly as possible the doctrine of the Church and then let his penitent see that his counsel is based on an interpretation of that doctrine.

The confessor cannot do everything. Unfortunately, people sometimes demand too much from him; he cannot change all the effects of their environment on their mind and will by a two-minute exhortation in the confessional. Yet, the confessor can do a great deal for people if he uses what I have called a dynamic approach. With patience, he can find out the possibilities of the penitent, and with an alert psychology, he will be careful not to impose too much on the penitent at any single time. His task is to help the penitent strive for and move towards perfection. It is an arduous task calling for great patience and humility on the part of the confessor. Finally, the goal of the teacher in the New Covenant is not to hand down decisions for another person, but rather to help him attain the maturity possible for him so that more and more he will be in a position to make his own decisions.

5. CONTRITION

The point has already been made that the most decisive action in the Sacrament of Penance is what Christ does through the power of the Holy Spirit. The proclamation of the good tidings of Messianic peace brings men to a deep understanding of the heinousness of their sins. The same proclamation moves men to repentance. At the risk of being repetitious, let me refer back to the account from the Book of Nehemiah: as the priests read and explained the Book of the Covenant to the people, they gradually understood the message; they began to weep and repent. From this repentance there sprang forth the joy of the Lord.

In the Sacrament of Penance, the most visible result of Christ's action is the sinner's repentance which renews him in his very spirit: "Blessed are the sorrowful. They will receive consolation" (Mt. 5:4). For the good tidings of Christ are what makes men repent, and from the act of repentance springs the "joy of the Lord that is our strength." That is why the priest must celebrate the liturgy of this great Sacrament in such a way that his ministry becomes the active instrument of the Holy Spirit who renews the heart and mind of the penitent.

There will be times when the confessor will have to determine whether a penitent has sufficient sorrow just as Our Lord sought to determine the faith of the father whose child was possessed by a demon. Our Lord asked the man: "Do you have faith?" The man replied: "I do believe, Lord. Help me where my faith falls short" (Mk. 9:24). The confessor's efforts with penitents should aim at awakening in them that sorrow which leads to peace and greater love. This takes one over and beyond the simple formula of sorrow. Leading the penitent to a realization of his sins by reminding him of the great motives which arise from faith in the good news is by far more important than moral reproof.

Sorrow is the penitent's basic disposition for growth. It is not something static which, once attained, leaves one satisfied. Sorrow submits to the process of growth. It is always within the confessor's task, then, to help the penitent come to a more perfect sorrow. As suggested in the *Rituale Romanum*, the confessor should always endeavor to move each penitent to a deeper sorrow by appealing to the motives for contrition: the mercy and the loving justice of God.

For those who have remained in the state of grace, in the love of God, it is relatively easy to make an act of contrition. They are "ontologically" disposed and the grace of the Sacrament further facilitates such an act. But for the penitent in mortal sin, an act of perfect contrition is a miracle. When such a penitent does elicit an act of perfect contrition, we are faced with the powerful action of the Holy Spirit creating light and life where there was darkness.

The penitent who has been living in mortal sin will generally come to the confessional with an imperfect contrition, or, as I will refer to it hereafter, attrition. The priest's manner of celebrating the sacrament should help the penitent become better disposed, at least to the point where he gratefully and joyfully receives the peace of God. Commonly, theology accepts the Sacrament of Penance as valid even if the penitent attains only an imperfect sorrow, providing he removes the obstacles that would interfere with the renewing action of the Holy Spirit. But the fruit of the Spirit is "love, joy, peace, kindness" (Gal. 5:22), not slavish fear. Neither the confessor nor penitent should be satisfied with attrition. Faith in the dynamic presence of the Spirit of Christ believes in a possibility for a deeper and more liberating sorrow. Attrition is good insofar as it brings one a step nearer to that sorrow which is motivated by gratitude, love and peace.

There is an old scholastic dictum: "The Sacrament of Penance transforms attrition into contrition" (*Sacramentum poenitentiae ex attrito facit contritum*). Is this meant only in the hidden judgment of God or is it a real transformation of man's mind and heart? Is there a kind of "ontological" presence of contrition and charity without a dynamic power to renew the way of thinking and acting? I think that God's word calls for real change in the whole reality of man although this may meet with obstacles of a psychological nature. The least we can do is to try to remove those obstacles which can be removed and strive toward a faith that is filled with love, one that finds expression in the love of neighbor.

The proclamation of threatening motives, such as eternal damnation, can lead the way toward contrition only if these truths are presented in their full theological context, *i.e.*, by his mortal sin and lack of penance, man rejects God's holy and earnest love for him. Fear of hell can become a cry toward God, a desire for reassurance of the beatifying love of God. The humble confession in view of God's mercy and the assuring word of peace manifest God's power to grant us a new spirit. Normally, then, when the liturgy is correctly celebrated and the Word of Peace has been communicated to the penitent, he now becomes capable of an act of perfect love of God. If he fails to make this act of perfect love, then he fails to obtain the full fruit of the Sacrament of Penance.

In order, then, to lead men from attrition to contrition, the confessor should remove threatening motives of a selfish nature and suggest or accentuate the positive and greater motives of gratitude and praise to the Lord because of His endless mercy. Perfect contrition stems from appreciation of the goodness of God who is all merciful and has shown his love in Jesus Christ: "Give thanks to the Lord, for he is good, for his mercy endures forever" (Ps. 117). If the aura of the sacrament, then, is a celebration of God's love and mercy, it is

easy—in man's real life and with the help of God—to attain
to true contrition. It is then the grace of the sacrament that
transforms the imperfect sorrow of attrition to the perfect
sorrow of contrition. However, this transformation from attrition to contrition is not done magically. True, it comes
about through the acting word of God, but it is related to the
priest's proclamation of the good tidings; the confessor's role
here is essential. The priest must attend to his function of
helping the penitent deepen his sorrow. In the communal
celebration of the Sacrament of Penance, the whole community contributes greatly through the active participation toward growth of love of God and contrition.

PURPOSE OF AMENDMENT

The penitent's purpose of amendment is the rich harvest of
his sorrow. It is completely dependent upon his sorrow for it is
impossible for a man to make the transition from, say, mortal sin to life in Christ simply by a firm purpose. If a man
has incurred a number of debts, it is not enough that he
promise not to incur any more. He must pay the debts he
has already contracted or, if unable to liquidate, be excused
by his creditor.

In relation to salvation, it is impossible psychologically and
ontologically to make a firm, efficacious purpose of amendment without repenting. Before a man proposes to change
his ways, he must be made to see how inept and sinful those
ways were, how wrong it was to say "no" to a call from God.
Only a humble recognition of one's wrongness will invite God
to create in him the possibilities of a new approach and to
open up a new path of life for him.

As a practice for confessors, I would suggest that where he
finds a man still attached to his sins, one not yet sincere in
his purpose of amendment, the priest's course of action should
not be simply a threat to withhold absolution. He should attempt to stir in the penitent's heart, as well as in his own, a
sincere sorrow for sin, perhaps by reciting some appropriate
spontaneous prayer with him. It may be the only way for a

confessor to reap the harvest of a firm purpose of amendment from his penitent.

ASSESSING THE PURPOSE OF AMENDMENT

In judging a penitent's purpose of amendment, the confessor would do well to keep in mind that even here the law of growth finds application. He will meet with some penitents who, while they are not scrupulous regarding the integrity of confession, are extremely precise regarding the statement of their resolution to amend. They might say, "Father, I cannot honestly promise that I'll never do this again. I still feel very much attached to it." It would be unfair immediately to conclude that such penitents have left the path of true sorrow. Very often, these are persons who are disturbed by the fact that their lower nature still craves satisfaction. They wish with their whole hearts that they could make the necessary promise, but their sincerity forbids it. They will not promise what they fear they cannot keep.

St. Augustine faced similar problems with Christians who wanted in the most sincere way to give themselves over totally to God's will, but who recognized their own weakness. They would tell the saint, "God asks us to do what is impossible for us." Augustine resolved their doubts with the Gospel of the merciful Samaritan. He would tell them how the Samaritan brought the poor, beaten wayfarer to an inn and paid for the man's room, and how he recognized that this man, even after the care given him, would still need a period of recuperation: "Take care of him, and whatsoever you shall spend over and above, I, at my return, will repay you" (Lk. 10:35). So it is with penitents. There are some who cannot rise immediately from their sickness, but need a longer cure before rising to full justice. Therefore Augustine would tell them (and he is quoted by the Council of Trent) to do what they could and pray hard for what they could not yet accomplish, because God does not ask the impossible of his creatures. There is no question of St. Augustine presuming that a short prayer always suffices to obtain a total change. He is trying to indicate that if a man is sincere, tries to do what he can, and at the same time prays, "Help me, O Lord, where my own freedom falls short," while he may not strictly be fulfilling the whole law, he is nonetheless, by his attitude, complying with God's command. For the moment, the Lord does not ask more from such a man.

I do not believe that one priest would ask another in confession to promise not to sin against fraternal charity in the future. Each knows how difficult this would be. Perhaps a saint could make such a promise. Yet, there are confessors who ask penitents living in difficult situations never to fall into a certain sin again. Some ask married people, for example, to vow or promise never again to yield to selfishness in the marriage act. Honest people will be hesitant about such a promise because they realize it may be impossible to keep. What the confessor might ask—it is only a matter of rephrasing—is that his penitent *try* not to commit this sin again.

The total situation of the penitent must come under consideration in the confessor's counselling. I will treat this at length when dealing with cases of recidivism and those in the habit of sinning (*consuetudinarii*). Psychology plays an important role in the guidance of such men.

A confessor is bound to meet with cases where absolution cannot be given immediately. But even in such cases, the confessor can still offer the sinner some consolation by proclaiming the peace of God, not in a sacramental way, but as a brother in Christ and as a preacher of the Gospel: "Do what you can now and pray hard to obtain the strength for what you are yet unable to do. The Lord is merciful to you. He accepts your good will and your praise." Far from laxness, this is a tremendous incentive for one to continue to be sincere and to pray.

In other cases, where the penitent is doubtful about his ability to conquer this sin in the future, the confessor might say: "If you are sincere in trying to do what you can, and if you continue to pray for what you cannot do yet, you can be sure that you are walking in the peace of the Lord." Prodigal sons returning to God from a great distance cannot be expected to adopt all the customs and mannerisms of the children of God. They come back to God as the product of a particular environment, and it is impossible for them to extricate themselves and fully counteract all the harmful influences that were internalized over the years. It takes time. Even so, the prodigal is welcomed back without delay; he is welcomed by a Father who runs out to him, kisses him and prepares a great feast in his honor. The kind reception tendered him will itself inspire him to do his very best, and this simply out of gratitude, without the need for great moral rebukes. As in the Gospel, let the penitent feel how much joy there is in heaven over his repentance. This will prove to be a great inducement for him to renounce past evil attachments and, in general, to guard against jeopardizing this obvious show of friendship and love.

The penitent being compared to the prodigal is now within sight of the Father. He has travelled a great distance and, like the prodigal son, has had to overcome, not simply his feelings of great guilt, but likewise a fear proportionate to—and in some cases far exceeding—that guilt. The fact that he is returning at all indicates that he has seen the foolishness of his ways. It does not mean, however, that he has a panoramic view of all that he must do to make his return complete. I am convinced that it would be imprudent, to say the least, to greet such a penitent with a barrage of demands regarding points that are beyond the scope of his present vision. Again, I am stressing the idea of growth. First, draw him away and sustain him from those failings that are in clear view. An example may serve to illustrate the method I am advocating.

In some parts of the world, particularly rural areas, there is a tendency to label certain forms of hatred or enmity as "noble." Very often, the same people who allow, even praise, this lack of charity would stand firm against contemporary suggestions regarding the innocence of premarital sex and other immoralities. Were they to commit a sin against the sixth commandment, they would humbly admit their guilt and show a sincere desire to change. But their vision of true Christianity is limited. I know of a particular case where a divorced man lay dying and wanted, more than anything else, to be reconciled with his wife for the injustices he had done her. The man's sister rushed off to the home of the former wife, who seemed to be a devout, practicing Catholic. To her embarrassment, the sister of the dying man was refused admittance into the house, being forced to speak to her sister-in-law from the street. The sister-in-law stood at the window listening. Her reply was simple: "I am a woman of character," she said. "I have no intention of so much as setting foot in that house, much less of forgiving him." How does the priest deal with such a penitent? The priest himself is quite aware of the place of charity among the virtues. The Sermon on the Mount (Mt. 5:43-48) pivots on compassionate love of neighbor, regardless of whether or not the neighbor is deserving of such love. There is no doubt that the priest is obliged, in the confessional, to urge his penitents on to charity. Yet, could the priest, hearing the story I just related being confessed by the wife, tell her that unless she immediately resolved to visit her former husband and assure him of her forgiveness her confession was of no avail? This woman has been brought up to believe in the justice of her refusal and a few moments in the confessional will not alter the training of a lifetime. As I see it, she should be admonished about her obligations to charity, but not pressed to a point that exceeds her present understanding; it is an emotion-laden issue for this penitent and her vision is blurred. In the exhortation, let the priest urge her to acts of virtue in areas where she recognizes weakness and is ready to exert efforts; she should be encouraged and even obliged, through an appropriate penance, to pray for greater readiness to forgive. Basically, the principle I am invoking here is familiar to all as "Make haste slowly."

For the sake of clarity, I would like to offer one more example. Let us consider the case of the woman who comes to the priest in confession and admits a strong personal enmity between herself and a certain co-worker. The priest, through questioning, finds that the reason for this deep bitterness rests on various suspicions: "I never liked the way she'd say good morning to me. She always seems to be looking down her nose," or "She's always trying so hard to please the boss and be noticed by the others. I think she might be trying to steal my job," or "She's so conceited that I can't stand her." I think that this particular case might be handled in the following manner, keeping in mind what I have said earlier about the law of growth:

PRIEST: Would you be willing, as a penance, to pray each day for this particular woman, until you can greet her in a friendly manner?

PENITENT: But Father, my dislike for her is so deep, I can't even say that I want to see her get to Heaven. If she treats me properly, I'll treat her properly.

PRIEST: Would you at least be willing to pray for her?

PENITENT: No, Father, I don't think I could be sincere in praying for her.

PRIEST: Then, at least pray for yourself. Perhaps you're in greater need of conversion than she is. Would you accept as penance to pray daily until the next confession: "Lord forgive me my hard judgments. Lord make me kinder"?

The attitude reflected here is one of understanding, one that suggests to the penitent means of moving in the direction of Christ.

A penitent's acceptance or refusal of a penance reveals a great deal regarding the penitent's purpose of amendment. And if a penitent is unwilling to make even the slightest movement toward love of neighbor, then it is hard to see how a confessor can properly declare God's peace and salvation on him.

PENITENTIAL GROWTH

A penitent may be described as reasonably well disposed when he is ready to accept a penance proportionate to his confession of sins. But it would be psychologically and pastorally wrong to maintain as an inflexible principle that those penitents who have stayed away for a long time and have serious sins to confess must receive a commensurate penance. As a young priest, I was sent into a parish where I was not known; the pastor inquired as to how I intended to handle confessions in which the penitent had been away for a year or more. Prudently, I believe, I turned the question back to him and he suggested his own method: "First," he said, "I begin with a strong reprimand. Let him think that I'm angry. Then I give a big penance." I wondered about this manner and decided, before I entered the confessional, that I would try a different approach. I did my best to make the penitent aware that I accepted him and his humble effort. When I found that the penitent obviously appreciated the kindness shown, I suggested that he take advantage more frequently of this wonderful Sacrament. I dismissed each with words of encouragement and a suitable penance. The psychology behind this method is quite simple: who wants to return to a place where he has been treated harshly?

The prodigal's father ran out to the roadway to meet his errant son and bring him home. A penitent such as the prodigal, coming to God from a great distance, will find it most difficult to accept the idea of frequenting the Sacraments, particularly Penance, if he receives the heat of anger instead of the warmth of welcome.

I have been careful above to state that I gave a "suitable" penance to each penitent, not in opposition to, but as a necessary qualification of, the "big penance" recommended by my one-time pastor. There are times when "big penances" should be dispensed and others when they should not. Ever mindful of the law of growth, the confessor seeks to make a prudential judgment in each instance as to the efficacy of a greater or lighter penance. In some cases, the penitent himself may request a "bigger" penance. I recall a certain penitent who returned to the Church after a forty-year absence. He had been a very convinced Communist. While he had done a great deal of good struggling to better social conditions for others, he likewise had done a great deal against the Church and his own conscience. In weighing the entire case, I decided in favor of a lighter penance. The penitent answered me, "Father, I won't accept that penance. I've brought here a heavy burden of sins and guilt. I want to make a more suitable reparation." I was delighted with his straightforwardness. I had obviously underestimated him. His response disclosed a much more sensitive character already being influenced by the grace of God. It would have been wrong on my part to insist that the penance I had at first offered was truly sufficient.

At other times, when I doubt the extent of a penitent's generosity, I offer a lighter penance prefaced by my fear of overburdening him. As tactfully as I can, I attempt to make him aware of the disproportion between the penance and the guilt. "God Himself will take care of things if a greater penance is needed." Hearteningly, many of the penitents react by saying, "Father, please, I would prefer a bigger penance."

To explain my position further regarding the apportioning of penances, I would refer the reader to the Council of Trent.[1] Trent insisted on some proportion between the sin and the penance. However, in explaining this, it stated that the pastoral aspect of confession must likewise be given consideration. Let the penance be assigned that will be in accordance with "what is helpful for these people." And so, sometimes we must hedge on the idea of proportion in order to perform the greatest pastoral good. This is not hard to accept when we recognize the law of growth and progress. Some penitents simply are not prepared to meet the demands of even a congruous justice because, having long been separated from God, their knowledge of God has suffered. Their sensitivity to the seriousness of offending an all-holy God has been blunted. Only later on, when their sense of balance has been restored, when they realize the goodness of God, will they respond properly.

Since I have made several references to the story of the Prodigal Son, I would like to conclude this chapter by retelling the parable of the long-offending sinner. The prodigal, separated from his loving father for a long period of time, obviously had forgotten the magnanimous nature of the man. For, when the prodigal decided to return, he expected he would be taken back, not as a son, but as his father's servant. We can imagine his surprise on seeing his father running out to meet him, arms outstretched, greeting him and leading

[1] Sessio XIV, cap. 8. Denzinger 905 (new edition, 1692).

him home. This first mark of forgiveness, moving as it was, touched off a series of actions that helped the son appraise the extent to which the separation from his father had impaired his memory of that benevolent man. "Fetch me a ring for my son's hand." "Bring me the finest robe." "Kill the fattest calf." Each new kindness gave the son a greater realization of his former folly, and each new kindness could not help but draw the son closer to the father. While the prodigal loved his father for taking him back so unreservedly, how much more intense that love must have grown with each new sign of affection on the father's part. Each affectionate move must have revealed another forgotten facet of the father's character. And it must have given the penitent time to reflect and to recognize all that he had forgotten about his most munificent Father.

6. ABSOLUTION

"Your sins are forgiven. The peace of the Lord is with you." In the Sacrament of Penance, these words are more than the words of man. They belong to God. Once more, as in the Sacrifice of the Mass, the priest summons Christ to action. For, unlike ordinary denotative words that simply "mean," the words of absolution actually produce what they mean.

To the confessor, a human agent anointed by the Holy Spirit, Almighty God has entrusted His own dignity as a Person who does what He says. In an attempt to protect that dignity, to avoid frustrating the action of Christ, the confessor must decide on the worthiness of the penitent: "Is this man ready to accept the message of Christ and all that it implies?"

On his part, the confessor must never deceive a person by proclaiming these words when he knows that the person is not prepared for such a message. He is obliged by his office to use the human means at his disposal to see that they can be sincerely spoken. To aid the confessor in avoiding unnecessary concern on the one side, and carelessness on the other, I would propose the following guidelines with reference to

absolution: (1) There is a presumption in favor of the penitent. (2) If there should, for some reason, be a presumption
against the penitent, then give him the opportunity to prove
himself. (3) If you must give conditional absolution, let the
penitent know why you are doing so. (4) If you must give
conditional absolution, be sure the penitent is aware of what
this means. (5) Never "refuse" absolution; rather, defer it or
postpone it. (6) Help the penitent understand the meaning
of absolution.

PRESUMPTION IN FAVOR OF THE PENITENT

In the past, people sometimes came under public pressure
to seek the Sacrament of Penance. A man who did not go to
confession during the Easter Season, for example, was treated
as a social outcast in certain Christian communities. And so
a number of people came simply to save face socially, lacking as they did the clear intention of converting their lives.
As a result, the moralists of the day wisely alerted the confessors to the prevailing conditions and the possible want
of sincerity in penitents.

For the most part, modern times have obliterated this form
of social pressure regarding the Sacrament. Today, if a penitent presents himself to the priest, there is a presumption in
his favor that he comes with good will. Neither his knowledge
about how to confess nor his honesty in confessing should
be questioned unless there are signs to the contrary.

I know that in some areas of Europe a confessor may still
encounter men who have been pressured into the confessional
by their wives, or girls by their mothers. An experienced confessor can generally sense when a person has been bullied
into the box. In my own experience, it sometimes became evident that a girl had just lost a quarrel with her mother as she
vented her anger on me. In such instances, a confessor should
not rule out good will, for it can lurk beneath a haze of lesser
motives. A little kindness and gentleness will bring it to the
fore. In similar cases, when an important matter is mentioned
by the person, a little encouragement from the confessor may

reap a fine reward: "You've already made a splendid effort in coming here today. I hope now that you'll allow me to help you." Special care should be taken with the person who shows only a minimum of good will. In such a case, and in accord with what I have already said about the law of growth, I suggest that the confessor be especially cautious not to demand a very detailed confession.

In the United States as well as in other countries, bridal party confessions may pose a problem to the principle that a presumption lies in favor of the penitent. At times, it is obvious that a member or members of a bridal party, waiting until the night before the wedding, come to confession under pressure and confess without any indication of good will. In such instances, the presumption that favors penitents is suspended and they must prove their sincerity.

Ordinarily, however, the confessor is safe in presuming that the penitents who come to him are honest and sincere. He might remind himself that his attitude will determine whether or not a penitent views the confessional in the proper light: a place where people can go to a man of God with the greatest confidence. Therefore, the confessor should greet his penitents with a deep respect and, generally speaking, with the conviction that they are deserving of their absolution.

The main condition for absolution is a manifestation of good will. If the confessor has no reason to suspect the contrary, then let him proclaim the word of God without any hesitation.

PRESUMPTION AGAINST THE PENITENT

Persons designated in moral theology books as *occasionarii* or *recidivi* or *occasionarii recidivi* do not have a presumption of good will in their favor. Though later I will treat each of these at greater length, it will suffice here to say that *occasionarii* are those who live in the occasion of sin. *Recidivi* are those who have a bad habit of sin and fall repeatedly. The *occasionarii recidivi* are people who freely remain in a proximate occasion of sin and consistently fail to do anything about it.

This state of affairs reveals an unwillingness to amend their ways, making them thereby seem neither worthy nor ready for absolution. However, a confessor must remain calm and patient with them, giving them time to think and pray. Though a presumption militates against them, the confessor, with the greatest gentleness, should let them know that he wants to give them a chance to prove themselves, that if he did try to absolve them, he would only be deceiving them. But distinctions and clarifications of these remarks are in order.

Often a prudent judgment can be made on behalf of people whose habitual mode of acting has greatly diminished their freedom of choice. In such cases, the confessor focuses his attention on whether or not these penitents are sincerely striving, even though little progress is being noted. A prudent judgment must be made regarding the lack of freedom and the particular difficulties surrounding each case. The confessor may be aided in his judgment by the sincerity of the penitent and by the frequency with which the penitent seeks out the Sacrament. In these cases, so much depends on the good will of the penitent. When a confessor detects this good will, his problem is no longer, "Can I absolve him?" but "How can I help overcome this bad habit?"

Other cases clearly rule out any presumption of good will on the person's part. I am thinking particularly of cases where there are voluntary and proximate occasions of sin involved. A man who commits adultery and freely continues to visit the home of the woman after his confession, or another man living in concubinage and making no effort to depart from his partner in sin, can hardly claim the privilege of presumption in his favor. After one or two trials, the person having been warned, the confessor must react firmly and decisively to the lack of improvement. All efforts to lead the penitent to a firm purpose of amendment having failed, the confessor must then defer absolution. The person leaves no choice in the matter.

There are many situations, however, in which a confessor on the point of deferring absolution may provide the person with an opportunity to indicate clearly his good will. This brings to mind a particular Easter confession that I heard. For three consecutive years I had been hearing Easter confessions in the same confessional. My third year, I happened to recognize a penitent who confessed frequent absence from Sunday Mass as the same person who had been coming to me each year with the same sin. Having assured myself that I was not mistaken, I reminded her that for the past two years she had been promising a greater effort. Even while I was speaking, she boldly interjected: "Why do I always find the same confessor in this confessional every year;" I hardly think it rash to say that her comment betrayed her lack of good will. As gently as I could, I told her: "I need your help. If you don't give me a sign that you are truly sorry for this sin, that you intend to amend your way of life, I can't possibly proclaim the Lord's peace to you. In fact, unless you give me a special sign of a firm purpose of amendment, I'll have to defer absolution." To obtain this special sign, I offered the woman a more difficult penance and awaited her reaction to it. My judgment of the presence or absence of good will on her part rested entirely on that reaction. I have used the following penances for cases of this nature: the promise to say a particular prayer or to do some spiritual reading each day over a certain period of time, or to attend Mass once or more often on weekdays.

Let me illustrate this approach to the person whose disposition is doubtful with one more example. Some theology manuals say that absolution cannot be given to a man who so hates another as to be willing deliberately to harm or defame him. Even in this case, the confessor should give the person a chance to prove himself. I would suggest that the confessor urge the man to join him in making an act of sorrow for sins. After this prayer, the next step is to test the man's good will. Again, assigning a difficult penance and assessing his reaction will prove most helpful in forming a fair judgment. In this particular case, I would not hesitate in asking the man to promise to return to confession as soon as possible should he sin against that other.

Obviously, there is no inflexible manner or penance for handling these cases. The confessor might simply tell the

person: "I am afraid that I'm uncertain as to your good will."
This will provide you the opportunity to explain to the person that absolution pronounced over one not properly disposed is really useless. This point made, the confessor might lead the penitent into a conversation, intent on gathering information to help him resolve his doubt. At times, in the course of the conversation, a person may tell the confessor bluntly that he has not really decided to change his life at all. Or it may also happen that the confessor discovers this person is really invincibly ignorant regarding the seriousness of his actions. In the latter case, the points made earlier relative to invincible ignorance come to bear. In short, a good confessor may find that his initial fear of having to defer absolution was unfounded.

CONDITIONAL ABSOLUTION

Should a confessor receive some indication of good will from a penitent, but not enough to completely dispel his doubts, he might still be able to absolve the man, though conditionally. In this case, let him reveal to the penitent both the conditions under which he is absolving and why he is absolving in this way. It may happen that a clear and kind explanation of why the confessor is absolving conditionally will be the very exhortation the penitent needs to remove the obstacle to a valid absolution.

Once the confessor has decided to absolve a man conditionally, some explanation of "conditional absolution" is in order. In a kindly way, the confessor might inform the penitent that he is prepared to give absolution insofar as it is in his power to do so, that is, insofar as the penitent is willing to receive it. Instruct the penitent that he will be truly absolved only if he has the intention, for instance, of avoiding a certain free and proximate occasion of sin; that if he lacks this intention, the word of God will be ineffectual for him.

It may happen that a person will express reluctance to fulfill the conditions laid down for his absolution. Automatically to refuse absolution to such a person would be an injustice.

A better understanding between the confessor and the party may still be reached, and the confessor would do well to explore this possibility. But should the confessor's attempts be frustrated, it would be advisable to tell the penitent that if, in the future, he should decide to fulfill the conditions laid down earlier, he would not need to reconfess his sins to him. He has only to present himself to the same confessor and say: "Father, I wish to re-submit in this confession what I confessed earlier. I now want to fulfill the conditions."

REFUSAL OF ABSOLUTION

Though it is a question of semantics, it would be psychologically wiser for the confessor not to say that he refuses absolution. It makes a great deal of difference to the penitent to hear that his absolution is "deferred," because the latter term is pregnant with hope. A flat refusal of absolution may so upset the person that he will never return to the sacraments.

In the case where the confessor is forced to defer absolution, he should follow this announcement with a stated understanding that he will be most pleased if the party return to him soon, ready to be absolved. It would not harm to add: "In the meantime, I'll pray for you. Allow me to give you my blessing so that the Lord will guide your steps and bring you back here soon." A little tact in the choice of words may sponsor an early conversion.

Let me offer just one example here with reference to deferring absolution. Admittedly, it may be a rare case, but it is well to consider it nonetheless. If an older priest who is not properly disposed, perhaps being unwilling to give up a free occasion of sin, were to choose a younger priest as confessor, the younger priest must not hesitate to defer absolution. Deferral would certainly be for the spiritual good of the older priest. In such a case, I would suggest that the younger priest ask his elder to read the tract on proximate occasions of sin and then return for absolution. Should he counter with, "Until now nobody has given me any difficulty;

you should be more respectful toward an older colleague," the younger priest might remind him that the confessor, regardless of age, is the representative of Christ: "I do respect you as an older priest, Father, but the question right now is whether you wish to receive absolution humbly as a pledge of new life."

A confessor should never confuse timidity with gentleness or meekness. He is the representative of God, the Holy One. His penitents must feel that there is an encounter with the Holy One and that it involves a serious commitment on their part. At the same time, he must convey his desire to help them.

If any priest has to postpone absolution frequently, he ought to examine the state of his own priestly life. Such deferral is not a sign of apostolic zeal. If the priest is a man of prayer, if he is sustained by the prayers of the people of God, if he is gentle, humble, and always attempts to arouse a deep sense of sorrow in his own heart as well as in that of the penitent, he will rarely have to defer absolution.

"YOUR SINS ARE FORGIVEN"

The confessor, whether in the confessional or in the pulpit, should try to give his people a fuller understanding of absolution. The focal point of instruction in relation to the Sacrament of Penance should be the meaning of absolution. Absolution means that a man receives the peace of Christ within himself. If he is in good faith, if he is willing to do all that he can and to pray for what he feels he cannot do, regardless of how weak that man is, he can rest assured that God's word proclaimed in the Sacrament of Penance will restore him and bring him the joy of Christ. Joy is the keynote in absolution: joy through peace.

I thank God that at last the penitent is able to hear the words of absolution announced in his own language. Every confessor, realizing the power and the beauty of the words he utters in this Sacrament, should make an effort to speak these words clearly and distinctly. They are the words of God: "Your sins are forgiven." The priest should relate these words to the actual life-situation of the person, so that his conversation with the penitent becomes part of the absolution.

7. THE PROXIMATE
OCCASION OF SIN

In the Sacrament of Penance, Christ's peace is a redemptive act carrying with it the mission to spread the message of peace and salvation within one's community. Christ says, "Be healed!" One would hardly be sincere if, understanding this proclamation and its ensuing mission, he were freely to continue living in circumstances conducive to relapse into sin. That is why more need be said regarding the relationship between the purpose of amendment and proximate occasions of sin.

VOLUNTARY AND NECESSARY OCCASION OF SIN

The concept of an occasion of sin is a relative one. What is to some a remote occasion of sin proves to be a proximate occasion to others. A set of circumstances or an environment is said to be a remote occasion of sin when the temptation aroused is slight and easily overcome by a particular person. However, should the temptation resulting from these circumstances or environment be strong and not easily overcome, it is designated as a proximate occasion of sin. A man must determine whether the occasion of sin is a voluntary or a necessary occasion. A voluntary occasion of sin is one that can be avoided by a person of good will. Such is not the case with a necessary occasion of sin.

It is humanly impossible to avoid all occasions of sin. But what a man can do is honestly to gauge his own strength in relation to the forces tempting him. He thus places himself in a position where he can prudently determine the risk involved and act accordingly.

CHRISTIAN OUTLOOK ON ENVIRONMENT

Theology manuals of the last century looked upon the environment as a possible occasion of sin. But to consider one's environment solely as a threat is hardly consistent with our mission as Christians to bring the freedom of the children of God into our society. It is a negative view that can likewise be harmful psychologically. Just as St. Paul urged the people to foster motives of gratitude and love for the Christian life, so should we cultivate the same motives for coping with the environment. St. Paul warned us of the danger of presenting to the people a lifeless collection of "do's" and "don'ts." He wrote: "Is the Law sin? By no means! Yet I did not know sin save through the Law. For I had not known lust unless the Law had said, 'Thou shalt not lust.' But sin, having thus found an occasion worked in me by means of the commandment . . ." (Rom. 7:7-8). Along with the law, you must suggest motives leading to a spiritual dying to self. If you fail to stir a man's heart with an incentive for a new life dedicated to God, the law will simply seduce him to curiosity about the thing forbidden. The same holds true with regard to outlook on environment. The priest, as confessor and preacher, has the obligation to teach men a Christian attitude about their environment, namely, one of gratitude and of responsibility.

Each one of us should learn to appreciate the blessings of his environment. Each one of us should weigh the reasons compelling him to gratitude, such as being born into this family, brought up in this neighborhood, associated with this parish. In one of our parishes in Europe, there were several poor families direly in need of financial help. As I was acquainted with a rather well-to-do Catholic gentleman who never missed Sunday Mass and who belonged to several Confraternities, I asked him if he would be willing to assist these people. He said, "No, Father. Why should I? What has anybody ever done for me?" I wanted to ask him if he had forgotten the opportunities opened to him by his parents; if he had deserved the million kindnesses and attentions heaped upon him by his family and friends. Instead, I only pitied him. I pitied his voluntary blindness to one of the greatest joys of life, the joy of knowing that other people care for you.

A man's gratitude for his environment will induce him to accept a greater responsibility for that environment. Real gratitude generates the desire to do something for the benefactor. In this case, a man who appreciates his society instinctively wishes to better it. For Christians, this means raising its spiritual level. If such a feeling of responsibility born of gratitude does develop, then things about us that might have constituted dangers become incentives to greater progress in responsibility.

But naiveté is not a characteristic that should mark a Christian's outlook on his environment. For the Christian to work effectively in society, he must be aware of its vices as well as its virtues. Only then can he properly immunize himself against the ills of the time.

Immunity is found in a closer union with Christ and His Church. For the Church of Christ is the "divine milieu" whose loving members, together with her teachings on love and salvation, ready the Christian for an apostolic career in the world. In his own day, St. Paul spelled out the Christian's problem in the world and what the Church could offer to help him tangle with it:

> Our wrestling is not against flesh and blood, but against the Principalities and the Powers, against the world-rulers of this darkness, against the spiritual forces of wickedness on high. Therefore take up the armor of God, that you may be able to resist in the evil day, and stand in all things perfect. Stand, therefore, having

girded your loins with truth, and having put on the breastplate of
justice, and having your feet shod with the readiness of the gospel
of peace, in all things taking up the shield of faith, with which
you may be able to quench all the fiery darts of the most wicked
one. And take unto you the helmet of salvation and the sword of
the spirit, that is, the word of God.

Ephesians 6:12-17

A Christian must first feel at home in the world of faith, of
prayer, before bringing the healing forces of light to a stricken
society. Only then can he come in contact with disease and
come away healthy, in fact, more than ever immune.

It is essential, then, that Christian education produce
mature men and women who understand the value of authority and personal responsibility. For these are the men and
women who will meet society head on and, by the strength
of their convictions, will help to brighten the nooks and
crannies of a secular city. You cannot prepare a Christian for
his place in the world by nourishing him on a doctrine of
blind obedience.

From the earliest years, a child must learn a hierarchy of
values, and be taught to appreciate the values in his religion, his family, and his environment. This respect for
values can never develop in a child whose parents fear admitting their occasional misuse of authority. "I was impatient.
I'm sorry." Why should a parent shrink from an avowal such
as this which, without disfiguring the parental image, helps
the child distinguish between the proper and improper use of
authority.

In the way of responsibility, the child should be encouraged, on his own initiative, to contribute to family life. He
should not be made to feel that he must always await his
parents' nod or beck. Nor should the parent who is asked:
"Daddy, why do I have to do this?" limit the child's understanding to "Because daddy says so." The young child is not
yet ready for deep and serious reasons, but an answer as simple as "Because I need your help" will not only please the
child, but give him insight into his place in the family.

The task of the pastor will be greatly simplified if the
parents have performed theirs properly. Just as the parent

encourages his child to play an active role in the family, so should the pastor try to persuade him to play an active role in parish life. Young people's participation in parish organizations will not only protect them from many dangers to which others fall prey, but will provide experience in effective parish life and a greater sense of responsibility. Training such as this is absolutely necessary both in the home and in the parish, for today's young men and women will have to withstand the shock of the discrepant values of the family environment and the business world. If they are brought up to be unquestioning conformists, they will yield to any strong influence, be it good or bad. Instead, their upbringing should lead them to a deep insight into values and to a maturity that will enable them to hold fast to the principles and convictions of their Christian training. We want them not merely to hold their ground, but to be leaders and shapers of opinion. The dynamic society into which we are sending them will be led only by dynamic people, people who can shoulder responsibility.

Along with the idea of educating Christians to an understanding of authority and to greater personal responsibility, the goal of the confessor should be to help his penitents form a mature conscience. He likewise has an excellent opportunity to teach them ways in which they might bring their influence to bear for the improvement of their social milieu.

On the occasion of a general mission, the confessors might try to make penitents more aware of their duty to serve Christ in the capacity of apostles. I know of one instance where the missionaries, through the combined media of preaching and the confessional, so inculcated the spirit of apostleship into the hearts of their hearers that each night the attendance grew visibly. It later became apparent that through the efforts of a handful of workers from a nearby factory employing close to a thousand people, the entire factory environment had been changed for the better. Unabashedly, this handful invited co-workers to attend the mission with them. They succeeded in convincing many who had stayed away from Church, from the Sacraments for various periods of time, of how happy they would be to return and experience the peace of Christ.

When the ordinary Christian bears witness to his faith, the result is generally most effective and far-reaching. For this very reason, it would be a splendid idea for a confessor, after arousing a penitent long-removed from the Sacrament to a sense of gratitude to God, to instruct him regarding his role as apostle for Christ. Let the penitent know that this is one way in which he might "do penance" and show his gratitude, by bringing some other person back to God, or perhaps simply by informing others that the Sacrament of Penance is truly a Sacrament of kindness and of peace.

If an apostolic spirit were developed in all practicing Christians, the world would soon witness a transformation. Such a transformation will take place when our pastoral objective centers on making Christians aware, not only as individuals but as communities, that they are the "salt of the earth," "the light of the world," and a leaven in their environment. The celebration of the Sacrament of Penance, while not the whole answer to this problem of instruction, can play a major role in disseminating this teaching.

However, should a man's environment be so polluted, or should the man himself be shaky from prior falls, only then must his strategy be one of flight. Admittedly, a person enjoying particular material advantages or cultural opportunities in a locality will be all the more reluctant to leave it. But a Christian must be ready, if necessary, to part with the pleasures of this life in order to protect his claim on eternity. The Gospel tells us that if a man's hand be a source of sin to him, it is better that he cut it off; if his eye be a source of sin, better that he pluck it out. Except in the extreme case mentioned above, this "heaven first" attitude is not at variance with involvement in the world. Far from it. Because of sin, St. Paul says, the world "groans in all its parts." The Christian is committed to see that the liberty and splendor of the children of God revitalize those parts (cf. Rom. 8:19-24).

OCCASIONS OF SIN AGAINST FAITH

A man's faith stands highest in the hierarchy of goods. Rather than expose his faith to unnecessary dangers, a man must be willing to sacrifice even his closest friendships. For, it is a fact that certain friendships between a Catholic and an unbeliever or a non-Catholic who is hostile to the Church can extremely imperil the Catholic's faith. Especially vulnerable would be the Catholic who is rather weak and easily swayed by others, whereas the other party is strong and dynamic. The same would hold in the case where the non-Catholic is highly intelligent and adept at argumentation and tends to use his talent in a way that spells danger to the Catholic's faith. It cannot be argued that the non-Catholic party poses no threat to the virtue of purity, and therefore, the friendship is all right. A sin against faith is by its very nature more serious than a sin against the sixth commandment. Where a friendship between a Catholic and a non-Catholic involves a man and a woman, should there be any indication of a possible marriage in the future, the Catholic must consider, before all else, whether such a marriage would constitute a danger to his (or her) faith.

With regard to faith and environment, *i.e.*, the work locale or the neighborhood, I would make the following distinction. Even though strong negative feelings against the Catholic faith are voiced in a particular place, if there are several committed Christians there willing to join forces, the possibility is great that through an effective apostolate, they will effect a general change of attitude toward the Church. The environmental threat to any one Catholic is minimized, so to speak, because of the mutual support accorded one another. The case is quite different if the believer is alone in such an environment.

Should the Catholic be a member of an organization which is generally hostile to the Church, as are some Masonic organizations, he would be obliged to terminate his membership. At times a Catholic will tell the priest, "I know I shouldn't belong to this club, but do I have to quit right away?" He may request breaking off gradually because of social or financial reasons, promising at the same time not to go to the meetings or not to read the club's literature. Generally, the man can be permitted to make a gradual withdrawal. He has no obligation to be heroic. (In the United States, most of the Masonic organizations are not hostile to the Church.)

OCCASIONS OF SIN AGAINST CHARITY AND JUSTICE

Environment can also occasion sins against charity and justice. A timely instance would be a locality where civil rights for Negroes are not recognized. One may have friends who feel that the colored people already have enough or even too many rights and that they are unappreciative of them. These friends evince bias by the fact that they stress only the vices and weaknesses of individual Negroes, ignoring completely their exemplifications of virtue. They blind themselves to the great injustices perpetrated against these people. Such a milieu definitely endangers the spirit of Christian charity and justice. If without sacrificing life or fortune the Christian can join groups seeking to convince racists that they are sinning against these virtues, he ought to do so.

Another instance of justice violation would be the case where one's firm derives its income through cheating or fraud. If the individuals responsible for such theft cannot be persuaded to act differently, the only choice for the Christian may be to leave the firm. By staying on, he conveys to others the impression that he favors the immoral practices, or, though he may oppose the practices at first, he runs the risk of compromising his own ethics and furthering the practice of injustice.

OCCASIONS OF SIN AGAINST CHASTITY

Because of his weakened nature and because of the selfishness which assaults him and poisons his environment, man often finds himself surrounded by occasions of sin against chastity. Admittedly, those who seek only the kingdom of God are protected by this very approach from the noxious influences of the world around them. However, one who unnecessarily exposes himself to temptation against chastity will almost certainly succumb. In the subsequent paragraphs, I will limit myself to signaling the more salient features in our contemporary society which endanger this virtue.

Today, the changing social patterns of youth are reflected in their own distinctions between *dating steadily* and *going steady*. In the first case, the youngsters reveal their wariness of entangling alliances because they are convinced that a relationship depends upon the emotions invested in it by each partner. "Dating steadily" consists of the frequent dating of the same two people without the element of exclusiveness or any immediate intention of future betrothal. It is simply the normal development of friendship between a boy and a girl, with no school pin or ring given as a symbol binding the two; there is mutual understanding that each has the right to date others. In our culture, this is a normal situation allowing young people to become well acquainted with several possible partners before a final choice is made.

In steady dating, the relationship is usually given all the solemn trappings of a demi-marriage; it involves a considerable degree of exclusiveness and often the explicit intention of future marriage. Parents and priests should not shirk their responsibilities by failing to point out to teen-agers that keeping company in this committed sense prior to the attainment of a reasonable degree of maturity foolishly limits their internal and external freedom in the choice of their future spouse. Exclusive company-keeping at too early an age often leads to premature marriage with all its attendant dangers for the future happiness of the couple.

However, these ideas should be part and parcel of a general religious formation of youth. Public opinion should be so shaped as to impart to young people a healthy attitude toward the whole problem of early dating; it would be healthier than clamping down on them after the damage is done. For the most part, the confessor's ability to be effective in these cases will depend largely upon whether or not our youth has been successfully formed and helped by healthy convictions and attitudes in his environment.

In general, if steady company-keeping has not led to warped sexual or interpersonal attitudes, or to such heavy dating that rightful duties are neglected, the confessor should not demand a break in the association. Nor is occasional superficial petting a sufficient reason for the confessor to discourage the friendship altogether. (Under the term 'superficial petting' I would include all forms of what is commonly called 'necking' as well as a certain degree of petting. The term 'necking' refers to displays of affection which accidentally may cause sexual stimulation, e.g., kissing and embracing. 'Petting' refers to any action which by its very nature and regardless of the intent of the agent tends to cause sexual stimulation. I would call a simple touch 'superficial petting' as opposed to mutual masturbation).

However, when steady dating among youngsters of fourteen and fifteen has already led to more than petting, the confessor should at least strongly urge the youngsters to end their association. Because of difficult circumstances that may be involved, I refrain from saying that the confessor should always demand an immediate break between the two. It is a fact that there are parents who encourage their children to keep steady company even at a very early age. Today's society also bears a heavy share of the blame because it encourages, and to some extent, pressures youngsters into going steady. The best that priests can do in this area lies in educating Christians to an appreciation of the values of matrimony and virginity. In this way, the foundation is laid for future generations of boys and girls who will grow up into a society formed by enlightened men and women. It will then be a much easier task to work with individuals who will not have to suffer the tension of hearing one thing from their priest and seeing another in the world about them.

At present, a confessor, recognizing the difficulties the young people face today, should try to convince them of the harm that they are doing to each other with respect to their future married life. Should the same ones return to him several times with the same faults, he must display the greatest patience. In the case referred to above regarding what I have called superficial petting, I believe that only when the confessor sees no noticeable effort on the patient's part to improve, should he try to persuade the penitent to stop seeing this boy or girl. But I do not recommend that the confessor threaten to withhold absolution unless a promise is given. The confessor should try to assess the intelligence and the psychological outlook of his young penitent. At times, even after the confessor has explained why their company-keeping or mode of action in dating is not right, he will find that the party is invincibly ignorant. The possibility of such ignorance is not unbelievable considering the particular environment in which the penitent finds himself. In such a case, the confessor should try to help the penitent make progress in other areas first. Only then will the moment to convince him of the existing danger be effective.

Another occasion of sin with regard to the sixth commandment might be *dancing*. Obviously, it would be a gross error to label all dancing an occasion of sin. The confessor must display a fine sense of distinctions in this area. Should a penitent confess sins committed as a consequence of dancing, the confessor might ask the penitent himself how this danger might be avoided in the future and then insist that he follow upon his own recommendation. If the sin is frequent and grave (if, for instance, a young man confesses that after almost every dance he attends, he ends up seducing a girl), the confessor should question the man's motives for going to the dance in the first place. Generally, this young man should be made aware of his obligation to give up dancing because of the real harm he is doing to himself and to others. Yet, local customs may complicate the situation. In the United States, as well as in many other countries, young people will be invited to certain celebrations where dancing comprises the major part of the entertainment. Very often a young man could not conveniently refuse to attend such festivities, for example, the wedding reception of a close friend, or the senior prom. Ordinarily a confessor should not insist too strongly that a penitent avoid dancing when there is a question of social honor at stake. At any rate, the confessor should be willing (and might even ask the penitent himself) to suggest possibilities whereby this young man can enjoy a reasonable amount of social life where dancing is involved.

For some, the period of engagement amounts to a necessary proximate occasion of sin. However, where the confessor has the opportunity to talk to an engaged party, he should not label the time of courtship simply as a time of sexual difficulties. This would be a very negative viewpoint which can only distort the true value of a propitious time. Let the confessor try, rather, to implant in the mind and heart of the engaged party an understanding of their betrothal as a time when each might learn the ingredients for love. Only a view combining an appreciation of marriage and an appreciation of the other person can provide a proper motivation for resolving, with mutual help, any sexual problem. Mutual respect, not fear, should be proffered as guideline. Nor should these positive ideas prevent the confessor from helping the party to learn the distinction between genuine tenderness and mere sexual exploitation. Finally, it is well for the confessor not to confuse the problem of an engaged person who accuses himself of having occasionally sinned with his fiancée with the problem of a young man who has no serious prospect of a future marriage committing the "same" sin with his steady date.

Under no circumstance can modern conditions of life justify a situation ethics which would allow, as Joseph Fletcher does, sexual intercourse between an engaged couple. A girl's fiancé has no more right to her body than he would have to the body of any other woman. The sex act by its very nature expresses the irrevocable and indissoluble bond between the couple concerned. Regardless of an engaged couple's present love for each other, they are not yet irrevocably and indissolubly united to each other in marriage. This argument, which is valid and true for engaged couples, has an even greater application against Fletcher's ideas about promiscuity, for a good reason.

But a confessor cannot brush aside the difficulties of modern youth lightly. Modern society is in a state of ferment. There have been tremendous changes in outlook and values. Even so-called Christian societies have not yet developed new, unchallenged customs which would help youth.

Perhaps the situation can be more vividly grasped by a contrast. In the eighteenth century, reacting against the extreme rigorism of his day, St. Alphonsus tendered the view that engaged couples should be allowed to see each other, in the presence of their parents, at least as many as three times, and more often in an exceptional case. His idea seemed rather loose to some moralists of his time who considered the period of betrothal so dangerous that they taught engaged couples should not see each other more than once before the marriage date. And even on this one occasion, the parents of the couple were to stay within eyeshot. But the moralists should not have to shoulder all the blame for this idea. In those days, the parents chose a partner for their son or daughter. Strange as it may sound today, these parents feared that if the couple came to know one another, one might refuse to accept the designated partner and all the family plans would be frustrated. At times, a girl married a man whom she met for the first time at the foot of the altar. Of course, rules such as these are scoffed at today. But let no one think that our own customs regarding marriage are perfect.

We have reasons to be thankful that the twentieth century has advanced so far in its understanding of the complexities of choosing a proper partner. Today's custom of encouraging the young people to get to know each other, to meet persons of the opposite sex and to make oneself aware of psychological differences between the sexes is very good. Young people should have ample time to observe each other and to find out whether the prospective partner is a person whom the other can esteem, respect and love.

In some areas, however, the opinion is quite widespread

that young people should have premarital sexual experiences. Knowing the influence that society's opinions can have over individuals, the confessor might very well meet with some who are invincibly ignorant in this respect. The fact that he or she will confess premarital sex as a sin does not necessarily preclude invincible ignorance. The penitent may confess because he knows that the Church forbids this action, but at the same time he may feel convinced in another part of his psychological make-up that premarital sexual experience is necessary. I know for a fact that in certain areas in Europe the practice exists, though the clergy have struggled against it for centuries, of marrying a woman only if she is expecting a child. The man, in these areas, wants some assurance that his wife will not be sterile.

In Africa there are tribes where the man accepts the woman as his wife only on condition that she become a mother. The marriage is not considered definitive until the girl becomes pregnant. Should she be found sterile, she is sent back to her home. These customs pose great problems for the Church. But we do not have to look to Africa for such customs. In America and in Europe as well, warped ideas about premarital sex and fertility likewise exist, though in a more sophisticated context. In view of social pressures, in view of the varying and complicated marriage customs that exist throughout the world, one thing is evident: priests and Christians who help to shape public opinion must make a united effort to point up to the average man and woman the difference between right and wrong in these matters. With these problems in mind, the confessor cannot help but be more patient with penitents whose environment contributes greatly to their faults.

Finally, with engaged couples, the confessor can contribute much to their future happiness by helping them to see the opportunity afforded them by their betrothal time to grow in love of God. He can likewise save them from many temptations by teaching them that a mutual experience of respectful love during this period will give them a deeper psychological insight into how good God is and how beautiful His love must be. Lessons such as these will give them a more profound understanding of marriage as a way of salvation.

EMPLOYMENT AS AN OCCASION OF SIN

Ideas about what constitutes a proximate occasion of sin, in practice, change considerably over the years. When it comes to judging whether certain professions are, in themselves, proximate occasions of sin, there is considerable difficulty. Years ago, strict moralists maintained that girls could not become hairdressers because this was regarded as a "dangerous profession." Older moralists forbade that a Catholic take on the job of housekeeper in a Jewish household, fearing that each Friday she faced a proximate occasion of sin to eat meat. I know of a pastor who only ten years ago threatened to refuse absolution to a woman unless she promised never to visit the homes of her non-Catholic relatives on Friday. Today, hardly any moralist would frown on a Catholic housekeeper in a Jewish home.

The Commandments of the Church oblige us only under certain commonly accepted conditions. They do not oblige absolutely. Still, I have heard of cases where priests have unreasonably insisted on the fulfillment of the law. One instance that comes to mind concerns a curate who tried to discourage several girls in his parish from attending a school for midwives. He told them such a profession might prevent them from getting to Mass on Sunday. He ignored their appeal that they were not seeking an occasion for missing Mass; in fact, they frequently went to Mass on weekdays. For the priest, the question hinged entirely on whether or not these girls would be able to fulfill the Sunday precept each week. He disregarded entirely the service that midwives can render to the people of God if they have been properly instructed in Christian morality. Nor did he seem aware that if he carried his approach to the Sunday precept through to its logical conclusion, he would have to forbid people to get sick over the weekend.

Nonetheless, there are some places of employment that are

proximate occasions of sin against faith, or justice, or purity. At times, then, the confessor may have to urge a penitent to give up his job. However, even though he may consider his advice in this direction necessary, he must not readily refuse absolution if the penitent is not convinced of this necessity. Often, the penitent does not view a confessor's advice as a question of obedience or disobedience to the Church. This is particularly true of people who do not have a regular confessor and who, going to one confessor one time and a different confessor the next, discover some wide variations in practice. These variations tend to promote the so-called crisis in authority. Once the penitent decides that Father So-and-So does not represent the Catholic Church, he waits for a confessor whose views are more in harmony with his own. For this very reason, confessors should aim at fostering in their penitents a greater personal responsibility. In the case at hand, the confessor might suggest to the penitent that he pray and reflect on the advisability of making a change in employment, but leave the ultimate judgment on this to the penitent himself. A respectful attitude on the confessor's part will reap far better results.

A PROMISE FROM THE PENITENT

At times, the confessor might ask the penitent to promise that if he continues to fall into some particular sin as a result of his employment he find another job. Psychologically, a penitent, having made a promise such as this, will try harder to improve. Though the results may not be immediate, and though he may have to renew his promise in subsequent confessions, the confessor should be patient. Possibly the man is not falling so frequently now as he might have fallen without the promise. Possibly, too, if he sees his own promise being violated time after time, he will find the courage to change to a different job. However, it would be wrong for the confessor to lay down as an absolute rule that if a penitent breaks his promise, perhaps breaking it several times, absolution must be refused.

Regarding a promise from the penitent, I would like to offer two cases, the first of an occasional drinker, the second of a chronic drinker.

If an occasional drinker, in spite of a promise in his last confession not to drink, should confess that he got drunk, this does not prove his promise was not sincere. His pledge indicated his intention to avoid taking a drink. Intention and fulfillment are two different things. The confessor, admonishing him gently, should ask him to renew his promise and to make a more determined effort to keep it.

However, if the penitent is a chronic drinker, the confessor would be wiser to ask him to promise, not to give up drinking, but rather to seek professional treatment. A chronic drinker is one who cannot overcome the habit unless he completely renounces alcohol. Very often such a man who comes to confession is extremely depressed over his own weakness and is suffering a great deal. As regards drinking, he lacks the necessary internal freedom to make a choice and to carry it out. But he can be persuaded that there are people capable of helping him. Again, the confessor should not threaten to withhold absolution if the penitent does not promise to seek professional help or, if after promising, he fails to do so. Truly, the obligation of convincing this man to apply for professional help belongs more properly to his family, or to the parish priest, or to some charitable organization.

If the chronic drinker is a bartender or a licensed liquor dealer, his work is a continual and proximate occasion of sin for him. Most probably he will not be rehabilitated until he gives up this profession. The confessor's most effective work with such a penitent, however, will be accomplished by a show of patience and understanding.

CONCUBINAGE AND OTHER OCCASIONS OF SIN

Other examples cited by the manuals as occasions of sin are concubinage and invalid marriages. It is well, even in our ordinary conversations, to keep the two distinct. Some are prone to refer to people living in an invalid marriage as "liv-

ing in concubinage." In fact, some years ago, the zealous
Bishop of Prato in Italy was sentenced to several months in
jail because he had declared that Catholics who were only
civilly married were living in concubinage. The civil authorities regarded his statement as a serious breach of decency.
Concubinage means the maintenance of a sexual relationship
without the intention of stability. A couple who present
themselves to be married, though perhaps invalidly, express
their intention of binding themselves to one another.

Concubinage is a term that in itself might easily be misunderstood by the average layman. For example, if a bachelor
or a divorcé employs a housekeeper and, from time to time,
sins with her, this would not bring the relationship into the
category of concubinage. In concubinage, though there is no
intention of forming a binding union, there is a semi-
permanent sexual relationship between the two. If a man
is actually living in concubinage, the confessor should insist
that he leave the woman, because his situation is a voluntary
proximate occasion of sin. In the case of the bachelor and
the housekeeper, there may be extenuating circumstances
to consider.

I would, then, caution the confessor against snap decisions. In my pastoral experience, I encountered several cases
when girls who had lived lives of sin, making their money
by wandering the streets, finally went to work as housekeepers. From time to time, they sinned with their employers, but
their lives as wage-earning housekeepers showed marked improvement over their past existence. In these cases, the employers proved to be fundamentally good men, even though
they were occasionally weak. If the girls had been forced to
give up their employment, they would probably have reverted
to their former ways. Though they were still falling, they
were gradually improving and regaining their self-respect. The
confessor should hold his final judgment in abeyance until
he feels that he has been apprised of the whole situation. The
character of the penitent, his psychological balance, the circumstances he faces, all should be brought to bear in making
a prudent judgment. Sometimes the best the confessor can
do is to tell the penitent that he himself is uncertain whether

or not it would be advisable to give up this employment. Then ask the penitent to continue to pray, to come to the Sacraments until both can decide on what the proper course must be.

INVALID MARRIAGES

Invalid marriages are quite a different problem. Such marriages, as I already explained, are not concubinage because the couple have formally bound themselves together as man and wife for the rest of their lives. Marriages may be invalid for various reasons. One of the most frequent reasons is that one of the partners was previously and validly married. Or, if the first marriage was invalid, it may happen that, for lack of sufficient evidence, the party cannot prove the point that made it invalid. Before such a marriage can be declared null, moral certainty regarding the existence of that point at the time of marriage is needed.

If the couple involved in an invalid marriage have no responsibilities, no children to educate, they should give up the proximate occasion of sin. If they are not able to live together as brother and sister, it is advisable that they separate, whenever this is possible. If, on the other hand, there are responsibilities, if there are children, then the proximate occasion of sin is often a necessary one.

Supposing a couple have been living together for many years and now one is ill. Then the healthy partner has a responsibility to the sick one. If the confessor insisted on separation from bed and board in this case, it would be cruelty toward the sick person, particularly when in such circumstances there is little chance of sexual involvement. Charity and the life they have led together oblige them sometimes to look after one another. This will especially be true where there are one or more children to be cared for.

With no possibility of reconciliation with the first spouse, a divorced man or woman living in an invalid marriage may be faced with the obligation of educating children. They may be living in peace and, humanly speaking, leading a good conjugal life. I feel certain that if a confessor insisted that this couple give up their relationship, in most of the cases only a greater harm would ensue. Not only would they in all likelihood refuse, but their attitude toward the Church would become more disturbed and more resentful. Their very first thought would be: "And what would happen to the children?" One alternative, however, for the confessor's dilemma is a consideration of a brother-sister relationship. There is no doubt that such a relationship would be difficult for the couple, but that it is not an impossibility has already been proved by others. I know of a number of cases where couples have lived in this way for many years. Even some younger people have succeeded in doing so. Through prayer, through self-control, through a true expression of Christian love and kindness, they have been able to arrive at perfect continence and thus are no longer living in a "proximate occasion" of sin. The question is: for what length of time must the couple be living in a brother-sister relationship before the priest can absolve them?

Many moralists say that normally a confessor should have the couple try out the brother-sister arrangement for several months before accepting their promise. However, no mathematical limit can rightly be set. The confessor's judgment should depend, not on mathematics, but on those facts indicating whether or not the couple is truly determined to try.

If the chancery has not reserved these cases to itself, the confessor can absolve the couple provided they show an extraordinary sign of conversion. But even though absolved, the couple must be reminded not to go to Communion in any parish where the invalid state of their marriage is known. Let me cite an example. During a mission, a couple may be moved by what they hear and inform the priest that they would like to try a brother-sister arrangement. I am convinced that a confessor often would be acting prudently if, in such circumstances, he trusted their good will and granted them absolution. In doing so, however, he should inform them that he is so acting because of the extraordinary signs of conversion shown. The confessor should also tell them that if they should fall back into sin, they should again try to obtain absolution revealing the reasons why they had received absolution in the first place: strong signs of repentance and the hope that the Sacrament would give them the strength they needed. Handling cases in this way, I often found that couples were deeply affected. Gratitude to God became a new source of power in their lives.

In some places, the bishop may have reserved cases of this sort to himself. The confessor, then, should be aware of the extent to which the bishop has done so. He may have reserved the regulation of the case only in the external forum. This would mean that the party absolved by the confessor could not be admitted publicly (where his case is known) to Communion in the diocese without the consent of the bishop. Confessors must strictly adhere to this legislation. It has reference to public order, and bishops have the right and the obligation to preserve public order in view of preventing scandal and uncharitable talk by people.

The bishop might also reserve the absolution of the sin to himself. This likewise is his right. It means that before the confessor can grant absolution, he must apply to the Ordinary. But Canon Law states exceptions to this. During a mission, missionaries as well as pastors during the Paschal season have the right to absolve from reserved sins (Canon 899). In other situations, the confessor may have to apply for faculty. But according to the wonderful wisdom of the Legislator, then, should the bishop refuse permission to absolve from the reserved sin, the confessor has automatically the right to absolve whenever the penitent has the necessary disposition (Canon 900,2). Nonetheless, the confessor cannot trespass on regulations regarding the external forum, and therefore, he would have no right to allow the penitent publicly to receive Holy Communion where his situation is known.

As a sort of pastoral addendum, I would warn priests who, in the course of distributing Holy Communion, find someone at the rail whom they know or believe to be in a bad marriage not to refuse that person the Sacred Host. Perhaps an incident will bring home the reason behind this warning. In a parish where I had preached a mission, a young couple came to see me. The woman had been married before and, though her first marriage was probably invalid, she could not get the pastor to help her with her case. She was about thirty years old and had one child. She and her second husband had already lived in perfect continence for two years. During that time, they had prayed together, even made spiritual reading together, and often went to Mass, not only on Sunday but during the week as well. Knowing the full details of the case, I gave the couple absolution, and told them that if they wished to go to Communion, it would be best to go to a parish where they were unknown. I felt certain that they would have been prudent enough to avoid any encounter with the pastor even if I had not warned them. Unfortunately for himself, the pastor noticed that this couple had come to me. The following day, while distributing Communion, he suddenly stopped over one woman and distinctly said, "You're living in concubinage. What are you doing here?" His remark was addressed to a woman who resembled my penitent. The woman was living in a perfectly good marriage.

Confessors must take into account recent discussions concerning divorce and remarriage (especially in the case of the "abandoned party," whose second marriage is tolerated by the Orthodox Churches), because these discussions are well known to many people and increase the possibility of a conscience in "good faith" on the part of people living in a canonically invalid marriage (because of a previous bond), but whose second marriage gives every appearance of being motivated by faithful love and a generous desire to fulfill parental obligations. When there is no danger of scandal to others, the confessor is not obliged to disturb the peace of conscience achieved by such a couple (cf. 297-300).

INVALID MIXED MARRIAGES

I am restricting myself here to a consideration of how to deal with penitents who live in an invalid mixed marriage. Should anyone be interested in a fuller treatment of the complex problem of mixed marriages, I refer him to my earlier work, *Marriage in the Modern World*.[1]

According to the new regulations, a mixed marriage contracted without observing the canonical form is still considered invalid. It is hoped that in the near future a more lenient practice proposed by several Council Fathers will be adopted. If so, a mixed marriage entered without dispensation and without canonical form will be regarded, not as invalid, but only as illicit. However, even today, the standing regulation makes the validation of mixed marriages possible if the Catholic partner shows good will. An invalid mixed marriage should be validated as soon as possible wherever the human conditions allow the hope of a stable marriage. It would be against common sense and especially against the ecumenical spirit to tell Catholics living in an invalid marriage that they should simply separate if the non-Catholic partner will not promise to give the children a Catholic education. The couple have a natural and Christian commitment towards one another and toward any children they may have.

However, there can be cases where a separation is advisable, for instance, when the non-Catholic violently and persistently hinders the Catholic from professing the faith and from living according to his or her own conscience.

The normal form of convalidating mixed marriages should be the *sanatio in radice* (cf. CJC Canones 1138-1141). The Holy See is quite generous in granting the faculty to bishops. The *sanatio in radice* means that the couple is dispensed from the canonical form of marriage and need not even renew consent, so long as the previous consent still exists. Through a juridical fiction, then, the marriage will be considered as though it had been valid from the beginning.

Even if the Catholic party cannot persuade the non-Catholic to consent to giving the children a Catholic training, steps should still be taken toward validating the marriage. The Catholic party must continue to do what he can regarding the education of the children without violating the conscience of his partner or of the children, and without

[1] B. Häring, *Marriage in the Modern World*, Newman, 1965.

endangering the harmony and stability of the marriage. The same can be said about absolving the Catholic party. Absolution must not depend on whether the Catholic succeeds in winning a nod of approval from his spouse to rear the children as Catholics. Only a Catholic who shows ill will in this matter and remains "contumacious" should have absolution deferred. But again, a careful distinction must be made between granting absolution and permitting the party publicly to receive Communion in a parish where others feel that the children are being deprived of the Christian witness from the part of the Catholic father or mother. In this case, charity dictates that the Catholic, at least until this wrong is righted or the people know of their good will, receive Communion only in a parish in which the case is not known.

8. MATERIAL INTEGRITY
OF CONFESSION

For many priests and many penitents the Sacrament of Penance has become a torture because of a lopsided emphasis on material integrity. Material integrity is only one aspect of the Sacrament of Penance. If the Sacrament is to be celebrated properly, it is essential to harmonize this aspect with the other even more important aspects of the Sacrament.

Normally, the penitent who has committed a mortal sin must reveal the kind of sin and the number of times he committed it. However, the confessor should beware of an exaggerated demand for number and species. Psychologically, such a demand may destroy, or at least dilute, the effect for which Christ instituted the Sacrament: the joy and peace of the penitent. For this reason, I will attempt, in this chapter, to place material integrity in proper perspective.

MATERIAL INTEGRITY

The Church law with regard to confession reads: "After Baptism a man who has committed any grave sins which have not been directly forgiven through the keys of the Church

must confess all these sins of which he is aware after a serious examination of conscience, and must explain the circumstances which change the species of the sin" (CJC Canon
901).

In speaking about the integrity of confession, we make a
distinction between material integrity and formal integrity.
Material integrity is a goal toward which every confessor
and every penitent should prudently strive. But—and the ad-
versative is important here—material integrity is to be sought
only in relation to formal integrity, and not for its own
sake. Basically, the term material integrity refers to a conditional obligation: what the penitent is obliged to do if he
can remember all his mortal sins, and if he is capable of distinguishing things which are essentially different, and if he
can do this without detriment to the more important aspects
of the Sacrament. At times material integrity is not possible or even not allowed.

The expression "formal integrity" refers to a confession in
which the penitent with good will confesses whatever serious
sins he can confess here and now according to his knowledge
and ability. In other words, it is the response to the concrete
will of God toward the limited human being. Formal integrity
for a dying man may mean that he is sorry for his sins and
manifests this sorrow as best he can, perhaps simply by a look.
Formal integrity for a man in a large hospital ward where the
beds are very close together may mean a general expression
of guilt and sorrow, lest the man expose his life to the ears
of other patients in the ward. Formal integrity may mean a
very short confession for scrupulous persons.

THE LEGAL AND THE IDEAL FULFILLMENT

Church law assumes that so long as a penitent is physically
and morally capable of doing so, he is obliged to confess all
certain mortal sins which have not yet been confessed. If he is
doubtful whether or not a sin committed is a mortal sin, from
the legal point of view, he has no obligation to confess it. On
the other hand, from the ideal point of view, moved by the

motive of an ever-growing love of God, he may wish to mention this sin and the doubtful state of his mind.

It is important, however, to keep in mind exactly what the legal obligation is.[1] The confessor is not free to impose more on the penitent. It would be very wrong, for example, to compel children to confess all venial sins for the sake of material integrity. No priest has a right to impose legislation not imposed by the Church. He might tell a child that it is a fine act of humility to mention all venial sins, but he should make it clear that there is no obligation to do so and that there should be no scrupulosity.

Similarly, it would be wrong to compel certain individual penitents to make materially integral confessions. For there is a principle which states: If fulfilling a positive law in a certain way would be harmful to a person, that person not only should not, but is even obliged not, to fulfill the law in that way.

There are surely times when a penitent is excused from satisfying the Church law of material integrity. I have no doubt that this is true in the case of a penitent whose past is cluttered with numerous sins against the sixth commandment. In fact, I will prove this by way of analogy.

Because he considered it too dangerous to awaken anew all the sexual faults and fantasies that might be connected with a person's past, Pius XII laid down the following as a rule with regard to treatment through depth psychology: "It is not permitted to awaken all the fantasies and memories of past sins if this would lead to new, unnecessary temptations."[2]

In view of this regulation which at times restricts a doctor's liberty to elicit complete information concerning a patient's sexual life, it seems to me an *a fortiori* conclusion to say that a confessor likewise may not urge a penitent to delve into his past to the extent of unduly reviving the temp-

[1] Cf. B. Häring, *The Law of Christ*, trans. E. Kaiser, vol. I, Newman, 1961, pp. 454ff.

[2] *On Psychotherapy and Religion*, an address of His Holiness Pope Pius XII to the Fifth International Congress on Psychotherapy and Clinical Psychology (April 13, 1953), Art. 24.

tation to former sins. Would not a penitent give a sufficiently accurate account of his past failures by confessing:
"Father, I've committed so many sins against purity, I don't
think I could begin to enumerate them. I just don't feel I
have the courage to reveal them all." The confessor can generally tell by the tone of the penitent's voice that what he is
actually trying to say is: "Father, whatever psychological balance and pride I have left will be completely destroyed if you
make me recall each of my sins against purity." I am convinced that it would be against the natural law for the confessor to persist in his demand that the penitent retrace his
impure fantasies, occasions of sin, temptations and actions
whereby he violated purity.

Each confessor should strive so to treat his penitent that
the latter, on leaving the box, would gladly pray in the words
of the psalmist: "What shall I render to the Lord for all He
has given me?" But if the confessor asks a person too many
questions, confession takes on an inquisitional tone and it
becomes psychologically impossible for priest and penitent
to give praise to God. In the penitent's anxiety to give an
accurate account of numbers and kinds of sin, he is likely
to be deprived, not only of the joy of the Sacrament, but also
of a firmer and more efficacious resolution to amend, a resolution that follows gratefully on joy. He will be left only with
the sterile satisfaction of having mentioned everything explicitly.

SPECIES AND NUMBER OF SINS

In general, Protestant and Orthodox theologians find many of
the distinctions of Catholic moralists regarding species rather
absurd. One of the greatest theologians of the Russian
Church, the famous convert Wladimir Soloviev, said that he
would never understand why Western theologians insisted
that fornication and adultery are "natural" sins while masturbation is an "unnatural" sin. Every sin, Soloviev points out,
violates the true dignity of the human person as well as the

friendship of Jesus Christ. Why, then, speak of certain sins as being in accord with human nature?

I sometimes wonder what moralists are trying to prove by dawdling over hairsplitting distinctions. Certainly they cannot expect the average person to understand these distinctions. Take the question asked in relation to the inferior species of sin. I have read one moral theologian who claims that masturbation by a married man is an entirely different species of sin from masturbation by an unmarried man. It would then follow that a confessor, in order to determine the species of sin, would have to ask anyone who confessed masturbation whether he is married or not. I have no objection to the question regarding the penitent's state of life being asked for the purpose of making spiritual direction more meaningful. Masturbation, insofar as it is a sign of infantilism or of a certain immaturity, can be an obstacle to happiness in married life. I am objecting to the line of thinking that requires this question for the sake of judging species, a line of thinking which leaves the confessor no alternative but to ask that question. More realistically, the same moralist says that he does not think that fornication would be a different species of sin if a condom were used. Unfortunately, in the next breath, he wavers and expresses some doubt about this opinion.

It is well for the confessor to remind himself that the Council of Trent, in legislating on the need to confess the circumstances which change the species of an act, could not have foreseen the exaggerations in which the moralists of the last century would indulge. The confessor should try to learn how the average person distinguishes sins. The latest scientific distinctions made by the moralists do not reach the ordinary layman. Therefore, the confessor, who himself might appreciate some of these distinctions, should not, generally speaking, ask more of the penitent who committed the sin than the penitent can distinguish.

All moral theologians agree that a penitent has only to confess a sin according to his understanding of that sin at the time he committed it. St. Augustine, for example, tells us that he was told by his mother that to have intercourse with a married woman was a much greater sin than with an unmarried woman. This, then, made a difference in his case, since it was what he understood to be so. If today a poorly educated man does not know the difference between adultery and fornication, and as a result does not mention the distinction, his confession is still materially integral. He confessed what he knew.

More important than a concern for complete accuracy regarding the penitent's self-accusation is the formation of conscience in the interest of future progress. In attempting to aid the penitent to form such a conscience, the confessor should abstain from all useless or tasteless questions regarding the sixth commandment. Nor should he allow the penitent to go into unnecessary detail. For example, if a man confesses that he has sinned against the sixth commandment with a girl, it will generally be clear from his words or from the tone of his voice or from the whole confession that he means a serious sin. Some moralists are of the opinion that the confessor should normally know whether the penitent means protracted petting with mutual defilement, or whether, in the case of intercourse, a condom was used; this opinion should be ignored. In so many of these cases the confessor will only provoke bewilderment or scandal by insisting on such distinctions, which actually contribute nothing to the conversion of the man.

As to confessing the number of times a sin was committed, the Church law says nothing explicitly. It only says that all mortal sins have to be confessed. Modern psychology teaches us that it is difficult for the average man to remember with accuracy the number of times he has done something beyond the count of seven. Keeping this fact in mind, the confessor is likely to be more understanding on the question of numbers, especially with the penitent who has been away from confession for a long time, or who has a habit of sin.

If a person is expected to recall the exact number of times he has committed a sin against the sixth commandment, he will have to review experiences which may readily produce impure phantasms and perhaps new excitation. No wonder, then, that after confession, we find a penitent falling back into his old habit of masturbation or succumbing to some other temptation. It is so senseless to expose a penitent to such a risk in order to find out exact numbers.

In some of the older moral theology books, the case of a reformed prostitute is considered. She is coming to confession for the first time after a career of sin. Note the emphasis on species and number in the series of questions proposed to the confessor: "For how many years have you been engaged in this trade? How many customers did you average per day? How many sins did you commit against nature? How often were your customers married men? On the average, how many of your customers were single men?"

Questions such as these are precisely the approach that I am attacking in this chapter. They may prove harmful to the confessor himself and are hardly beneficial to the conversion of the poor penitent. Further, in the particular type of case just mentioned, psychologists teach us that prostitutes in general are frigid when plying their trade, but once they decide to reform, they experience great difficulty in overcoming temptation related to their former sins. The type of questioning that certain moralists suggest can, in my opinion, only harm such a penitent. A reforming prostitute is known to feel deeply frustrated about her loss of dignity. If the priest questions her in the confessional in the manner suggested, he is likely to destroy the last vestige of dignity which she feels she has. It is sufficient for such a girl to make clear what she has done in some general way. This takes care of everything. Legal distinctions should not be asked for. Rather, the confessor should stress the great honor which the Lord is about to bestow upon her, that of becoming a child of God and living in a life of grace. In short, the confessor should help her realize, and even feel, that a new era is opening for her.

PROPORTION AMONG THE VARIOUS ROLES

In the past, there has been a tendency to overemphasize the confessor's role as judge. Unfortunately, the meaning and the structure of the Sacrament of Penance as a liturgy were sometimes lost in the din over the juridical aspects. Today, more and more theologians, prompted partially by the spirit of the times, are stressing the need for a greater concordance among the various roles that must be played by a confessor. As the representative of Christ who is the quintessence of the roles of Priest, Judge, Healer, and Redeemer, the confessor must direct the penitent toward a fuller Christian life. As a fellow-Christian, he should strive to persuade the penitent to join with him in the praise of Almighty God.

If the confessor harps on material integrity, scrupulously ferrets out numbers and species, he may seriously jeopardize the benefits of the Sacrament for the penitent. No doubt, before long he too will be as frustrated as his penitent. For he will be abdicating his role as peace-bringer and even, to some extent, as priest, whose office it is to promote an attitude of worship and praise of God.

CONCLUSION

I hope I will not be misunderstood. In this chapter, I am not encouraging a bare minimum fulfillment of the law. But there will be times when acceptance of the minimum in legal matters is in the best spiritual interest of a particular penitent. Ordinarily a man will not even ask whether he must confess this or that sin. He wishes his confession to be as fruitful as possible. He will be humble, honest, frank, and will endeavor to open his soul to the purifying action of God in the most complete way.

No confessor can impose spiritual growth like a law upon his penitent. But, at the same time, no confessor should shrink from encouraging his penitent gently to a higher life. He may tell the penitent, for example, to try to make his examination of conscience not only in the light of the Ten Commandments, but in the light of the New Law to love one another, in the light of the Sermon on the Mount. To teach a penitent openness according to the law of grace, to inspire in him a deepening sense of continual conversion, is a most noble task for a confessor. Only in this way will a penitent perceive the wrongness of his sins and, in a true spirit of atonement, humbly confess them even though they may only be venial. While it is true that a minimum fulfillment of the external (written) law suffices for everybody, the minimum is only a beginning for those who believe that they have a vocation to sanctity: they look to higher demands of humility without being blocked by legal scrupulosity. These results will be more easily obtained if the individual confessions are integrated into a communal celebration of the Sacrament of Penance.

9. THE CONFESSOR AND MATERIAL INTEGRITY OF CONFESSION

First Principle: *Within the Sacrament of Penance, the confessor's role insofar as the material integrity of the confession is concerned, is to supply help when the penitent is unable to fulfill his obligation.*

Today's confessor should not mechanically follow rules laid down by moralists of the eighteenth or nineteenth century with regard to the questioning of penitents. It would be foolish to take indiscriminately even what St. Alphonsus, the Patron of Confessors, had to say on this topic. For the most part, St. Alphonsus dealt with illiterate people, shepherds and fishermen who had little or no instruction whatever in matters of faith. He prudently geared his ideas about questioning to the needs of his time. To apply these questions inflexibly in the totally different circumstances of the twentieth century would almost certainly cause serious offense to penitents.

Within the Sacrament, the obligation to material integrity lies chiefly with the penitent. The average well-educated Catholic of today knows that he must confess all his mortal sins. I think it is safe to say that most people in North America and in Europe who go to confession on a fairly regular basis (more than once each year) are very much aware of their obligation to a materially complete self-accusation. In fact, many do more than is necessary in this regard. To presume that most penitents are ignorant on this point leads, not only to unnecessary questions, but to unnecessary offense.

Outside the Sacrament, the priest has the obligation properly to instruct his people concerning the manner of confessing. In so doing, he should present the average layman with a more balanced view between material integrity and the other aspects of the Sacrament. In addition to such things as catechesis, pamphlets and the *speculum conscientiae* (longer or shorter texts telling one how to examine his conscience), an excellent means of promoting fuller knowledge of confession is a Bible Vigil on conversion to God, or the communal celebration of the Sacrament of Penance with readings and a homily before the individual confessions.

Second Principle: Omne factum praesumitur recte factum. *There is a presumption in the penitent's favor that, in confessing his sins, he does so sincerely and properly.*

Unfortunately, scrupulosity or inadequate training causes some confessors to commit, at least objectively, a sin of suspicion. The penitent should be questioned about his intentions only if there are reasonable grounds for it. This is true regardless of what sins are being confessed, but particularly for sins against purity. In 1943, the Holy Office issued a strong warning against unnecessary questions about the sixth commandment. Even if the confessor has a slight doubt, the presumption still favors the penitent; no questions should be asked. A penitent who comes to the confessional with confidence must be received with confidence.

A distinction should be made, however, between those who confess regularly and those who do so infrequently. It is often evident that the latter are not properly prepared for an integral confession. Frequently these penitents indicate in their own way that they want the confessor to help them by questioning them.

Obvious as it may seem, the rules of courtesy oblige even

more in the confessional than they do in everyday life. Unfortunately, there are examples of confessors flagrantly disregarding these rules. One such example was presented to me by an acquaintance of mine, an intelligent and respectable gentleman holding a governmental position. He told me that because of the pressures of his work he sometimes got to confession only twice a year. However, each Sunday he went to Mass and Holy Communion. But in one of his Easter confessions, without any reason whatsoever, the confessor, on hearing that he had been away from confession for some time, asked him if he had committed any sins of sodomy. I think that objectively, at least, the confessor committed a serious sin. He certainly transgressed the law of common courtesy.

Third Principle: *Within the Sacrament, the primary responsibility of the confessor is to look to the formal integrity of the confession.*

It would be a grave mistake for the confessor to be so concerned about material integrity as to jeopardize the formal. The confessor who pressures his penitent for material integrity in the course of confession may easily arouse the penitent's resentment or shame to the point that the latter refrains from including certain sins.

If it should happen that a confessor fears, because of indications given him by the penitent, that the confession lacks formal integrity, he should gently ask the penitent whether he would like to be helped. "Do you mind if I ask you questions?", "Do you feel that you need any help?", "Do you feel that you've made a complete confession, or would you like me to help you by asking questions?" would all be acceptable queries in this case. If the penitent indicates that he does mind, then the confessor should go no further. Generally, however, if the penitent has hemmed and hawed, and a discreet question is courteously put to him indicating the confessor's intention to be of service, the offer is gratefully accepted.

It would be well for the confessor to review his method of questioning from time to time. A well-phrased question presented properly will evoke a docile response from the penitent. Gradually, no offense will be taken if the confessor prefaces his question with, "Did you have a temptation to . . . ?" For example, if the confessor suspects, because of the nature of the confession or indications during it, that a penitent may be withholding the fact of an abortion, he should say, "Did you have a temptation to seek an abortion after the sexual relationship which you have just mentioned?" So presented, the question makes it easier for the penitent to admit to an abortion if that be the case, but, at the same time, the wording is inoffensive enough to forestall astonishment or scandal on the penitent's part. In fact, it may happen in cases of this sort that the penitent will respond: "Yes, Father, I did have the temptation but I did not yield to it." And the confessor will have performed a real service to the penitent by helping her to relieve her conscience of the fact that she did entertain such a thought, even though no external act was committed.

But again, it is most important to show kindness and respect for the conscience of the penitent. The confessor must not try to impose on a penitent what the penitent cannot understand or cannot sincerely accept. Though a certain moral doctrine may be clear in his own mind, the confessor should not impose his opinion on a penitent whose conscience has not reached the same clarity of thought or who is unable to make or grasp the same distinctions.

Fourth Principle: *The sixth commandment is not the punctum puncti.*

The confessor is obliged to accord a proper place to all the commandments of God. He should place the commandments within the proper framework of primary obligations: faith, hope, charity, and the virtue of religion. These constitute the foundation of Christian ethics. The sixth commandment must be treated only in relation to these religious aspects of our life.

Generally speaking, it is a mistake for the confessor to begin direction by asking questions about the sixth commandment, even though eventually he may have to do so. The confessor should see to it that his comments on chastity are carefully integrated with the basic virtues of Christian morality. In presenting questions, gentleness should be the hallmark of the confessor. When a penitent requests the confessor to question him point by point, the confessor, broaching the subject of chastity, should proceed from the less serious to the more serious. For example, he should ask first whether the penitent is having difficulty with bad thoughts, rather than start abruptly by asking whether he has committed bad actions. If the confessor must also refer to deeds (at times, the penitent, given a lead, will continue on his own), then he should ask first about matters of rather widespread difficulty, which are relatively less shameful. Only when he finds that the penitent is deeply involved in a distorted sex life should he ask about other problems of a more shameful nature, and then chiefly with a view to necessary help toward perseverance.

The Young Christian Workers were asked one time to take note of what was being said about priests by the employees of one of the largest factories in Munich. They found many employees whose gratitude to the clergy was reflected by the respect with which they spoke of them. However, one of the grievances most frequently heard was that priests in the confessional often seemed too curious, particularly about the sixth commandment. The complaint came from a cross-section of Catholic factory-workers, even from the more devout. Possibly, it would be more accurate for them to blame not so much curiosity on the part of the confessor as faulty training. In the past, many people, including seminarians, were taught Christianity in a way that focused on chastity as though it were the principal commandment.

This poll among the factory hands in Munich is only one example of the extensive complaints regarding questions on purity. The instruction from the Holy Office warning confessors against asking too many questions about the sixth commandment was one of the most necessary admonitions given in the last thirty years. How many married people were tortured with unnecessary questions in the confessional!

Only when there are good reasons for doubting the formal

integrity of the confession, should the confessor bring up the subject of purity. If the confessor doubts whether or not he should ask questions in this area, it is better for him to refrain from inquiring. This is especially true for young priests. People seem to be more sensitive and more resentful when young priests question in this area than when more experienced confessors do so.

Fifth Principle: *To avoid causing harm, a confessor can often be excused from questioning, even if he has good reasons to doubt the material integrity of the penitent's confession.*

This principle, commonly accepted by moralists, pertains to questions about any commandment. Whenever questions would do more harm than good to the community or to the individual, they should be omitted.

So far as the community is concerned, a knowledge of social psychology and the actual situation prevailing in a town or parish may be indispensable. At times, missionaries may be invited into a parish where the parishioners, because of previous unpleasant experiences with some priest, are particularly resentful of questions. It will be the task of the missionary to detect such an attitude early and to alter his approach accordingly.

I remember preaching a parish mission with one of my confrères who, beyond doubt, is a prudent man. In the ordinary situation, he could not be said to exceed the general rules governing the questioning of penitents, yet, for that very reason, the people of this parish avoided his box. The people, it turned out, were hypercritical because of past unpleasant experiences, and after the first handful had confessed to him, they spread the word that he was another grand inquisitor. When the missionary confessor—or any confessor— notices a particularly strained atmosphere between him and the penitent, he would do well to limit his questions to what is absolutely necessary, and even then, he should first ask the penitent's permission to question him.

I have no doubt that in certain areas of South America where the priest is able to visit a town perhaps once a year, he has to—and is even expected to—help his penitents confess by reviewing the commandments with them, questioning them point by point. If that same priest were to come North to one of the big parishes and use the same approach in the confessional, he would offend many people. The reactions of penitents differ greatly from area to area, even within the same country. The confessor must be ready to cope with any social situation because the effectiveness of his ministry depends so much on the way people react.

Obviously, consideration must be given not only to the attitudes common in a given place, but also to the attitudes of each individual penitent. A man's attitude can often be detected by the way he speaks—loudly, softly, haltingly—and even at times from the way he breathes. These things give the confessor a working idea of the type of penitent he is dealing with, whether the person is phlegmatic, sanguine, scrupulous, nervous, timorous. If the confessor has a great love for people, if his hours in the confessional are more than mere routine to him, he will instinctively respond to all these things. Should he find himself confronted by an excitable person in the confessional, he will know enough to postpone questioning until he has won the penitent's confidence. At times, he will even refrain entirely from asking questions if he senses that this will give the person greater courage and love for the sacrament. This will especially be the case where the penitent has neglected to mention the number of times venial or doubtfully mortal sins were committed. If the confession involves mortal sins (with some certainty) and there is no special circumstance excusing the confessor from asking about the number of times a sin might have been committed, he might carefully frame his question along these lines: "You have humbly confessed these sins, but perhaps you have forgotten that you should also confess the approximate number. May I ask, did this happen once or many times?" But often it may be better not to ask at all.

Sixth Principle: *Internal sins are often implicitly confessed in the confession of external sins. The confessor should not inquire about things that are already implied in context.*

This principle applies in the following examples: if a man confesses that he has gravely offended another person several times by saying unkind things about him, the confessor may be sure that the penitent has had unkind thoughts about that person. Or, if a penitent confesses that he has committed adultery five times, the confessor can be sure that the penitent has entertained impure thoughts even more often. Sins of thought and desire have to be confessed, but they can be and often are implied in the confession of external sins.

There is some problem when no external sin is confessed. Just how far can and should the confessor go with questions concerning internal sins? If the penitent is a good Christian, a fact generally revealed by the confession, the assumption should be that he has not consented to bad thoughts deliberately and freely. In such cases, it would be imprudent for the confessor to ask about internal sins. If the penitent is a lax Christian, again determined by the confession itself, and if there is reason to doubt the formal integrity, the confessor, after noticing that no external sins are confessed, may sometimes adroitly remind him of the obligation to confess bad thoughts, desires and purposes that were deliberately and freely entertained. But generally it is better to refrain from questioning.

Seventh Principle: *If there is need for questions but time is scarce, those questions necessary and useful for the penitent's contrition, purpose of amendment and future spiritual growth prevail over those related only to the material integrity of the confession.*

If a confessor is overly concerned with material integrity, he may pass up the opportunity to talk with the penitent on those matters which would reorientate his spiritual life, especially questions about faith, hope and charity. The best traditional teaching has always insisted on this point. Father

Francis Connell, for example, admonished confessors to "follow a just and moderate course, avoiding both undue exactness and unjustifiable laxity in seeking to obtain material integrity" (*Spiritual and Pastoral Conferences to Priests*). Instead of spending time and energy only in securing integrity according to exact, and very often all too exact, theological rules, it would be more advisable to arouse in the penitent sentiments of deep sorrow and of trust in God's mercy and to invite him to join the confessor in praising God for His saving justice and mercy. The most noble mission of the priest, to instill joy and peace, must not be blocked by a meticulous concern for a wrongly understood material integrity. The confessor must know his various roles and fulfill the requirements of each with great sensitivity to the individual penitent. This does not rule out all necessity for questions, but the various roles of the confessor as messenger of peace, as teacher of the new law, as servant of the high-priest Jesus Christ will remind him that his major goal is the penitent's conversion and growth as an individual and a social being.

In the case of an invincibly ignorant penitent who cannot be enlightened on a certain point, the confessor might persuade or assign him some spiritual reading. If there is some evidence for suspecting that the penitent may be in a near occasion of sin, the confessor might say: "I have no reason to doubt that you've made a splendid confession. Perhaps you will allow me to ask, in order to make sure that you're on the road to progress: is there any special difficulty in your life that you would like to speak about?" Very much depends on the way the question is asked.

In the case of a man apparently well disposed, the confessor might take a more positive and direct approach in presenting a plan for the penitent's advancement. For instance, he may ask, "Until now, have you tried at all to improve your environment? What do you think you could do among your friends and neighbors to help shape better opinion on matters of religion and morality?"

A confessor might unwittingly neglect to trace a problem to its source. Let me explain what I mean. A young girl of the upper social class confessed that she had procured an abortion. The history of her case, I think, was far from unique. She had sinned with a young man who, at the time, she believed was going to marry her. But the romance suddenly tapered off. When the girl discovered she was pregnant, she ran to her mother to ask what she should do. Her mother did not say a word; she simply gave a slight shrug of the shoulders. This reaction confused the girl at first and she thought that perhaps her mother had not heard what she had said. The girl repeated that she was pregnant. Again the mother shrugged her shoulders. This time the girl understood. She realized that if she did have the child, her mother wanted no part in helping her. Under these circumstances, the girl's chances for bringing up the child decently seemed nonexistent. She ran off and found herself an abortionist. In this case, the girl's mother certainly was more responsible for the crime than the girl herself. I believe, then, that it is more important to seize the proper opportunity of asking mothers what kind of advice they give their daughters on birth control than to ask the young daughter the same question. But better than questioning in the confessional is a proper effort to instruct the faithful outside the confessional.

Both modern sociology and pastoral theology, in the light of the constitution *The Church in the Modern World,* acknowledge the importance of sound public opinion. Each Christian should make it his business to try to change an erroneous public opinion. Consequently, it is helpful at times for a confessor to inquire whether a penitent is supporting certain warped ideas, or how he reacts when confronted with these ideas by others. In general, people do not consider that these are points for confession. Many pious persons could confess more than the fact that they were distracted in prayer.

Grandmothers and other relatives should be taught how to speak about such matters as marriage, large families and sex. We tend to overlook the importance of proper education in this area. Naturally, the confessor must exercise prudence in bringing this point to a penitent's attention, but if the penitent is pious and obviously has a great respect for the confessor—and many have—the confessor need have no fear that the person will be insulted or threaten to stay away from confession. The rule should be: ask those who show that they can take it. But even here the confessor must always ask with the greatest respect. Oftentimes when these penitents, in response to the confessor's query, say that they have failed the Church regarding the way they have spoken of, or neglected to speak about, certain things, their fault is chiefly one of inadvertence. The confessor, then, by reminding them of their obligation, has given them a further means of advancement.

This topic reminds me of the day I met a friend with whom I had spent some time in Russia. Both of us were delighted to meet again, and my young friend lost no time in telling me about his good wife and three wonderful children. In the course of his proud stories about the children and the things they say and do, he suddenly became depressed and said sadly that he and his wife could not have another child. I asked if it were a question of health. "No," he said, "we're both very healthy. And it's not money either. We're pretty well off. It's just my mother. She gave my wife so much trouble after the second child, and even more trouble after the third." The young man's mother had heard some talk in the neighborhood that her son could not control himself, and that as a result his wife was pregnant almost every year. Where she had every reason to be proud, she felt ashamed. As a result of this gossip, she warned her son and daughter-in-law rather violently not to have any more children. "Is your mother a Catholic?" I asked. "Oh," he answered, "she's a very good Catholic. She goes to Mass and Communion several times a week, and never misses a First Friday." If only my friend had realized his obligation to instruct his mother, or his mother her obligation to instruct her gossiping neighbors!

I recall a similar story of another friend where the outcome, happily, proved quite different. This young man and his wife had six children. He told me that his mother-in-law made a terrible fuss after each child was born, particularly after the third. In fact, she threatened never to visit the family again if they had another child within the following two years. "So," he said, "I told her, 'You've always been welcome here, you know that. But if you continue with this kind of talk, then the case will be different. This is my family, and if God sends us more children, then we'll be happy to accept them.'" Obviously hurt by his directness, the mother-in-law stayed away for quite some time. However, when she finally resumed her visiting, when she met and fell in love with the new members of the family, she had to admit that of all her children's homes that she went to, none delighted her more than this. In fact, she complained that her other sons and daughters who had one or two children would be better off with larger families. She felt that her other grandchildren were too spoiled.

This same friend gave me a rather interesting epilogue to this story. Though he did not say so himself, it was evident from this story how well he had trained his own children to appreciate each other. Several times a year the various aunts and uncles visited with their families. He often overheard his nieces and nephews boasting to his own children about how many presents they had received at Christmas and on their birthdays, in the way children are prone to boast. But on one Christmas visit, one of his nephews, an only child, in front of the entire family of relatives teased one of this man's sons about the scarcity of toys the son had received, and went on to enumerate all his gifts. Suddenly, the man's oldest boy came to the rescue. The father told me that he would never forgot how proud he felt when he heard his son say, "But we have a Bernard, and a Mary, and five brothers and sisters. That's better than a lot of toys."

Surely the pulpit can and should promote the idea of the people's obligation to shape a more healthy public opinion about Christian doctrine on a far broader and more frequent scale than the confessional. Still, if through their preaching and missions priests have alerted the people to the opportunity for this apostolate, then the confessor can all the more easily remind his penitents of their obligation.

While I would by no means limit the following idea to penitents whose confession may be materially imcomplete, I offer this general rule: when the confessor must prudently refrain from asking questions necessary for a materially complete confession, he should compensate for this omission. A particularly profitable compensation would be to educate the penitent with regard to greater responsibility in the apostolate, and especially in the formation of a sound and healthy public opinion of Christian doctrine.

If good penitents recognize and perform this obligation, then many more people will realize what is sinful and what they have to confess. In short, the Sacrament of Penance will play a still greater role in the conversion of men to Jesus Christ.

10. THE FORMATION OF
A CHRISTIAN CONSCIENCE

This chapter is divided into three parts: (1) an explanation of what the term "conscience" means along with basic principles flowing from this concept; (2) the formation of conscience in relation to man's faith; (3) the formation of conscience as knowledge and as a creative power.

MEANING OF CONSCIENCE

Today the word "conscience" has a broader meaning than the old scholastic term "conscientia." In scholastic terminology, *conscientia* referred simply to a man's judgment on how he is to act here and now if he wishes to please God. The modern concept of conscience comprises both this notion and the scholastic concept of *synteresis*, *i.e.*, that disposition which enables, in fact urges, a man to form a correct judgment of conscience and to act upon it. In this sense, conscience refers to more than the individual act. It is the fundamental capability of man to determine and to experience dynamically his obligations toward God, or, a capability that allows man to understand the call of God and to respond to it. That call is generally mediated through the teaching and the witness of the Church, through the needs of our neighbor, and through the gifts that God has bestowed on the individual. While it is an evil to distort a single act of conscience, *i.e.*, to make a wrong judgment in a particular situation, it is a still greater evil to distort or destroy conscience as a disposition or moral capability.

The Thomists regard this capability known as conscience from a different point of view than does the school of St. Augustine (which includes St. Bonaventure). While many Thomists stress the role of the intellect in the work of conscience, the Augustinians linger on the role of the will. The Thomists see conscience as the capability of having a correct insight into what is good, a series of self-evident principles. The Augustinians, who assert the primacy of love in their analysis of what man is, maintain that conscience is the very depth of the soul (deepest *scintilla animae*). It is that power in man that is directed and touched by the *ordo amoris*, the order of value, of love. It is the channel whereby God as Infinite Love, wishing to make men sharers in that love, communicates with the individual.

The difference between these two schools of thought is not so great as it may seem at first glance. Good Thomists, while emphasizing the function of the intellect, would not deny that the practical judgment of conscience includes an act of the heart and will of man. And the Augustinians, for the most part, agree that conscience is not simply an act of the will and heart alone. Both see the work of conscience as an act of the whole man.

Conscience arouses man and urges him from the very depth of his being toward the real good. It produces a joint seeking of the good by the intellect and the will, not as simply juxtaposed, but as internally integrated faculties.

Man is made to the Image of God in mind, in will, in his power to love. But man mirrors that Image most perfectly when the penetrating desire of conscience issuing from his being unites intellect, will and love, and strives to keep them united in the daily discovery of the good.

In God, despite the distinction of Persons, there is absolute unity between the Word and the Spirit of Love. Man is created to the image and likeness of God, and ideally, he too enjoys this unity of his being, though in a finite way, in his search for the good. However, in man there can be a reluctance on the part of the will to join with moral intelligence. Further, man can be even more unlike God in that his heart and will can be misled.

The formation of conscience, therefore, cannot be restricted simply to instructing the intellect. Formation of conscience involves the formation of an entire personality, a personality which, through its internal unity, will pay witness to the Mystery of Unity in God Himself. The emotions, the affectivity, cannot be neglected in this formation. Affectivity fosters the unity between the moral intelligence and the moral will.

The effectiveness of the confessor in helping a penitent to form a proper conscience will depend largely on how well integrated the confessor's own personality is and also on his understanding of the necessity for an integrated approach. He must educate the penitent to seek a unity of intellect and will and heart in his life. He can never be content to provide only knowledge of what should be done. Rather, he should seek a way of introducing knowledge that will touch the *scintilla animae*, the innermost depth of the heart. This he will achieve by helping the penitent translate the new information into personal terms, by finding applications of the proposed values in the penitent's daily life. Only then will a penitent feel attracted by this truth.

BASIC PRINCIPLES

If the confessor wishes the penitent to form his own conscience properly, the confessor must himself bear witness to the fundamental love of God and of neighbor.

A man who does not love suffers from a sort of spiritual blindness. He can neither see nor appreciate the basic truth that all things reflect the Triune love of God. Love is the magic reality that restores vision. The confessor lacking in this love but directing penitents might be likened to the blind man leading the blind.

One who knows all the casuistic solutions to theological problems can never apply them effectively to real life if he does not love. He can instruct the intellect of others, but he cannot help to form a conscience in the full sense.

If a confessor has a properly formed conscience—a term that implies the notion of synteresis—he will not only exercise mature judgment in his own everyday life, but will communicate to others the great reality of true love through his whole attitude. Being attracted to the good in his own innermost being, he will bring to the penitent the tidings of God's all-embracing love in such a way that the penitent will feel the joy and the peace of the Sacrament and likewise be moved in the depths of his own being.

THE CONSCIENCE AND THE GOSPEL

The confessor must convince the penitent of the necessity of continuing the search for a fuller understanding of the religious and moral life. If a man thinks only of what he must do to avoid mortal sin, he still reveals the mentality of a slave, untutored in the liberty of the Law of the New Testament. He will never enjoy the fruits of liberty until he learns the Gospel as a new way of life. This learning applies to much more than the isolated rules of casuistry. He must try to understand how he can please God, how he can express his fidelity to the New Law, the full Law of the love of God and neighbor, in all things, through all the virtues and through the fulfillment of all the commandments. In short, he must seek to comprehend the meaning of faith and its demands.

ALERTNESS TO THE KAIROS

St. Paul expresses a fundamental attitude of the Christian conscience in his Epistle to the Ephesians: "Use the present opportunity to the fullest" (5:16).

For the formation of conscience, it is not enough merely to know abstract principles. A typically Christian virtue is vigilance for and awareness of the present opportunity. This concept of *kairos*, the hour of grace that God prepares, is one of the profoundest Biblical concepts. God reveals to the Christian the needs of others and gives him special gifts whereby to alleviate those needs. But only through vigilance can a man grasp the challenging call of the hour.

In His own life, Christ spoke of His hour as not yet come or as having arrived. Frequently He exhorted his disciples to be watchful and ready. The parable of the wise and the foolish virgins is a call to watchfulness. For the formation of conscience in the fullest sense, a man must appreciate the fact that God has prepared the present opportunities to do good. A Christian conscience means, then, a loving awareness of the present needs of the community and of one's neighbor.

PERSONAL AND COMMUNAL RESPONSIBILITY

A Christian conscience does not imply the mechanical application of general rules. Instead, a man in his innermost being tries to grasp what the present will of God is for him within the community of the Church, in the family, in society, in the person-to-person encounters. His response is expected to be a function of the individual gifts bestowed upon him by God. All individual gifts are given for the common good, for the community or common life, for the common attainment of salvation. One can be said to have a Christian conscience if he approaches his moral problems and, above all, his relationship to his neighbor from the viewpoint of the gifts of God, using those gifts in the best interest of the community.

The confessor's constant endeavor should be to educate the penitent to live according to his own conscience. The great temptation today is to yield blindly or instinctively to the pattern of one's environment, or to the life style advocated on movie and television screens. Today, motion pictures and television have an uncanny influence over many of our young people. They are continually confronted by a celluloid world setting prime value on the beauty and pleasures of the body. Worse still, many of these celluloid heroes portrayed by the actors are either violent individuals or simply freelance lovers, and the cameras manage to catch only the comic effects of their escapades.

There is, then, an urgent need to help people form a mature conscience. The man who has a properly formed Christian conscience experiences the freedom of the children of God. This experience fortifies him against mediocrity and self-centeredness, and makes him less likely to fall prey to the unenlightened patterns of his environment. He recognizes that his contribution to his environment will serve the common good only so long as he preserves his own personality and lives according to his own conscience as a Christian.

THE SIGNS OF DISCERNMENT

All the criteria for true morality or true life must finally be subsumed under the following criterion: "Am I making a positive contribution to the common life of the community or society in which I live, and to the Church at large?" (cf. I Cor. 12; Eph. 4; Gal. 5:19-24).

If the confessor desires to help his penitent form a Christian conscience, he will teach him to distinguish between a selfish love and a self-effacing love of God and neighbor. Only the unselfish lover will sincerely search for the will of God. As he grows in the joy of faith and the knowledge of revelation, he will seek new means of expressing this growth in his daily life, regardless of self-sacrifice.

If the penitent's faith in eternal life alerts him to the present opportunities for the practice of virtue, that penitent truly fits the description of the vigilant disciple. His uniqueness as a person will express itself in a fully developed, responsible regard for the common good.

FAITH AND PRAYER

Christian formation of conscience is based on the spirit of faith. St. Paul writes: *Quod non est ex fide, peccatum est* (Rom. 14:23). This quote may be rendered in English as "Everything which does not arise from the conviction of conscience is sin."

The judgment of conscience must come from the depths of one's faith. Hence the demand that Christians be men of prayer. Only a man who habitually seeks God's guidance through prayer will know exactly what God expects of him: "Watch therefore and pray."

Only prayer can sensitize a man to the apostolic possibilities of the present situation. For help and guidance from above, prayer is necessary. But simple repetition of accepted formulas or lip service paid to God is not truly prayer. In prayer, a man meditates on the wonderful law of our God and the good tidings of Jesus Christ.

A man given to meditation can really understand the call of faith in life. Therefore, a typically Christian formation of conscience includes an effort to deepen one's faith. Once more, we are not referring to bare abstract articles of faith that can be memorized, but to a real, joyful understanding of the faith. Joyful because it belongs to the conscience of the whole man. This certainly implies that the emotional response is also of great importance, but only as a part of a well-balanced personality. Emotion and intelligence thrive on the dynamism generated by their mutual contact. But apart, that dynamism must quickly fizzle out.

The man with a true conscience not only understands but actually feels his indebtedness to Christ and, led to action by the power of his conviction, he begins a process of perpetual action and reaction, his convictions inspiring deeds, his deeds strengthening his convictions.

It is simply belaboring the obvious to say how necessary it is that the confessor be the integral man, his prayer life nourishing his faith, his faith increasing his joy, his joy brimming over so much that it touches the life of his penitent and in turn moves him. While word of the Messianic peace and of reconciliation must be communicated with some solemnity, it is important too that it come to the penitent aglow with the warmth of a joyful heart.

DEEPENING SENSE OF CONTRITION

"I have not yet reached perfection, but I press on, hoping to take hold of that for which Christ took hold of me" (Phil. 3:12).

The closer a man draws to God, the more aware he becomes of his many imperfections. Man's condition is that of the traveller following the ever-receding horizon of perfection.

None of us can assert that his conscience is perfectly formed, not even the moral theologian with a thousand pages of principles and cases to his credit. Knowledge does not guarantee good will. Nor can good will substitute for knowledge.

Our nature yearns for the perfect harmony between intellect and will. When a schism exists between these two faculties, man becomes a sort of spiritual schizophrene. The remedy for such a condition need not be delayed. In fact, a confessor should urge his penitent that any time there is opposition between intellect and will, any time the penitent falls by refusing a grace, he should immediately have recourse to an act of contrition. A true formation of conscience involves this deepening sense of contrition in a humble encounter with Christ.

A great deal can be learned about a penitent if a confessor were to ask him: "When you committed these sins, did you ever think of making an act of sorrow?" We may encourage ourselves along with the penitents: "If we're careful to make an act of contrition, an act of confidence in God after any fall, we can be certain to meet in Heaven."

In his Diary, Pope John writes about immediate recourse to contrition in a touching way. He says that if, after failing God in any way, he made a quick act of sorrow, he found that he could proceed joyfully, as if Jesus had given him a kiss. Besides being in accord with the best tradition of the spirituality of the Church, this is one of the most practical expressions of Pope John's spirituality.

11. GUIDING THE FORMATION
OF CONSCIENCE

At times, because of faulty training, certain penitents seem to be interested only in knowing whether a sin they committed is mortal or venial. They show surprise at the confessor's admission that he cannot give a definite answer regarding the subjective guilt of a particular act. When such a penitent presents himself, the confessor should seize the opportunity to help him form his conscience for the future. This formation will involve the consideration, not simply of the gravity of an act, but even more an orientation for the future in the light of beautiful aspects of the Sacrament such as the forgiveness of God and love of neighbor. However, training of a mature conscience includes the presentation of certain criteria for determining the seriousness of the act.

In judging the gravity of the offense, the penitent must first of all determine what his fundamental attitude was at the time he committed it. "Did I will, consciously and freely, to prefer my own egoism or any created thing to God? Did I feel that I was deliberately separating myself from God? Did I fully realize that I was resisting the will of God?" There may be times when the external act itself is a slight violation of the law of God, but the man's internal attitude is a decisive declaration of contempt for God's will. Such an internal attitude (a fundamental option) renders the affront serious.

If the penitent pleads innocent to a contumacious attitude, then the criteria lead him to consider the relative importance of the action itself. Such a probe can only result in a rough estimate of the guilt incurred since a multiplicity of factors went into making this particular action what it was.

Where, exactly, does the dividing line between a mortal and a venial sin lie? No blanket answer can be given. The boundaries between a mortal sin and a venial sin vary from penitent to penitent, and even vary within the same penitent from time to time. For the penitent does not always have the same attention and awareness of the gravity of his actions before God's holy will.

One of the great traditions of the Church holds that the basic reason why an offense against God can be a slight sin at all is not because of the relativity of matter, but because of man's impaired nature, resulting in his imperfect knowledge and the frailty of his will. An angel cannot commit a venial sin. An angel sees at a glance all that God's holy will asks of him or commands him to do. A refusal in his case would constitute a total refusal of God's holiness. The Church Fathers thought that Adam could not have first committed a venial sin. His first sin had to be mortal, they said, because of the extraordinary degree of his freedom. In a discussion on lying, St. Augustine posed this question: "Is the lie of a perfect man a mortal sin?" He and after him many other theologians incline toward the opinion that a man who is perfect in knowledge and freedom would clearly see that this lie could not be reconciled with the love of God and its demands. And so, it would be a grave offense. However, the ordinary man of general good will does not commit a mortal sin when the matter is relatively light.

Age may also be a factor in determining whether a sin committed is mortal or venial. The confessor should not judge a child's transgressions in the way he might an adult's. My personal opinion is that a child, generally speaking, does not commit a mortal sin before the age of twelve or fourteen. It does not follow, however, that all the moral actions of children are to be ignored by the confessor. In all likelihood, these actions will provide the pattern for future moral decisions and so the child should be carefully weaned from objectionable habits and given direction that will serve him better in the development of moral freedom and joy later on.

The question of whether a particular act is or is not a mortal sin is often raised when a penitent wishes to know, not whether he has sinned mortally in the past, but whether he can commit this same act in the future without fear of serious sin. In short, the penitent is hoping to elude the demands of God's will without committing moral suicide. This is a very dangerous attitude. A deliberate escape from the holy will of God amounts to flight from the fullness of life itself. A man's only refuge in such flight must be sheer legalism. In freeing himself from God, then, he enslaves himself to the law. Kindly but firmly such a penitent must be brought around to a better frame of mind. He must be taught to see that the question should not be, "Is this a mortal sin?" but, "Is this the right response to the loving will of God?"

Sometimes a penitent will ask whether an act is a mortal or a venial sin because he is in real, honest doubt, especially about the obligation to confess before receiving Communion. There is no great problem for the confessor here. If the penitent is a person of good will, a bare doubt as to whether or not he has sinned seriously should not deter him from receiving Communion.

There are times when a penitent might suffer from a perplexed conscience. In a given situation, he may have thought that any option open to him involved sin, mortal or venial. In his anxiety he judged that one choice would involve only venial sin, and so he selected the lesser of two evils. If the penitent saw no better solution, he is not guilty of any sin at all. For he believed he had no freedom to choose anything but sin. In aiding such a penitent, the confessor must gain a clear picture of the case in point, and show him that in this case, as in all cases, a person always has the choice of a right course of action, is never forced to choose sin, whether mortal or venial. It is a question of helping a penitent come to a better understanding of morality and law.

THE SACRAMENTAL FORMATION OF CONSCIENCE

The formation of conscience by the confessor must be constructive. The Sacrament, in destroying the effects of past sins, should likewise help to destroy the affection for these sins by deep contrition and firm purpose of amendment. An ever-growing sense of charity and social consciousness should replace the sinful affections. For the formation of conscience must always be guided by the principle that all gifts of God are given in view of the common good, not in view of a self-centered search for salvation or perfection. A confessor who limits his task to a cataloguing of sins and obligations is practicing moralism in the worst sense. As a messenger of peace he should rather point out to the penitent God's wondrous interest and activity in the whole of Christian life: what He did in the Sacrament of Baptism; what He fulfills in the Sacrament of Confirmation; what He grants in the Sacrament of the Eucharist; how He restores and strengthens the life of grace in the Sacrament of Penance. The grace of God offers the Christian more than assistance to fulfill the commandments. Through the action of the Holy Spirit, this grace purifies the heart and motives and will of man and promotes a grateful, "sacramental" response in the life of the penitent. But for grace to produce such a response, the penitent must be alive to the fact that God has freed him from the shackles of sin and in their stead, offers the liberating ties of love and gratitude.

The sacramental formation of conscience must be directed especially toward forgiveness and love of enemies. For Our Lord says:

> If you only love those who are your friends, what reward can you expect . . . be all goodness just as your Heavenly Father is all good.
>
> Mt. 5:46-48

In the Sacrament of Peace, Christ teaches us: "Be compassionate as your Father is compassionate" (Luke 6:36).

St. Thomas discusses the absolution of a man who, having confessed a sin of hatred of his neighbor or enmity, later returns to that same sinful attitude militating against his former detestation of this sin. Would his sin remain forgiven? He answers that whatever God has once forgiven remains forgiven, but the whole heavy burden of his past sin and the forgiveness of God weighs upon the renewed attitude of hatred.[1] Our Lord illustrated this very point in the gospel of the good King and the unforgiving servant (Mt. 18:21-35). The penitent, then, should be made aware of the fact that it is his experience of the kindness of God that obliges him to a greater, more merciful and patient love of neighbor.

The primary action governing the penitent's life is grace, that is, the gracious action of God in man's soul and heart and mind. From this it follows that he does what he has to do in response to the gifts of God, and in view of both the present manifestation of God's goodness and his final hope, eternal life in full revelation. It is not right to celebrate the liturgy of this Sacrament without calling the penitent's attention to this reality. The confessor's admonition would remain pure moralism divorced from the sacramental action of Christ, and would hardly aid in the formation of a mature Christian conscience.

THE ECCLESIAL FORMATION OF CONSCIENCE

The doctrine which the priest teaches is not his own. He has no right to adjust moral theology to his personal way of looking at things.

In the confessional, the priest represents the Church. His primary consideration should be whether he is being faithful to the teachings of the Church even though his direction of a penitent may humiliate him in view of his own shortcomings.

Lack of success in the confessional does not necessarily indicate a failure on the confessor's part to respond to the full

[1] See St. Thomas, *Summa Theologica*, Q. 88, art. 2-3, P. III.

responsibilities of his role, though it will often result when the confessor neglects to unite himself with the Church in proclaiming the "law of the Spirit." This law urges the confessor to help a penitent to love and to understand the doctrine of the Church as the doctrine of Christ and to realize what this doctrine means for him here and now. A good ecclesial approach presupposes a good grounding in ecclesiology, that is, a knowledge of what the Church really is. Every confessor should make it a point to read carefully the constitution *Lumen Gentium*, which sets forth the Church's present understanding of her own nature.

Some mistakenly think that the ecclesial formation of conscience means teaching simply the positive laws of the Church, *e.g.*, no work on Sunday and the like. On this basis, some of the older prayerbooks devote a whole chapter to examination of conscience. In fact, I remember one rather widely used prayerbook of Irish origin that based the gravity of sins on a rather strange principle. Under mortal sins it listed: eating meat on Friday, servile work on Sunday, missing Mass on Sunday, coming late (*i.e.*, after the chalice has been uncovered) to Sunday Mass, not supporting the Church, and sins against the sixth commandment. Then there followed a catalogue of some 72 venial sins that included: not praying, not making an act of faith, hatred of one's neighbor, injustice, and so forth. On the whole, the author of that book seemed to assume that the most important laws were those which the Church had imposed upon herself. After these, some consideration was given to lighter faults, namely, faults against the laws revealed by Almighty God and written in man's heart. I characterize this as a wholly mistaken ecclesial approach. The Church's primary task is to proclaim the word of God, to proclaim the Gospel as fundamental law. The confessor's task, then, must be to set the natural law, "the signs of the time" and the positive laws of the Church in their proper relationship to the law of Christ.

The penitent who has had his conscience formed according to the law of Christ will regard the Church as a Mother whose first consideration is for the welfare of her children. The law of grace which she proclaims is not a law that kills. It is a law that gives the penitent an insight into the heart of God, a God who is both father and mother to His people. In teaching the positive laws, the confessor must help the penitent understand that the Church imposes these laws only out of her motherly love and consideration. One must not follow them literally if to do so frustrates the intent of the law.

LOVE OF GOD AND NEIGHBOR AS SYNTHESIS

The Ten Commandments are not the best representation of Christian morality. Now that Christ has come, Christians are expected to accept the Gospel as the chief norm of their lives. To do otherwise is to ignore the fact of the Incarnation.

St. Augustine, one of the first Fathers of the Church to take the Ten Commandments as a basis for a short presentation of Christian morality, carefully laid down the fundamental conditions for the use of this approach. He insisted that the Commandments be presented within the framework of the New Covenant, that account be taken of the Sermon on the Mount and of Christ's great law of love. And in all of his works, Augustine particularly stressed the operations of the Holy Spirit as the essential aspect of New Testament law. Everyone, then, is expected to fulfill the command to love God and neighbor, "According to the measure of Christ's gift" (Eph. 4:7) through the action of the Holy Spirit.

In countries where people may be accustomed to examining their conscience by a consideration of the Commandments, the confessor must be most careful to furnish the penitent with a fuller understanding of Christian life. I tried to meet the customs of different countries in my work, *The Law of Christ*, by providing two distinct formats. In the English edition, for example, in volume II, I interrelated the life of communion with God with the first three Commandments. In the third volume, love of neighbor is developed through a specific consideration of each Commandment that looks to our fellowship in Christ (III-X). However, the French edition follows an entirely different format because of the different catechetical tradition already prevailing in that country.

It is agreed that external format in the presentation of moral obligations is by no means the most important consideration. The spirit with which a man should meet his obligations, namely, insisting on the primacy of love of God and of neighbor, is the most important consideration. And along with charity, faith and hope, it must be recognized as part of the foundation of a Christian life.

God has communicated a loving revelation and promise to man. Faith and hope urge man to respond to this revelation. And even when man does respond, his response originates not from his own human and weak love, but rather from Christ's love urging him from within. These are some of the many and beautiful aspects that should be presented to a penitent in the formation of conscience. For the more a confessor can make the penitent aware of the loving kindness of God, the greater the incentive he provides for a return of that love.

12. THE FORMATION OF CONSCIENCE: FAITH, HOPE AND CHARITY

THE VIRTUE OF FAITH

Faith, not the sixth commandment, is the *punctum puncti* in the formation of a Christian conscience. It is the doctrine of the Church that faith is the foundation, source and root of justification. Hence, if our *praxis confessarii* is to be orthodox and faithful to the doctrine of the Church, our greatest attention must focus on a deepening and purifying of that virtue in the penitent.

SACRAMENT OF FAITH

Sorrowful confession is not simply a telling of one's sins, but also a profession of faith. It is important to draw the penitent's attention to this point, especially if he has not been to confession for a long time. For if the penitent's awareness to the implications of his confession is enhanced, the Sacrament becomes the more meaningful to him. And so, the confessor might reassure him that, contrary to the inclination to evil expressed by his sins, his humble telling of those sins has once more given expression to his faith. In effect, his confession amounts to a renewed allegiance to the goodness and holiness and justice of God's law. He further demonstrates his belief in the power of the Lord who, through the ministry of the Church, makes him free from his sins.

The penitent must now learn to sustain this profession of faith through a carry over in behavior when he returns to his family, his work, his recreation. In concrete terms, this means the attempt to incorporate his humble acknowledgment of God's will into his everyday life, never hesitating to proclaim the truth to those who, for one reason or another, confuse right with wrong. Such fortitude gives others occasion to reappraise their own faith and standards of morality.

At times the confessor will have to call a penitent's attention to a need to deepen his knowledge of faith. A very practical way for the confessor to do this would be to assign, with the penitent's approval, a penance such as a daily short reading of Scripture or another spiritual book, or even of the diocesan newspaper, presuming it is good.

But growth in faith is not simply a question of knowledge. Even before the penitent leaves the confessional, the confessor must make him realize the significance of his absolution as a great message of faith and hope. The confessor can do this by celebrating the Sacrament in such a way that his own faith finds resonance in the heart of the penitent. The faith of the whole community helps and strengthens that of each member on the occasion of a communal celebration of the Sacrament.

Formation of conscience in faith is successful if the penitent recognizes that his life should be a joyful response to the revelation of God's salvation. Bearing this in mind, the confessor may encourage him especially to attend to those aspects of his faith which bring him joy, *e.g.*, aspects related to his family life.

By faith the Christian is called upon to be a light shining in the darkness of the world. It is not enough that he does not deny or disown His Master. He has the further obligation of leading others to the happiness he has found. This duty particularly presses upon him with regard to his proximate environment. The Sacrament of Penance, as a Sacrament of Faith, invites him to fulfill this obligation in reparation for his sins.

What environment could be more proximate to a penitent than his own home? Without denying the need to admonish married people at times on matters pertaining to conjugal chastity, I say that confessors will obtain better results—even with regard to chastity—if they concentrate their greatest effort on deepening the couple's faith. Help the couple look to their family life as a vocation to grow together in faith! If they understand that they have a mutual responsibility to exalt the events of daily life in the light of faith, they will surely grow in the knowledge of Our Lord Jesus Christ and in a deeper understanding of the mystery of marriage.

Parents have the wonderful vocation of looking to the sacramental education of their children. Through baptism, they introduce the child to the realm of faith. By their example, they teach the child how to live that faith. The regular confessor of a good married couple about to have a child might encourage them to celebrate the baptism in a way that will bring edification to the rest of the family as well as to the neighbors. I heard once of how a simple farmer approached his pastor and said: "Father, I came to arrange for the baptism of my eighth child. After the baptism of my other children, I always felt something was wrong. The ceremony was performed almost in secrecy, as though we should be ashamed of giving another child to Christ. This baptism I would like to make as joyful as possible. Could the bells be rung? Could you invite the members of the parish to take part if they wish? In this way, I'll be able to share my joy with everybody. I want the people to sing and praise God because a new child has been born into this parish." The man's sincerity so moved the pastor that he wholeheartedly supported the suggestions. In fact, the pastor admitted that he decided then and there to examine his conscience on the practice of baptism in his parish. His reflection on what this simple farmer had said led him to conclude that he had failed his people with regard to the celebration of this great Sacrament of Faith. I am not recommending bell-ringing at every baptism. The point I am making is that pastors with a little imagination might devise ways of making the Sacrament more meaningful to the entire parish. In one place, the pastor welcomes the children to be baptized that Sunday by including their names in the Prayer of the Faithful prayed by the entire Sunday congregation.

The confessor himself should carefully consider ways in which he can develop his own faith with regard to baptism, and so help his penitents to develop theirs. When he has occasion to baptize a child, he might capitalize on the occasion and remind all present that the word of God about to be spoken in this ceremony was once spoken to them at their baptism. He might remind them of the grace being offered to them who join in the liturgy of this Sacrament, to testify to their own faith by joyfully reciting the Creed together, and finally to carry this renewal into their daily lives. As confessor, he can urge the father and mother to assist at the ceremony and meditate on the implications of the message conveyed by the liturgy regarding the Christian education of their child. In baptism, through the ministry of the Church, the Heavenly Father acknowledges His claim of this child: "He has now become my beloved son!" The parents of that child can no longer limit their responsibility to training the child in the formation of good habits: "Do this, but avoid that." It is their privilege to explain continually by word and deed the total meaning of this sacramental proclamation of good tidings.

Some parents feel that if they send their child to a Catholic school they are fulfilling their obligation for providing a Christian education. This is not so. Pope St. Pius X, who made seven the average age for receiving Holy Communion, made it quite clear that normally the parents should accept the most rewarding task of preparing the child for the reception of the Sacred Eucharist. If the child is instructed only by the priest or by the nuns, if the parents abdicate their duty entirely, the child, in the depths of his subconscious, will tend to associate these things more with the school and the sisters and the pastor than with everyday life.

A child is a natural hero-worshiper and his earliest heroes

are his own father and mother. If they play a major role in readying their child for the sacramental encounter with Christ and go to Communion with the child, not only periodically but frequently, then their child will take the good tidings of this central sacrament of faith into his heart. Religion will become a way of life for him, not something tacked on during school hours.

The confessor should frequently counsel young parents regarding their vocation to be the first heralds of the faith to their children (cf. *Lumen Gentium*, Art. 11). He might recommend to them good books and periodicals that will guide them in the spiritual upbringing of a child. He should indicate his own willingness to explain any doubts they may have. In helping parents help their children, the confessor will be strengthening the faith of all concerned. Such pastoral effort likewise helps the parents to overcome any temptation to practice birth control in the pejorative sense. Once the parents become aware of the precious things they can bring to their child, things that all the money and college degrees in the world can never bring, they will not ask so easily: "Why should we have more children? What can we possibly give them?" From that very query, perhaps from their partner or from a neighbor, will flash through their mind some of the finest moments of their life. They will remember the day their child was baptized, and how they stood by and happily listened to the liturgy and the response it evoked:

"What do you wish from the Church?"
"Faith."
"And what does faith give?"
"Eternal life."

They will remember the exciting days of preparing their child for Communion, and the joy in that child's eyes and in their hearts the morning he approached the altar with them. These thoughts would quickly dispel the temptation to practice selfish birth control. For selfishness of this kind results mainly from a lack of faith. It is the materialistic person who concludes: "I can give them nothing." For parents who have been vitally involved in the sacramental education of their children, faith is much more than abstract knowledge. It is an actual experience.

There will be times when the confessor will be in a position to suggest to parents how to educate their children to a proper prayer life. He should warn them to avoid giving the children the impression that prayer is a mechanical process that we are called to by the clock: "Now it's time for all of us to say prayers." Rather, the parents should introduce the child to prayer life by first speaking of the goodness of God, and all that Jesus has done and continues to do for people. The father, as leader of the family, might proceed to consecrate the events of his family's day through a personal prayer offered in the presence of the others, thanking God for His favors and asking forgiveness for the way he and his family have failed Him. Such prayer will be a profound experience for the children.

The custom of family hymn-singing is closely related to family prayer. Many families have begun to revive the custom of singing God's praises together. In his letter to the Ephesians, before speaking on the mystery of married love, St. Paul exhorted the faithful: "Speak to one another in hymns and songs" (5:19). There are Catholic villages where a man, walking the streets in the evening, hears the sounds of religious song faintly carried to him from the houses in the area. In his own day, St. Alphonsus made a special effort to promote this custom in his missionary work. He composed many hymns from the popular tunes of the day and taught the faithful to sing them, not only in church, but in their homes and in the fields. Today, the spirit of hymn-singing is particularly being revived through the Cursillo Movement where it has met with an energetic response. Singing can be a wonderful expression of joyful faith, and God wills that our faith be lived in joy.

The pastoral plan of every priest, then, should be geared to the growth of his people in faith. This plan will be incomplete if he limits its expression to his preaching and catechizing. A personal suggestion for strengthening his faith offered to a penitent in the Sacrament of Penance will be the best means of maximizing the effectiveness of the preaching and catechizing ministry.

THE VIRTUE OF HOPE

Chapter five of the Vatican Council's Constitution on the Church, *Lumen Gentium,* entitled "The Universal Vocation to Sanctity," expresses the ideal of Christian hope in a very wonderful way. Each one of us, we are assured, has been called by God to holiness, and the way to attain this holiness lies in the faithful acceptance of the very circumstances of life in which one finds himself.

The confessional gives priests many opportunities not only to exhort a penitent to believe and hope in the general call to sanctity but also to help him understand his particular call. Heartened by this doctrine, a penitent is more likely to renew his firm resolve to strive toward this sanctity.

If a penitent still wanders on the path of legalism, sometimes the best counsel the confessor can give is to remind him that God's promise to save the sinner was not extended to the man who simply seeks to avoid mortal sin. Rather, God has called all men to sanctity and promised His assistance to those who set that as their goal. Having so informed the penitent, the confessor might follow up with a penance: to pray each day for stronger faith and hope regarding his vocation to holiness. Or, an alternative penance might be to ask the penitent to examine his conscience on this point at the close of each day, asking himself: "Was I guided today by the faith and hope that I profess? Were my thoughts, words and deeds befitting a man called to sanctity?"

Christian hope is put to the test by suffering. In the eighth chapter of his Epistle to the Romans, St. Paul tells us that we have received in our hearts the Spirit that cries, "Abba! Father!" and he testifies that we are children of God, God's heirs together with Christ, provided we are prepared to suffer with Christ. The exhortation to trust in God, then, is in order when the penitent reveals his distress and difficulties. Let the confessor explain to the penitent, in a manner that will meet his understanding, that God is trying him and that by accepting these sufferings he will draw nearer to God. As St. Paul explained it:

> But if we are sons, we are heirs also: heirs indeed of God and joint heirs with Christ, provided, however, we suffer with him that we may also be glorified with him.
>
> Rom. 8:14-17

The confessor should assure the penitent that by accepting his crosses he will deepen his spirit of hope and secure for himself a sure pledge of God's promises and fidelity.

Perhaps no time is more auspicious for the confessor to speak of hope than when his penitent comes to him depressed by a habit of sin. I remember a young teen-ager saying to me: "Father, explain to me how God can be Love. How can I believe that God loves me when I can't keep myself in the state of grace for a single week even though I pray and really want to be good?" Stung by his own inability to overcome his difficulties when he wanted so much to forge ahead in friendship, his heart wondered if God was not rejecting him despite his good will. By wavering in his belief that God is Love, the boy was undergoing a strong temptation to lose hope. He was trying hard to overcome masturbation which today is so common a trouble for boys. Time and time again his confessor had stressed the seriousness of this offense against Almighty God. Though the boy sincerely wished to draw near to God, his absence from Communion was more and more frequent. No wonder he was discouraged.

I feel very strongly that the boy's regular confessor should have adopted a different approach in his case. Instead of stressing the seriousness of the offense, he might have emphasized the importance of overcoming this temporary difficulty. He might have congratulated the boy on the wonderful display of good will. Here was the perfect time to instruct him in the law of growth: "So long as you can honestly say that you are trying, so long as you continue to pray for help to do what you can't do as yet, then be assured that you are in the grace of God. It may be a long, hard battle, but you will succeed." One should not be surprised if a penitent such as this boy begins doubting whether or not he still has good will. To forestall such doubting, the confessor might instruct him that a test of good will would be: faithfulness in coming to confession, cheerfulness with others, daily prayer, and a serious effort to employ the means suggested to him by the confessor for overcoming his habit. Often, too, it will strengthen the boy's virtue of hope and his psychological energies if the confessor invites him to go to Communion without previously going to confession. This procedure is especially recommended if the boy is in a school or seminary where everyone goes to Communion and where his frequent absence from the altar rail or frequent confession before Mass may be a cause of embarrassment.

This same approach is likewise valid when dealing with married people who are striving and praying ardently to achieve perfect conjugal chastity but who have been failing. So long as they show good will, they must be absolved; this opinion is based on traditional principles. But apart from the question of absolution and the actual discussion of some aspects of contraception in difficult cases, I would like to say a word about the possibility of their receiving Holy Communion without confession. Let me set the stage with two actual cases.

On the very same day I received two letters postmarked from two different towns in Spain. The first letter was from an elderly man whose daughter and son-in-law had six children. They had conscientiously educated these children into the faith and had personally prepared the two older children for Holy Communion. After giving birth to her last child, the mother was told by a Catholic doctor that she should not have another child for some time at least. In fact, the doctor warned her that if she did not space the next child, her family might well find itself motherless. The letterwriter vouched for the efforts of this couple to rearrange their conjugal life so that they might live according to the teachings of the Church. Although they loved each other truly and prayed hard, they had not yet been completely successful in observing the Church's norms on conjugal chastity. They feared to go to confession, and still more to go to Communion. As a result, the children started wondering and questioning why their parents no longer approached the altar with them. The troubled father asked what, if anything, could be done for his daughter and her husband. The second letter presented a case very similar to the first.

In answering these letters, I did not raise the whole issue of theological discussions on the subject but I made an analogy. I told my correspondent that even though a priest realizes that the greatest commandment is charity, he sometimes fails to practice this virtue. Yet the priest does not hesitate to receive Holy Communion, and even to celebrate Mass without first going to confession. He renews his love for God by an act of contrition and continues striving toward perfection. I could not see why each married couple in the above-mentioned cases, provided they had the same good will that the priest has with regard to charity, should not go to Communion after an act of contrition. But I call attention to the details of the case I presented and remind the reader that I am applying the principle of the law of growth explained in an earlier chapter.

People who have good will, who are striving and praying to be better, must above all be given hope. It is a well-recognized psychological principle that a habit cannot be broken overnight. If, then, a man of good will is doing what is humanly possible for him at the time and is calling upon God to further support him in his efforts, what more can be expected? How can any confessor say with certainty: "Every time you do this, it is a mortal sin." Christ said that the greatest commandment is to love God. Can a confessor truly be fostering love for God in the hearts of these people if he continually condemns their efforts and starves their hope?

Naturally, hope must be presented in such a way that it does not promote tepidity or laxness. But the confessor need not fear that he will be the source of his penitent's tepidity and laxness if he directs his attention to strengthening the man's faith and good will. If a penitent believes wholeheartedly that God is love and that it is possible for him, weak as he might be, to remain in the state of grace, then he will surely grow in all the virtues.

Christian hope is an eschatological virtue that encourages a man to seize the present opportunity that God has prepared for him. Education in Christian hope, then, means education in *vigilance* and alertness: how can I use this present opportunity to the best advantage? A confessor will promote hope by assuring his penitent that if he generously uses the present opportunity of grace with regard to other commandments and virtues, he will surely be freed from distress with regard to the one commandment which, because of a habit or perhaps of a special problem, is so difficult for him.

INVETERATE HABITS AND HOPE

According to legalistic moralism, a poor penitent needs only good will and prayer to cut off the most inveterate habit instantaneously. Practically speaking, such a theology equates the man long accustomed to intemperance or swearing or masturbation or sodomy with the man who may have an occasional temptation in one of these directions. If man had absolute freedom, then a moral imperative imposed on him at any time could be perfectly observed, presuming he has good will. Obviously, this sort of freedom could belong only to a God-Man. But oddly enough, there were some in the last century who did posit this freedom in every ordinary individual. The juridical moralist, at least in practice, accepts this erroneous notion.

While it is true that man is morally free, psychology has taught us that many people labor under the influence of some emotional disturbance or pathological urge. Such people do not enjoy full freedom of choice. Yet some confessors piously tell penitents without any discrimination: "If you pray to God and receive the Sacraments, you can be sure of avoiding this action again." But this is true only if the situation and the penitent happen to be "normal." If there is a habit of sin or a general trend in the whole environment in the direction of "abnormality," then in many cases this amounts to a sickness, to an evident lack of sufficient psychological-moral freedom.

The confessor will only succeed in destroying divine love and hope in his penitent by adopting the notions of juridical moralism. Rigorism is not based on truth and will not bring joy or courage or strength to penitents most in need of them.

God is all-powerful. There is no doubt that He can, by a miracle immediately and completely free a man from the influence of a habit. But ordinarily God chooses to give men the good will to pray, to strive for progress according to psychological laws. I wish to make it absolutely clear that what is being said here in no way derogates from the doctrine that man, while unable to avoid all venial sin throughout his life without a special grace, can avoid all *subjective* mortal sins. However, the type of person now under consideration is the individual with an inveterate habit of sin who now wishes to stop sinning. If this man prays and has good will, even though he may objectively commit the same sinful act, I maintain that it is at least doubtful whether there is subjective mortal guilt. Due to the contributions of psychology in the areas of habit and free will, moralists can no longer maintain without qualification that so long as a man calls upon God for help he can avoid all acts which objectively are mortally sinful.

With regard to man's ability to avoid mortal sin, the Council of Trent quoted St. Augustine: *Deus impossibilia non jubet sed jubendo admonet facere quod potes et petere quod non potes*. "God does not impose impossible things, but by giving his command, he admonishes you to do what you can and to pray for what you cannot do (yet)." The Council was well aware of the context of this remark (*De Natura et Gratia*, cap. 43, CSEL 50, 270; Pl 44, 271). St. Augustine was using the parable of the merciful Samaritan and wrote that when the Samaritan brought the injured man to the inn, he paid for the care which was still necessary for the man's recuperation. The injured man was not healed immediately. The same is true of those who break away from a sinful life. They cannot ascend to justice as rapidly as they fell from it. But they are asked to do the best they can and to pray for grace to do what they cannot yet do.

The man who is honestly striving to overcome a bad habit

of sin will not be sinning gravely at all if his action results from the habit rather than from a weakening of purpose to amend. He should be encouraged, then, to check himself on three points: "Do I have good will? Am I praying and doing my best in this area and others where I enjoy more freedom? Do I renew and fortify my efforts when I fail?" Such an examination of conscience will ward off the temptation to say after a fall: "I have already committed a mortal sin. It doesn't really matter if I commit more. They'll all be taken away in my next confession." The fact that he can believe he is still in God's grace, despite his obvious habitual weakness, is a great incentive not to relinquish his efforts. God is rewarding his good will. The penitent now views God as a friend, as an ally who understands and who cares.

The confessor, as the representative of Christ, should encourage the penitent who, though weighed down by the burden of a bad habit, is struggling to keep his eyes focused on God as a gesture of Christian hope. He should not hesitate to comfort this poor man by telling him, "We can't say definitely whether you have committed a mortal sin or not, but there is good reason to doubt grave sin as long as you have good will and pray. It should be a great relief for you to know the Church's teaching on this point, that unless we are sure of having committed a grave sin, we may go to Holy Communion. As your confessor, then, I see no reason why you should not go to Communion, even without confession, if you can honestly say that you are trying your best. Make a sincere act of contrition and approach the altar with confidence." That penitent will leave the confessional marvelling at the patience and nearness of His God to him.

LOVE OF GOD

To form a Christian conscience in the love of God implies that the confessor is making some aspect of the Great Commandment to love more meaningful in the life of his penitent.

The first and basic aspect of Christ's command to love is: "Remain in my love. Dwell in my love as I am dwelling in the love of my Heavenly Father." Regardless of a man's good deeds, if that man is in serious sin, no action of his can be said to glorify God. This is the hard fact that must be communicated to people: the realization of the sterility of a life without friendship with God. To live in God's love is the most fundamental demand of charity. Without it, man has alienated himself from His Creator and Redeemer. The implications of such an alienation are staggering. In the absence of God's love, man cannot see the deeper meanings and values in the ordinary tasks of life. As for his faith, he is a blind man who is groping past the opportunities of love that Providence places on his path.

The confessor, then, will inform the penitent of the urgency for him to make a deep act of sorrow after committing any fault that is or may be mortally sinful. Caution him against probabilism in this greatest question of life: "Am I in God's love?" With regard to doubtful sins, a man may heed the law which states that he is not obliged to confess such sins. But, by divine law, by this highest law to remain in God's love, a Christian is obliged to follow the way which makes him more certain of God's friendship (*pars tutior*). Therefore, he should not let a day pass without atoning for his faults by an act of perfect contrition.

Whenever a person doubts whether he is in the state of grace, he should immediately make an act of perfect sorrow. This obligation arises, not from any written law stating he must confess this sin as soon as possible, but from the urgent appeal of the New Covenant to dwell always in the love of God. Christ continues to offer the world the good tidings supplying sinners with His grace either to make an act of contrition or to confess their sins with a contrite heart. Confession is only obligatory if one knows with moral certainty that he has committed a mortal sin.

Each confessor must make his penitents aware of the fundamental need for them to be in a state of grace when they partake of the Eucharist, the great sign of the Covenant of Love. The whole celebration of the liturgy then will further strengthen and deepen their sense of sorrow for sins and increase their love for God.

The confessor must also form the conscience of his penitent to an awareness of the obligation to grow in the love of God. The Great Commandment is a dynamic commandment. To abide by it, it is not enough for the penitent simply to avoid doing what likely would destroy the love of God in him. He must make constant and positive efforts to grow in that love: "Love the Lord with your *whole* heart and your *whole* mind." He should be helped to find ways in which he can increase his gratitude for all of God's daily gifts: for providing food for him and his family, for the solace and joys of prayer, for the kindnesses extended to him by others. In proportion to his awareness of all he has to be grateful for, so will love increase within him.

The confessor's role is to guide the penitent through the various pathways to holiness, lighting his way to Christ by helping him to develop a fuller prayer life. He may claim the title of "Spiritual Father" only insofar as he takes time to encourage his penitents and bring them to a better realization of faith, hope and charity, to a better appreciation of personal and communal prayer. A great part of St. Alphonsus' *Praxis Confessarii* is devoted to these very points.

Contemporary theologians who know only of St. Alphonsus' *Theologia Moralis* consider him a legalist, but this is not so. His positive approach to moral theology appears in his work entitled *The Great Art of Loving Christ*, written as a commentary on the thirteenth chapter of the Epistle to the Corinthians. It begins with the words of St. Augustine: "Have true love and do what you will." His spiritual approach is specifically expressed in his *Praxis Confessarii* where he places great emphasis on the obligation of the confessor to strengthen the prayer life of the penitent and to help him follow his vocation to holiness.

Apart from his moral works, St. Alphonsus wrote many books on the love of God. As a point of interest, he published a small pamphlet on the love of God called, "Darts of Fire," the ideas for which were rescued by St. Alphonsus from a work which appeared on the Index of Forbidden Books. Alphonsus changed some objectionable points and then sent it to press.

The whole Christian life should be seen in the light of the Covenant of Love. In the Sacrament of Penance, Christ assures the penitent of his participation in this convenant. The purifying action of Christ in the other Sacraments continues the work of conversion, moving the penitent to a still closer union with God. The Sacraments are among the greatest manifestations of God's love. By approaching them, the penitent confirms his allegiance to God and manifests his desire to fulfill his part of God's covenant.

It is a grave misconception of the Sacrament of Penance to consider it merely as a sort of punishment for the penitent sinner. Penance brings about or increases conversion to God's covenant. This can hardly be called punishment. It would be well for confessors to emphasize this fact, replacing any distaste the penitents may have for the Sacrament with a realization of its benefits. The confessor's spiritual direction and penances will greatly influence a penitent's attitude toward confession. The aim of every confessor should be to instill in his penitents motives for gratitude. As confessor, his goal should be to send his penitents back into the world asking themselves: "What can I give to the Lord for all that He has given to me?" The evocation of such a response will attest to the penitent's readiness to grow in faith, hope and charity, and the proper formation of conscience.

13. FORMATION OF
CONSCIENCE: RELIGION

At the source of all sin and perversion is the refusal of man
to adore God:

> Knowing God, they have refused to honor him as God, or to
> render him thanks. Hence all their thinking has ended in futility,
> and their misguided minds are plunged in darkness. . . . For this
> reason God has given them up to the vileness of their own desires.
> Rom. 1:21-25[1]

Conversion means restoration to the dignity of a worshiper
of God. The Sacrament of Penance can be viewed as a re-
storative since it revitalizes man's attitude with regard to
glorifying God. It is a sacrament of faith, assuring the penitent of the most fundamental truth of salvation, that Christ
is his Savior. As liturgy, the Sacrament of Penance is an
act whereby Jesus Christ, the High Priest, incorporates the
prayer of the penitent into His own sacrifice, into His own
adoring and redeeming love of the Father. Thus the mercy of
God is exalted.

In view of Christ's action, the penitent who receives the
Sacrament of Penance with faith, hope and love is united

[1] See also Genesis 3-4.

with God in Christ. So united, he perfectly hallows the name of God. Since the proper celebration of the Sacrament of Penance consists in an act of religion, the confessor should not only sensitize the penitent's conscience as regards this virtue, but he should above all join with him in the praise of God's mercy.

In this chapter, I will discuss several aspects of Christian life whereby a man may render greater glory to God through the practice of the virtue of religion. Penitents need to be well-informed of these aspects if they are to transpose into their everyday life the praise given to God in the Sacrament of Penance.

CELEBRATION OF THE LITURGY

All the people of God are invited by the compelling love of Christ and His Church to take an ever deeper part in the celebration of the liturgy. Evidence of the urgency of this appeal came at the promulgation of the Constitution on the Sacred Liturgy, the first document of Vatican II to be issued. As Pope Paul has said on several occasions, the liturgy is one of the great sources of the spiritual and pastoral renewal of our times. One cannot be a good Catholic if he is unwilling to put into practice such important principles as those found in this conciliar work. At the end of the first session of the Council, Pope John said that it was the work of Divine Providence that the Council began its deliberations with the renewal of the liturgy. Confessors must enlighten their penitents who balk at renewal by looking back to a silent or dead liturgy; it serves only to disturb their peace of mind and to endanger the unity of the pastoral action of the Church. Of course, the reluctance of older people to applaud the changes is understandable. With the greatest patience, confessors of the elderly should explain the reasons behind the changes.

Unfortunately, there are pastors and priests who have hampered the movement for renewal. While we can sympathize with the personal difficulties encountered in adjusting to change, it is their clear duty to support, not to hinder, the changes advocated by the Council. Therefore, confessors are under obligation to inform pastor and curate penitents who are careless about carrying out the Constitution on the Liturgy that, should they adamantly oppose the updating recommended by the bishops, they are not worthy of receiving absolution. Priests who disobey or make only external changes while publicly manifesting their reluctance should be earnestly admonished by their confessor. If these priests seek and find another confessor who thinks as they do and are absolved, it is doubtful whether the absolution could save them. I know this stand will surprise some, but priests, by reason of their office, have a major obligation to lead the people through this rather difficult period of transition. Those priests whose ill-will keeps them from intelligent cooperation in the renewal are opposing the authority of the Church and to a certain extent preaching the false message of the "God is dead" theology.

SUNDAY MASS OBLIGATION

A confessor who wishes to impress his penitent with the importance of Sunday Mass will reap little success if he presents the value of the Mass in the form of a threat: "If you deliberately miss Mass on Sunday, it is a mortal sin. It means that should you die before going to confession or making an act of perfect contrition, you'll be sent to hell for all eternity." At best, this method will keep some people plodding into churches on Sunday, but it will hardly enlighten them as to the benefits they can derive. More instruction should be given both in the confessional and from the pulpit outlining clearly the beauty of the Mass, making it a desirable burden accepted not simply out of duty but out of love.

How appalling a situation when priests tell seven- or eight-year-old children that they are obliged under mortal sin not to miss Mass on Sunday. These children, in my opinion, are incapable of committing a mortal sin. But even aside from this point, the approach runs counter to good psychology:

it discusses the Sacrament of the Eucharist and presents the Sacrifice of the Mass as a dangerous test of obedience rather than as the dynamic symbol of unity and love. How can priests expect children to grow up with a real desire for the Mass when all they ever heard about Sunday service was, "You'd better go or else!"

It is also difficult for adults to appreciate Sunday Mass if they never heard of Mass as a visible sign of a community united in faith, hope and joy. And even after exposure to this teaching, how can they be convinced if their priests celebrate the Mass in a slipshod fashion. After all, these priests are the men who tell them how valuable the Mass is.

Several years ago I began helping out on weekends in a parish in Rome. My first Saturday in the confessional revealed many devout penitents who began their confession by expressing their gratitude to God for having preserved them from serious sin. They then proceeded to enumerate their minor encroachments. It surprised me time and again to hear confessed as "minor offense" the sin of having missed Mass once or twice. In fact, in a number of instances the penitent admitted that this was an habitual fault. At first, I presumed these penitents had good reasons for missing Mass, but almost as frequently as I asked, each would sincerely reply, "No, Father. It was nothing but laziness." Many went on to express precisely why they could not accept the fact of a grave obligation to attend Sunday Mass. Some admitted that they did not feel they were really invited to Mass as long as the priest turned his back to them and muttered in a language they could not understand. They continued their list of grievances by saying that obviously the Mass did not mean much even for the priests since they rushed it, and the pastor preached at most of the Masses from the Gospel right through to the consecration. Sermon topics, to a large extent, alternated between money and politics and back to money again. The penitent would finally conclude with, "I can pray better and spend a happier Sunday by staying home."

The following day, I was told by the pastor not to worry about a sermon that he would preach during my Mass. That first Sunday, he preached from the Gospel right up to consecration. At my second Mass, he did not leave the pulpit until communion time. Worse yet, his sermons on that first Sunday as on succeeding Sundays had little or nothing to do with the liturgy at all.

Before leaving the rectory to return home, I saw the pastor privately and told him that I found saying Mass during his sermon very distracting. He laughed and told me that I would get used to it. The following Sunday, I again took him aside and told him that I was scrupulous about this matter of distractions during Mass. He was amazed to hear this, but replied that since I was a moral theologian I could easily overcome my scruples. He again assured me that I would get used to the rumpus during Mass. Finally, on the third Sunday, I bluntly presented my case: "Father, as you know, I am a moral theologian. I feel that I am violating the principles of moral theology and hurting my own good name by celebrating Mass here. You have me offering the sacrifice of the Mass before these people while you draw their eyes to the pulpit, forcing them to listen to something totally incompatible with the day's liturgy. If you still feel you need my assistance on weekends, I'll gladly give it, but I will preach a homily after the Gospel of the Mass." Somewhat apologetically he answered: "Well, Father, I feel that since we oblige people to come to Mass on Sunday under pain of mortal sin, we have an obligation to entertain them." He indicated that he did need a priest for the weekends and would appreciate it if I continued coming. From then on, I preached at the Masses I said. However, the pastor maintained his usual practice at all the other Masses. Since then, the pastor has gone to another parish and most of the grievances regarding Mass no longer exist at that church. But you see how the example of priests can tend to deform the consciences of people!

There is no doubt as to the seriousness of the commandment of the Church to attend Mass on Sundays and holy days of obligation. But simply presenting the legal intent of the legislator is not sufficient; instruction on the value of the Mass must be given. If maintained at the verbal level only, instruction remains lifeless. Priests are expected to proclaim what they preach about the Mass in their manner of celebration. Let the people experience for themselves the joy and the unity of their Mass. Let them hear the liturgy preached to them, and soon their opposition, their boredom and their spiritual insouciance will cease. If priest and community together did their very best to celebrate the Mass as requested by the conciliar Constitution, they would surely open the heart and mind of those whose faith in the Mass is wavering. Proper instruction, of a verbal and experiential nature, will convince every Christian of normal intelligence that he is offending God gravely by staying away from Mass on Sunday without a good reason. He will recognize his Sunday opportunity for what it truly is, an invitation from the Great King to come to His banquet. Perhaps the most beautiful example of the Mass as a banquet was given at the Last Supper where Christ, the Son of God, the Lord of all the earth, had invited his chosen ones to partake with Him. His speech, as Host of that supper, was the most condescending and humble speech that a God could address to His creatures: "With a great desire I have longed to eat this meal with you." He then bade them—and us—to repeat this meal again and again ". . . in my memory."

The lopsided insistence on the sheer legal aspect of Mass, coupled with negligence in the liturgical formation and celebration of the sacrifice, is a reason why so many Catholics often miss Mass, come in late, or attend Church services in a perfunctory way, or out of fear of mortal sin and hell. The task of forming a true Christian conscience is an uphill struggle because so-called "leading moralists" have permeated the Church with legalistic thinking. Sunday Mass and Sunday repose have assumed a desiccated juridical complexion.

Barely eighteen years ago, I attended a lecture by the famous moralist, Father F. Hürth, whom Cardinal Ottaviani called "the pillar of the Holy Office." Father Hürth was discussing the following case: "A priest in a mission country is able to pay only a single annual visit to the outposts of his territory. He requests permission from the bishop to binate should his visit fall on a weekday. Unless he can binate, whole groups of people will be deprived of Mass throughout the entire year. May the bishop grant the priest's request?"

I will never forget this question. The response of the famous counselor of the Holy Office and teacher of thousands of future priests and moralists was unbelievable. He said solemnly: *Respondendum est: Negative! Quia nunquam et nusquam in Ecclesia fuit lex assistendi Missae die feriali. Ergo, nulla est ratio iterandi Sacrificium Missae.*—"Since the Church has never known a law requiring people to assist at Mass on weekdays, there is no reason at all for bination." There were about six hundred seminarians and priests from all over the world in the aula at the time. I thought that they would cry to heaven and shout that their faith had been outraged, but no one seemed to be disturbed. What he said was simply accepted as the normal thing.

This is a typical example of the juridical approach to moral theology. Father Hürth's answer took no account of the fact that the Christian, through baptism, is wholly oriented toward the great sign of the New Covenant. It seems to me that some consideration should be given to the fact that Christ Himself said, "Do this in memory of Me," and "The bread which I will give is my own flesh. I give it for the life of the world" (Jn. 6:51). Can Father Hürth's answer find a comfortable place in the framework of Christian belief which states that the celebration of the Eucharist is the greatest joy of Christian life? All these points were overlooked. There was a law. The law said this could not be done. The law is inflexible. Unfortunately this juridical spirit has long reigned in pastoral work.

Priests will never succeed in instructing the faithful to love their religion if they continue to underscore the argument that such-and-such a law binds under mortal sin. Ironically, because of this emphasis in the past, Sunday Mass has become, for some Catholics, a sort of servile work, a lack-luster duty completely devoid of joy.

A few years ago while travelling from Cologne to Brussels, I met two young Belgian soldiers. They sat opposite me on the train, and during the course of our conversation which, as I recall, was on religion, one of them said: "I'm a Catholic, Father, but I've lost my faith." Then the other young man spoke up. "I still believe, but my family and I don't go to

Church any more." I asked him if he had any reason for staying away from Mass. He answered frankly: "My family and I feel God just wouldn't oblige us to take part in the kind of Mass we have in our parish. The priest talks to God in a foreign language. All we ever see is his back. It's a sort of big secret between the priest and God. They just don't need us people." He went on to say that he was convinced that more than half of the people who still went to Mass in Belgium disliked their Mass intensely. "They just go because they fear hell." And even today, with most of our altars turned to the people, with our priests praying in the vernacular, many people still shuffle into the Church on Sunday more concerned about their "obligation" than the joy of praising God. The bare precept feature has yet to be eradicated. Confessors and preachers must meet the challenge and re-orientate the faithful to a positive and joyful Christian life.

One of the confessor's obligations is to assist his penitents' formation of conscience with regard to attending Mass. But he is likewise obliged, as pastor or curate, to take a hard look at the schedule and liturgy offered in his parish. He may find that certain structural reforms are mandatory. For example, in many parishes, the Mass schedule is too tight; there is a Mass every hour resulting in serious parking problems. In some places, the liturgy has been reduced to a thirty-five or forty-minute maximum. Such a schedule creates an automat atmosphere in a Church: a vacant seat is quickly taken by the next customer while the ushers try to keep the crowd moving. There is no time for a real homily, no time to do things as they ought to be done for the Mass to be a real spiritual experience for the people, serving to increase their faith. If this is the case, it would be better to request from the bishop authorization for evening Masses not only on Sunday, but also on Saturdays so that the schedule would allow for better spacing.

If the chief devil wanted to advise his squadrons well—to borrow a comparison from C. S. Lewis—he could not give more effective counsel on how to destroy the faith of Catholics than to tell them to persuade the clergy to "celebrate" Mass and the other parts of the liturgy negligently and mechanically. Add to this a persistent thundering from the pulpit and emphasis in the confessional that missing Mass is a mortal sin. These are the ingredients used in aborting the liturgy, the great source of joyous faith.

Canon Law permits a pastor to dispense individual parishioners and even individual families in the parish from Sunday Mass for a just cause (cf. CJC Canon 1245, 1). In our age of fewer priests, bigger parishes and greater emphasis on personal responsibility, more and more the faithful will be deciding on their own whether, on specific occasions, they have a just reason for not attending Mass. Therefore the confessor should not chide a penitent who decided that a sufficient reason existed for his omitting Sunday Mass, particularly when it is obvious that, had he asked, he would have obtained a dispensation from the pastor. In my opinion, if in the course of a year people occasionally miss Sunday Mass for some reason, though not a compelling reason, they can normally and legitimately boast of a good conscience. This is especially true of those who go to Mass several times during the year on a workday, for such people sufficiently indicate that there is no lack of good will or of high appreciation of the Eucharist.

The Church rightly gives great value to Sunday as the celebration of the resurrection of the Lord and as the day of common and public worship. But this would not prevent the Church from being more flexible perhaps in the future by allowing the faithful occasionally to commute the Sunday Mass to a Mass during the week.

SERVILE WORK

The early Church did not forbid certain kinds of servile work on Sunday. In fact, a meticulous casuistry on this point was expressly forbidden by several synods: they merely held that the faithful must keep themselves free on Sunday to listen to the Word of God, to celebrate the Eucharist and to pray. The Rule of St. Basil states that the abbot or superior of a monastery can provide some work on Sundays for the brothers who cannot read, otherwise they could become lazy and succumb to temptation.

These historical circumstances have to be taken into consideration. Father Huber of the Accademia Alfonsiana published a book entitled, *Geist und Buchstabe der Sonntagsruhe* (1959), in which he showed that in times of great fervor emphasis was always put on Sunday, the day of the resurrection, as a day of joy and community worship, but very little emphasis on the matter of servile work. He then points simply to the insistence in teaching that the faithful not allow greed or avarice to interfere with the holiness of the day. But in times of decadent theology, preachers began to boom the casuistics of servile work, and distortion became inevitable. In the early Middle Ages, Ireland and France adopted a rather stringent attitude in this connection. The rigorism then spread throughout the germanic world. The *Lex Alemannorum* and similar legislation of the newly baptized German tribes threatened the transgressors of the Sunday repose with the most horrible punishments. A Christian who had been warned several times about violating the Sabbath rest could even be sold into slavery. Gradually legends about the fate of people who failed to observe the law grew and spread. The true meaning of Sunday had begun its long slide into the shadows. The same decadent spirit can be detected in certain nineteenth- and twentieth-century theology manuals. The resultant confusion in the people's mind regarding their Sunday obligation not to disturb the Sunday rest is not surprising. That is why the confessor of this early postconciliar period must be prudent in dealing with this matter.

SELF-DENIAL

A truly Christian conscience distinguishes between the essentials and non-essentials of Christian life. Mortification, self-denial, penance in a broad sense—all are essentials in Christian morality. The apparent danger that Friday abstinence might become a purely legalistic observance, *i.e.*, people might obey only the letter of the law, prompted the bishops in many countries of the world to suspend this law. It is their hope that people will come to a greater realization that a Christian's commitment to self-denial cannot be satisfied by a meticulous formalism. A lobster supper on Friday night could hardly be considered penitential. Today, with the practical absence of meatless Fridays, Christians with a well-formed conscience will be brought to realize the necessity of some more essential forms of self-denial.

The old law of Friday abstinence never paralleled, in terms of equal obligation and importance, the Church law to hear Mass on Sunday. Sunday Mass holds greater claim to our attention because it is essential to our faith, a sign of our lasting commitment to the covenant of love. It was never simply a positive law. Abstinence, on the other hand, is merely a positive law of the Church from which whole nations have been dispensed.

In times past, abstinence had far greater meaning than it has in the twentieth century. It was originally a common act of religion and a very obvious testimony to a person's spirit of self-denial. The Friday meal consisted of little more than bread and herbs. As time progressed, the bread and herbs were replaced by thousands of other things, particularly for those whose wallets or credit cards allowed a fish dinner such as to whet any appetite.

Today, with the practical abrogation of Friday abstinence in the United States, the bishops of the country have handed to the faithful themselves the responsibility for some form of penance. In view of the Passion of our Lord, every Christian is obliged during his lifetime to practice self-denial. He owes it to himself to consider "sacrifice" in examining his conscience with respect to the demands of his vocation to holiness: "What sacrifices are inherent to Christ's great commandment to love my neighbor? Am I ready to perform these sacrifices? Am I willing to share my wealth with those in my country who are needy? Am I willing to share with the poor people all over the world? Do I impose upon myself strict rules of temperance in smoking and drinking and in all those things which would endanger my internal freedom or scandalize my neighbor?"

Ash Wednesday and Good Friday are the only days specifically mentioned where fast and abstinence must still be observed. But discussion over how many ounces of meat one may eat on these days without seriously violating the precept should not arise. Such discussion was considered apropos for a Christianity in infancy, but not for an adult Christianity.

The confessor, then, should be careful to help form the consciences of his penitents with regard to this obligation to self-denial. In the lifetime of many of these penitents, self-denial has meant little more than Friday abstinence, which many performed in the best of faith. They may fail to understand fully the change in the law or the new responsibilities laid upon them by the change. The confessor can be most valuable in giving them a new appreciation of their Christian commitment.

HABIT OF SWEARING

The confessor must sometimes advise his penitents in relation to swearing. Victims of this habit or of blaspheming, which is even worse, should be exhorted to strive energetically to overcome their habit. They should be led to understand that the habit is contrary to the vocation of a Christian, whose highest goal is the glorification of God through fraternal charity and worship. The confessor may ask the penitent: "Would you accept the penance of saying three 'Glory be to the Father' or three 'Blessed be God' as often as you swear?" Counsel should follow that the penitent examine his conscience in the evening on the fulfillment of this little penance. In such cases, the penance is a reminder of the motives which help to overcome the habit. But the confessor should tell his penitent: "If you forget to do as I have recommended, it is not a sin. I hope that it will help you cut down, and perhaps do away with, your habit of swearing, but just remember that your good will is what really counts, even if you forget to say the prayers." The penitent could then be advised to keep up the practice of saying the short prayers (which express his worship) as long as necessary.

SUPERSTITION

Another matter that may sometimes claim a confessor's attention is superstition. Especially likely is this to be true of certain parts of South America, but it is also true of areas in the North. The confessor should make an effort to acquaint himself well with the parish so that if it is necessary he can wage battle on the serious forms of superstition and not waste his time with minor forms indicative only of a vein of human weakness. Superstition is one form of ignorance that makes Catholics look ridiculous, and makes real witnessing to our faith incredible (cf. Pastoral Constitution on the Church in the Modern World, Art. 19-21). The confessor must delicately strive to instruct and to reform the conscience of a superstitious person.

14. FRATERNAL
CHARITY

The Sacrament of Penance is, by its very nature, an efficacious sign of unity, reconciling as it does the penitent with the family of God. It effects a return to or growth in fraternal charity as one draws nearer to God. In the formation of conscience, fraternal charity becomes a focal point since it is directly related to the commandment of the love of God. Our Lord Himself clarified the commandment: "Thou shalt love thy neighbor as thyself" when, in celebrating the new covenant "in His blood," He said: "Love one another as I have loved you" (John 15:12). While love of God can be distinguished from love of neighbor, they cannot be separated. One cannot love the heavenly Father without loving Christ, and one cannot love Christ without loving his neighbor. "If a man says, 'I love God' while hating his brother, he is a liar. If he does not love the brother whom he has seen, it cannot be that he loves God whom he has not seen. And indeed this command comes from Christ Himself: that he who loves God must also love his brother" (John 4:20-21).

THE ALL-EMBRACING COMMANDMENT

In the formation of conscience, it is most important for the penitent to realize that love of God must be manifest in love of neighbor. If he sees his neighbor as the image of the loving Christ, he will also see in him the invisible God. He who truly loves his neighbor can be sure of having the love of Christ in his heart. The commandment of fraternal charity is the great, the all-embracing commandment. The confessor would be allowing a conscience to be erroneously formed if he sanctioned the penitent's view of fraternal charity as a commandment added to all the others. Spiritual anarchy would reign were Friday abstinence, attendance at Sunday Mass and tithing to be equated with the great commandment of brotherly love. The confessor must help the penitent realize that the twofold commandment embraces all aspects of life; it helps produce all virtues. Should one virtue be lacking, the absence, or a marked weakness, of fraternal love can be detected.

Fraternal charity relates to all the commandments, includes all the virtues, permeates all the forces and powers of the soul. It encompasses all men, even the greatest sinners. Faith, hope and charity lead us to the image of Christ in our neighbor, though it may be distorted by sin. Love, rooted in faith and hope, recognizes him as one who, with us, was redeemed by the blood of the Savior. But for the very fruit of redemption in us, how could we believe in our vocation to holiness which presupposes full solidarity with our brothers and sisters in Christ?

SIGNS OF TRUE LOVE

Use of one's neighbor as an occasion of merit is no indication of true love. Even in contemporary manuals, one may find examples such as this: A man standing on a bridge sees a fellowman drowning. It occurs to him that he could dive in and save him. But, according to divine law, love of self is stronger than love of neighbor; therefore, he deems it wrong to risk his life for that of another. However, it would be meritorious for him to take this risk. After lengthily weighing the pros and cons, he concludes that the order of love allows him to take the risk, and he plunges into the water. He may fail to save the man as a result of this complicated accounting system. Even if he did pull him out alive, he would not have displayed love of neighbor. He was using his fellowman as a means of increasing his own merit.

The same can be true of almsgiving and other deeds supposedly on behalf of one's neighbor. Their value is diminished if the dignity of the person concerned is not taken into account. It may seem that as others accept our gifts we receive the merit, but the reality of the situation is different. To love someone means to extend a warm heart, to revere him as a person. It is offensive to the beneficiary of our gifts to be considered merely an object of "gain" of merits instead of a person created in God's image.

REDEEMING LOVE

Fraternal love is essentially a redeeming one if it is to follow on Christ's injunction: "Love one another as I have loved you." He loves us as children of the heavenly Father. Similarly, fraternal charity must be characterized by apostolic-mindedness and animated by missionary zeal. Such love applies not only to priests and religious, but to all Christians alike.

It would be a misconception to think of fraternal love as only one notch above the humane dispositions of kindness and gentleness. To call it supernatural would be mocking fragmentation of the great commandment. A religious was once heard to say, "My love for this confrère becomes ever more supernatural," when he meant "stay away from me"; he was using 'love' without any connotation of affection or warmth. To love our brothers in the Lord means to love them with the wholeheartedness of the Lord.

A redeeming love means that all the powers and passions have been stripped of selfishness. Redemption does not bypass creation. God has redeemed whatever he has created, including our passions. Redeeming love means a fully human love; it must include all our powers to love. It must embrace the beloved in the entirety of his being, of his life. If we show no interest in his values and miseries but only in evangelizing him, the Gospel will not mean life to him. We must love him seriously in all aspects of his life. Fraternal love cannot be a redeeming love unless it is a helpful, active human love.

If we are insensitive to their daily life, interested only in preaching supernatural life and the love of God, our hearers will be deaf to our message. Take only the example of a wife whose cooking varies from can-opening to TV dinners, who neglects the household, is irritable but who conscientiously gives the husband a lecture on Christian living every evening. What better way of instilling a distaste for religion. If on the other hand, she were kind and helpful, created a cheerful home atmosphere, cooked delicious meals, engaged sympathetically in conversation, she would be in a more favorable position to discourse on Christian living.

Redeeming love must also be an incarnate love, one that permeates the whole life. In the formation of conscience, it is necessary time and again to remind the penitent of the importance of kindness. Gentleness and consideration for one another are much more important for those living under the same roof than is concern for strangers whom we meet only occasionally. To be totally lacking in kindness toward our nearest neighbors, the members of our own household, is a perversion of right order.

THE LAW OF GROWTH

We must bring the penitent and ourselves, too, to the full realization that our love of neighbor is not yet perfect, and that we are still blind to many aspects of this virtue. It may happen that while our love is efficacious and sincere, it fails to permeate the whole of our lives. Fraternal charity must be the integrating element of our Christian life. One can always grow in generosity and warmth. If a penitent is satisfied with himself and claims that all is well regarding his love of neighbor, we cannot call him a liar, but we can pray God to remove his blind spot and to grant him the grace to realize that his love is still very imperfect. His attitude is like that of the Pharisees. If a person never has anything to confess against fraternal charity, it is obvious that either he does not fully appreciate the importance of the commandment of fraternal love or he does not examine his conscience in the light of the New Law. If he confesses eating meat on Lenten Fridays, missing Mass on Sunday, but has nothing to say about fraternal charity, there is reason to believe that love of neighbor plays a minor role in his life. It is a good sign when a person humbly and sincerely accuses himself of sins against fraternal charity. The confessor can assure him that he is making progress and that his eyes are open on the great realities of life.

Our Lord Himself tried to remove the blindfolds from the eyes of the Pharisees and the doctors of the Law in relation to the law of charity. They were neither merciful nor kind; they neglected the primary commandment of love while remaining inflexible about the observance of such trivia as tithing for the smallest things.

THE TEST OF CHARITY

The hallmark of fraternal charity is love of one's enemies, of those who are cause of grief and affliction for us. One cannot be content with the negative aspect of doing them no wrong; love of enemies implies a typically redeeming love. We must help them overcome their difficulties concerning ourselves. They admittedly suffer with respect to us in spite of the fact that we may have done nothing to provoke this attitude. Guilty or not, we have an obligation to help them overcome their animosity. "If you bring your gift to the altar and remember that your brother has some grievance against you, first leave your gift at the altar and go to be reconciled with your brother" (Mt. 5:23). Does this enjoin us only if we have wronged our neighbor? Not at all! Whenever we find him in some kind of spiritual difficulty due to our mode of operation or because of lack of love on our part, we must come to his assistance. If we have positively caused the trouble, then we must be doubly helpful and seek his forgiveness. The Lord teaches us in the Sermon on the Mount that the spirit of the new covenant calls us to be all goodness as the heavenly Father is all goodness, and that his mercy extends to both the sinner and the just man (Mt. 5:48). "Your heavenly Father himself is kind to the ungrateful and wicked. Be compassionate just as your Father is compassionate" (Lk. 6:36). As St. Paul forcefully points out, the Lord died for us although still sinners, without any merit on our part. Thus our Redeemer has set us an example: "Love one another as I have loved you."

Our charity is truly tried when we must extend a loving hand to those who really hate us and sin against us. It is not unusual for confessors to encounter penitents in the confessional who harbor wrong ideas on this score. They seek self-justification by considering only their neighbor's wrongs. What should the confessor do in such circumstances? He must begin with the commandment to love our enemies. Even when our neighbor is wrong, we need to love him in truth; this is an opportunity offered by God to test our love. However, it would be wise for the confessor to display caution in not confirming the penitent's negative judgment on his 'enemy' without substantiating evidence.

Take the case of the good wife who imagines that she is being victimized by her husband. She is confirmed in her delusion by confessors who assure her that her role is to suffer as a "victim" at the hands of her husband. It so happened that the last confessor knew her husband. He told her she could never be grateful enough to God for her good spouse; God had made him kind and patient with her eccentricities. Of course, this came as a shock to her because it deflated her blown-up image of herself as a persecuted woman. Her husband was naturally grateful for what the priest had said.

In her case, the contessors were not helping her in confirming her paranoid ideas and leading her to believe in her own great patience. She was able later to admit that she no longer annoyed her husband, and that furthermore, he was a good man. It is helpful at times to indicate to these people that others may be suffering considerably at their own hands.

If the penitent's presenting complaint is that he is being wronged by his enemy, the confessor may begin by the principle that God is offering him this trying situation to test his love of neighbor. He may point out to the penitent the example of the heavenly Father's goodness to all. He should try to convince the self-righteous person that his attitude may be pharisaical. The confessor would do well to guard against the other extreme, telling the person that he alone is wholly wrong in the situation. He could inform the penitent that experience teaches that both sides usually share the fault. Experience further teaches that those who pass up the opportunity to help their neighbor because they were previously hurt by him are usually at fault themselves. Confrontation with these truths can often redirect the individual and set him aright on the path of fraternal charity.

FRATERNAL CHARITY VIOLATED

The relationship of uncharitable thoughts to the practice of fraternal charity seems to elude many penitents, if one is to judge from the few accusations on this count. Penitents profit by being reminded that the Lord uttered the saying: the mouth speaks from the fullness of the heart. If the heart is pure, words and actions will be pure, and the reverse holds true. Then again, if a person entertains uncharitable suspicions, it will not be long before the unkind thoughts are voiced. Sinful thoughts are not the exclusive domain of impurity, and penitents must be persuaded of the need to control their thoughts in relation to fraternal charity. Its practice will follow more readily and painlessly.

Some people waste considerable time thinking up ways of avenging themselves on their neighbor. They are frantically preoccupied with conjuring up stinging remarks and sharp speeches for the opportune time. They become completely frustrated when the occasion fails to arise. However, the nurturing of such thoughts is very wrong. Even priests, nuns and monks are found on occasion to harbor such thoughts and desires; it may even be that the fertile period for such cogitations is meditation time.

Other penitents come to you claiming that they will forgive but never forget. A case in point is that of a priest who had been ordained for fifty years and whose bishop had offended him forty years back. He constantly kept referring to the incident. When asked by a confrère, "Do you forgive him?"—"Certainly, I forgive him, but I'll never forget." The truth of the matter is that this is not forgiveness.

A sincere confession may help to eradicate bad habits, but man does not operate in a vacuum; bad habits must be replaced by good ones. The thirteenth chapter of Paul's first Epistle to the Corinthians can serve to guide our efforts along this line. It proclaims the qualities of true charity, the "signs of discernment." "There is no limit to the hope of charity" (13:7). Hopelessness should never enter the considerations of a Christian. There is no limit to endurance; charity can always do something and suffer for the eternal salvation of others. Positive thinking breeds hope for the best and is of great value when we seek to bring joy, consolation and comfort to those who are frustrated. In examining his conscience, a Christian may ask himself: "Do I feel for and with others? Am I aware of the sufferings and difficulties of others? Do I make an effort to brighten the day of one burdened by the vicissitudes of life?"

SCANDAL AND THE SOCIAL MILIEU

A priest's effectiveness in preaching on confession or in hearing confessions will be greatly enhanced if beforehand he actively seeks knowledge about the moral climate of the area. What are the prevalent temptations? What is the attitudinal stance on social issues of the so-called pious individuals? For instance, warped attitudes were revealed in a sociological survey asking among other questions: "What is your attitude toward unwed mothers?" The consensus was that unwed mothers were despised by those who considered abortion a normal solution; they were also scorned for their apparent ignorance in the use of contraceptives. The most shocking fact was that the so-called pious souls by their loveless contempt for unwed mothers made the pressures even more unbearable. Such an attitude on the part of sanctimonious individuals very often drives unwed mothers-to-be to seek abortions.

In another survey, a well-intentioned priest (a pastor) mentioned that he observed a useful custom. "No unwed mother is allowed to be dressed in a white gown when she is married." Two sisters happened to be married in a double ceremony. One wore white and the other was obliged by the pastor to wear colored apparel because she was pregnant. It was public knowledge, however, that the girl in white had had at least three abortions. The sister in colored dress was in much better standing. Through such conservative and narrow-minded views, the overly pious give scandal and cause crimes to be committed.

Perhaps a confessor would do well to shock such people if he has an opportunity to do so, just as people have to be shocked into the realization that they share in the responsibility for renewal decreed by the Second Vatican Council. For example, how can such people claim to be obedient sons and daughters of the Church if they oppose the Church's teaching?

One of the most insidious scandals of our time is the mediocrity of many Catholics, particularly priests and religious; it is all the more so when mediocrity is praised as the ideal. For example, one sometimes hears Father X praised because he is able to say a weekday Mass in fifteen minutes and a Sunday Mass in twenty; isn't it too bad that other priests didn't try to get the people out of Church on Sunday instead of dragging things out? A serious examination of conscience is in order with regard to public worship. Many of our parishes are a scandal to those devout Protestants who long ago learned the meaning of public prayer.

AGGRESSIVENESS

Finally, I would like to say a word about aggressiveness and fraternal charity. Educators, sisters, and particularly priests must learn to appreciate the importance of self-control and better still, to exemplify it in their daily behavior. Those who devote their lives to spreading the Gospel scandalize others by their impatience and lack of self-mastery. This applies in the confessional, the pulpit and the classroom.

Self-complacent individuals are quickly offended when others refuse to accept their ideas or dare to propose changes. Oftentimes, the aggressiveness that characterizes certain teachers and preachers of the Gospel stems not so much from zeal as from feelings of personal affront. They take out their frustrations on the faithful by reprimanding them very severely, when in reality they themselves have transgressed the law of God by their lack of self-control.

15. THE FOURTH COMMANDMENT

The Commandments pertaining to one's interpersonal relationships will now be discussed in the light of love becoming incarnate and finding expression in the various dimensions and areas of life. First consideration will be given to the fourth commandment, not merely as a moral imperative, but primarily as a catalyzer of social charity. Every societal agency: family, school and Church, as well as the different sub-groups of society are communities which, in different ways, should reflect brotherhood in Christ.

FAMILY LIFE

The preparation of young people for marriage has, for too long, remained an area of serious neglect in the formation of conscience (cf. Constitution on the Church in the Modern World, Art. 49, 52). The many failures attendant upon "rushing into marriage" bespeak the lack of preparation from the moral and religious point of view. The high rate of divorce and the alarming instability of family life attest to a want of Christian social responsibility.

Our sophisticated technological society may be highly advanced in push-button areas, but the damaging lag in areas such as education for freedom and responsibility may sabotage a whole civilization. Take only the parent-child relationship that is still viewed, in many circles, through Victorian and pre-Victorian eyes. Some parents go on treating their teen-agers as children, their young men and women as teenagers. Some refuse to have their children's friends in their homes. Others act as if youth needed to be watched constantly. Such attitudes are likely to bring about two harmful reactions: either a child becomes slavishly obedient to his parents or he exhibits explosive rebellion. In the first case the child is robbed of his energy and freedom to develop his own personality and his consequent emotional deformity will render him inadequate to the challenge of productive living. In the second case, the parents' influence and prestige no longer reach the children, who are totally unprepared for exposure to the prevailing patterns of the world. More often than not, the latter group nurtures a negative attitude toward all authority.

Parents will profit by being reminded that the successful education of their children will be effected through example far more than through bare rules and restrictions. Parents are the first identification figures in a child's life, and whatever they are and stand for will serve as a basis for the growing child's value system. Their authority must be maintained, of course, but it must be a loving authority, an education toward maturity. Authority will be in the service of love if it expresses humility toward God and children. It is an authority that will help the children to distinguish between right and wrong, between virtue and vice.

Some parents take for granted the child's acceptance of them as "heroes." They seem totally unaware of the harmful effects of their inconsistencies in discipline and in other areas of general everyday living. Think only of parents who are extremely tolerant of bad manners but equally intolerant when a lampshade gets dented. The anarchic state of the parents' sense of values is sadly revealed. Good education, if it is to go by that name, means instruction by words and deeds in setting up a hierarchy of values. Training of a child's will becomes an impossibility without training in values. That is why parents gain by being challenged, occasionally, on the nature of their reprimands: are they the result of irritation or do they stem from the parents' desire to help their children grow to maturity?

Parents fail occasionally by contradicting one another, at times in a violent way, in the presence of the children. Quietly and calmly discussing differences in front of them, however, is not catastrophic. The children have a right to know that their parents are not infallible and that they learn in patient discussion. What better way of informing children that the parents are partners, and as such, try to reach solutions for common problems? But it is harmful for one parent to give an order to the children and have the other parent come in and contradict the order; children are then placed in a built-in conflict situation. Sociological studies indicate that inconsistency of discipline in the home increases the likelihood of delinquency, a serious social problem.

Because of the structure of society today, the father's working eight or more hours a day, the upbringing of the children is left largely in the hands of the mother. However, a father who, because of his workload, completely abdicates his role in the child's life is making a serious mistake. He is the father and partner of his wife in the education of the children. He cannot be content to be the provider for the family; he should be an element of joy and stability within that household. If to his wife and children he becomes the man behind the newspaper or the man watching television, if he is simply the man who brings in the money, then he has forfeited the most rewarding aspect of fatherhood. It is a sad home indeed where a father is too tired to sign a report card or listen to his son's experiences in school; where a husband takes his wife for granted and forgets to compliment her on her work, her cooking, or fails to ask her how things are going with her and the children.

TV AND THE FORMATION OF CONSCIENCE

The widespread use of television poses serious problems with regard to the education of consciences. Parents, of course, should exemplify wise choice of programs, teaching children all the while to be discriminating in their viewing and not to welcome everything they see on TV. The impact of TV on American viewers is ascribed to the "intimacy" of the medium; TV stars become guests in the living room. Parents should guide their children in selecting their guests carefully.

Of course, we cannot presume to educate consciences in this matter if we take in all the soap operas of the week, if we have not made an effort to discipline ourselves through a balanced TV diet. The average American child has been found to spend more time before a TV set than he does in school. Parents seem not a bit perturbed provided the children are "seen and not heard." Family life suffers because it is dominated by the picture-and-sound box. TV becomes especially disruptive when no time is left for conversation between parents and children. Such time is needed for parents to discuss the values of the programs, for them to help children judge programs objectively. Confessors would do well to remind parents of their obligations in this area.

ATTENTION TO VOCATION

Another aspect of family life that the confessor might helpfully bring to the parent-penitent's attention is the aspect of the child's vocation. It is important for parents to ask themselves from time to time whether they are doing all they can to guide and encourage their child in the choice of a vocation. Parents should seek opportunities for discussing the values of different callings, of different professions, with a view to their importance to society in general and to the Church in particular. Special encouragement might be given the child when he lights upon the profession that his personal talents seem equipped for. Parents of course must promote religious vocations, but they must always be utterly scrupulous about their children's freedom: they must not stifle a child's possible vocation to the priesthood or to the religious life; on the other hand, they must not push them or force them to enter seminaries or monasteries against their will.

There are other areas in which the alert confessor may be of great service to parent-penitents, making them more alive to their duties in relation to their children. If the confessor knows the environment of the family, he will be in a position at times to offer pertinent cautions to the parents. For example, if he is aware that within the immediate neighborhood teen-agers engage in pot-smoking or glue-sniffing and he is also aware that his penitent has one or more adolescents in his family, he might recommend that the parent sit down with the children and warn them of the dangers involved in addiction and caution them about the common means used in enticing them or getting them "hooked." If he is the regular confessor of this parent, he may call attention to the fact that his penitent is too strict and tends to blame his child whenever things go awry. Or he may realize that the parent tends to overlook the good qualities in his children, consequently discouraging and frustrating them. The confessor is in a position to warn, also, against the excessive praising and extolling of their children, which may lead them to believe that they are somehow superior to others.

The formation of conscience in parents cannot be promoted by merely asking questions. Positive suggestions to cope with individual situations have to be offered. Confession gives us a good opportunity to stress the matter of the sound education of children. For example, a confessor may offer as penance to a parent: to make an examination of conscience on what could be improved in the proper education of his children. One of the most important questions a parent can ask himself is: "Am I educating my children to a social, open-minded attitude, to be helpful to one another, to the family, to society?" Are the parents educating them to their supernatural responsibilities?

EDUCATION IN OBEDIENCE

Education in obedience poses a special problem in our day. In a closed society, as in the past, when society was subject to the severe control of uniform patterns, it was less harmful to have children educated to an external, almost uniform type of obedience. This was not Christian obedience, of course; it was training in conformity. Were this to be tried today in our open, dynamic, pluralistic society, the results would be disastrous. The principal means by which parents can educate their children to obedience and responsibility are by example and by inspiring sound motives; by listening to their questions and answering them honestly as best they can; and above all, by understanding their children. For instance, it is wrong for parents to insist that children conform to certain religious patterns of behavior without inspiring in them a true religious spirit. I am not against the teaching of religious practices, but the fundamental obligation is to instruct the children in spirituality. All the virtues are gifts of God and have to be acquired in personal responsibility, but much depends on the parents.

In dealing with children and young people, the confessor must help foster proper attitudes toward their parents. To reduce everything to obedience would be fatal. The first response of children should be love, gratitude and deep religious respect, because parents represent for them the authority of God. Children, and particularly adolescents, must learn to be respectful in their thinking and actions; they must be taught the primacy of the heart. Children tend to reciprocate these attitudes when they are held by the parents.

Oftentimes, the confessor will have to tell the young penitent that if he hopes to better his relationship with his parents and make home life happier, he will have to curb any resentful thoughts he may be harboring in his mind, and any tendency toward snap judgments about their motives in dealing with him. The source of many family quarrels can be traced to distorted thinking and judgment. The confessor might encourage the young penitent to meet the challenge of respect presented to him even in the chambers of his mind.

A failure to make distinctions is one of the great temptations to which youth is subject. In the formation of their consciences, young people must be helped to be humble in their judgments, to know their own limitations; at the same time, they should learn discernment and personal thinking, to display a sense for proper distinctions in the complex life. The confessor might ask a young penitent to observe himself over the course of a few days and to take note of his tendency to make strong, unqualified judgments, particularly on his parents.

Many of the older generation should recognize that they are really "old-fashioned" in some respects. I am convinced of this with regard to myself. The experience of Vatican Council II proved to be an eye-opener for a good number of us. Some generally thought to be "pioneers" or "avant-garde" thinkers had to be converted from regressive opinions. Others who were thought to be excessively conservative in some matters, were nevertheless very open and liberal when it came to certain modern ideas. Labels of "liberal" and "conservative," "hep" and "old-fashioned" should be avoided in general everyday life because most of us are a perplexing mixture depending on our various experiences.

Adolescents, above all, must avoid the temptation of being too categorical in their judgments, but parents must display patience when the children do because it represents their attempt at appearing mature. Here also the confessor can be of great help. It would be tragic if children grew up without any training in making critical judgments, merely accepting as true whatever they were told by parents, teachers or clergy. But they should learn to treat their own thoughts as problems, as hypotheses to be tested, not as final categorical pronouncements. The young need training in the exercise of discretion. It is an old tradition of moral theology, both in the East and West, to place emphasis on the science of discretion which analyzes motives and actions, distinguishing true love from its counterfeit.

THE OPEN FAMILY

Many questions are related to family life or the fourth commandment. Well known are the duties relating to older members of the family, such as grandparents. But confessors must show the faithful that 'love of neighbor' is not limited to the immediate realm of the family, even though the family is the ideal place to learn about that love. Man lives not only in a family but in a manifold social world. The family itself must be modelled after an open community. Not only must the children learn to love one another, to be kind and respectful to their parents, brothers and sisters, relatives, but they should realize that the family as a whole is part of a social life, the life of the neighborhood, the town, the school, the state and the world at large. It belongs in the realm of formation of consciences to make people aware of their responsibilities with respect to the various groupings of society.

CIVIC MORALITY

Just as modern society has had to concern itself with so many problems and obligations that formerly belonged to the family, so the formation of conscience must now concern itself with the citizen and his life in society. Therefore, confessors cannot go on repeating the maxims of moral theology appropriate to a former age but must think of the formation of conscience in terms of social responsibility. Christians must be taught that they have an obligation to concern themselves with the problems of the community and country: cultural, social and economic. It is wrong for the Christian, who claims to be "the salt of the earth," to limit his vision to his own family or to the affairs of his own social class or neighborhood.

The steadily increasing influence of government on all levels of human life affects one's environment, for better or for worse. Incumbent on the priests, then, as preachers and confessors, is the responsibility of promoting civic responsibility. One cannot, of course, in his priestly role, urge voting for a particular person or party. His role consists in forming consciences in such a way that a good Christian becomes an enlightened citizen living up to his social responsibilities. The common good requires honorable and capable men in government. No one, therefore, is innocent of sin who knowingly votes for an office holder who is dishonest or who seeks personal aggrandizement at the expense of the common good. Such voting behavior would betray the Church's efforts to create and to sustain a divine milieu of love and justice.

Patriotism is definitely a matter of concern in the formation of conscience, but confessors must be careful to inculcate a patriotism that extends to the whole family of God, not merely to a narrow part of the whole. As the world becomes smaller and smaller, our obligations to neighbor tend to increase in scope. For example, few would deny that in our present-day America the problems connected with social and racial integration are of paramount importance for the solutions of other problems concerning international life.

INTERRACIAL HARMONY

It is impossible to examine one's conscience nowadays without taking interracial matters into account. "What have I done to promote social and racial integration in my own social circles?" At times, even pious Catholics claim exclusive rights to the "good qualities" and regard everybody else as inferior and unfit for full assimilation into the mainstream of American life. This is especially true along color lines. Prejudice closes one's mind to objective facts. There can be little doubt that the Negroes in America, by and large, are a traditionally religious people with a great capacity for faith. This must be admitted even if their expression of faith differs from the way in which white men express theirs. Colored people are known for their extraordinary patience: they were patient as slaves, and they are still patient in spite of the long period in which their rights as citizens have been neglected, not to say outrightly denied.

It is very important, in the formation of a Christian conscience, that confessors bring their penitents to view things positively. If the civil rights movement, for example, has suffered reverses and obstructions of all kinds, it is because of the tendency of so many to see only the negative in the opponent. If one Negro gets out of hand, the entire race is censored. It is a form of immaturity to generalize from single incidents. The heart of the matter is that too many white people still continue to look down on the Negro as intrinsically inferior. One will not promote social justice and integration if he does not first of all admit equality of men under God.

What can the individual white person do to aid the Negro cause? Suggestions that the confessor might offer in view of formation of conscience in this area would be: not to go to bars, restaurants, theaters and clubs where colored people are excluded. When they have a choice, they should patronize places which foster integration. It would be the penitents' way of protesting segregation by proving that the segregationists' present policies and attitudes are self-defeating. If parents have a choice, they could witness to the sincerity of their faith by placing their children in integrated classrooms rather than in segregated schools, or in the case where integration has not yet been achieved, inform the local school authorities of their support for the cause of integration. Penitents may be encouraged to use their influence on friends and neighbors in bringing them to the Christian attitude of accepting all people. It might be added that the promotion of social and racial integration in one country inevitably helps the cause of peace and freedom throughout the world.

INTERNATIONAL BROTHERHOOD

We cannot expect to promote peace and freedom if we advocate discrimination within our own country or state or neighborhood; this is tantamount to Pharisaism. Peace is built up

by words and deeds. If nations, like individuals, were respectful of each other, then there would be no wars. Christians
are duty-bound to help promote international understanding
by training themselves and others to focus attention on the
positive qualities of other nations. While we cannot praise
Communism as a system, we can show discretion in our judgment about individuals in the system and what they are trying
to do. Not everything about Communism is bad. Then, too,
not all Communism is the same. For example, Communism
in Poland is not the same as Communism in East Germany.
The latter is still dominated by Stalinism and tends to suppress many human rights. The former has compromised
some of the basic principles of the system and has sought to
reconcile these principles with national or social needs.
Some few Poles are real Communists, but the majority are
not Communists at all. They call themselves Communists in
order to deflect attention from themselves and get along with
the powers that be. Again, Communism in Czechoslovakia is
considerably different from Chinese Communism. Furthermore, we must not confuse a nation with its political system.
As Christians and realists, we must recognize these distinctions; otherwise we are not promoting peace and understanding but fostering disharmony and rivalry.

As Pope John has reminded us, we must distinguish between the economic-political system and atheism, between
the system and the people. My four years' experience in Russia
during the war only confirmed what I always heard and believed: the Russians are a great-hearted people, traditionally
devout and hospitable. As a priest and member of the Medical Corps, I had an opportunity to deal with many Russians.
I can vouch for the statement that it would be a grievous mistake to identify the sins of a few with an entire populace.
Such injustice has nothing to contribute to the desired peace
on earth.

In many places today, it is not only risky but a matter of
life and death to express disenchantment with the communist regime. Christians should be taught as a point of conscience that if they have to speak out against Communism,
they should never fail to express their deep appreciation of

the religious qualities of the Russian people. The Russian authorities must be made to feel that we entertain only the most friendly attitude toward the Russian people. The same should apply when speaking of China and Chinese Communism. We must give them no grounds for complaint against us in the interest of promoting a friendlier atmosphere. Confessors should insist that this is a matter of conscience not only for journalists and politicians, but for all Christians insofar as they contribute to the formation of the public opinion.

RESPONSIBLE MEMBERS OF THE CHURCH

Confessors have a formidable task ahead of them in reforming the consciences of Catholics regarding their attitude toward the Church. All too many lay people think of "the Church" only in its juridical structure, failing to realize the import of the definition of the Church in its membership. They have not grasped the fact that they—the whole people of God—are the Church. For the layman to labor under this misconception can only encourage lethargy and apathy.

Not all Catholics have yet understood or even studied the teachings of the Second Vatican Council in terms of the right understanding and self-definition of the Church. Everyone can gain from reading and re-reading the Constitution on the Church. The Second Vatican Council also gave us a clear evaluation of the role of the laity. Unfortunately, these documents have not found their way onto the reading list of enough Catholic homes. If the laity is to be given a better understanding of their Church, if they are to be awakened to the responsibility that they must share in the mission of this Church, then they will have to be informed and reminded about the Constitutions and decrees of the Vatican Council. Confessors might, for the sake of making the conciliar documents better known, suggest that certain penitents read one of them as their penance. Those of particular interest to lay people would be Chapters 2, 4 and 5 of the Dogmatic Constitution on the Church, the Decree on the Laity, the one on the Church in the Modern World, and the one on the Lay Apostolate. Confessors should not argue that this is an unrealistic penance. "We'll only disturb their consciences, because they won't read the decrees anyway"; "most of our people wouldn't be able to handle a penance like that"; "they wouldn't even know where to find one of the decrees." Such arguments underestimate many of the laity and encourage others to the type of apathy the Council has attempted to dispel.

There is no doubt in my mind that ecumenism as promoted by the Second Vatican Council would make much greater progress if priests and lay people alike took more time to examine the Council's decrees. The confessor, whose interest must be the proper formation of conscience, cannot ignore the decrees of the Second Vatican Council in his work as counsellor. To do so would be crass negligence.

16. THE FIFTH COMMANDMENT AND THE FORMATION OF CONSCIENCE

All the commandments promulgated on Mount Sinai need to be explained and applied to our own period of salvation history. And so the fifth commandment, in the perspective of the New Testament law, is viewed as a consequence of the great commandment of love of neighbor.

In seeking the contemporary answer to the age-old question: "Lord, who is my neighbor?", new vistas appear on the horizon. Our neighborhood is now international, crossing all racial barriers and encompassing all believers and non-believers; every man is my neighbor. Although the Old Testament "Thou shalt not kill" has evolved from the negative to the New Testament affirmative "Thou shall love," our world has not fully grasped the message. In many instances, a deep-seated hatred has yet to become love, violence to become compassion, before men can find peace on earth. Men must first find Christ and His love in their own hearts.

MODERN WARFARE

In modern times, a confessor may well be asked by a sincere young man whether or not he may serve in the armed forces with a good conscience.

Traditionally, moral theologians have supported the fighting of a just war. This means that a government may request its citizens to fight and even sacrifice their lives in the defense of the common good and freedom of the country. Any citizen may then respond to this request with a clear conscience. However, if a man is convinced that a certain war is unjust and, nevertheless, takes part in that war, killing other people, he is a murderer. This, too, is the traditional opinion. In the latter case, a private citizen who questions his government's right to demand service or the justness of the war must make every effort to form an upright conscience in this matter.

With regard to atomic or nuclear war, the question is quite different. It would be most difficult if not impossible to justify supporting such a war. The evils of atomic warfare would always be greater than the sacrifice of a part of one's civil and political rights. When Nikita Khrushchev was still premier of Russia he said, with regard to an atomic war, ". . . the survivors will envy the dead." To drop A-bombs or H-bombs on cities can never be morally justified. Furthermore, I believe that a soldier who obeys his government in such a command is positively guilty of murder a thousand times over. I feel that the people of the world who were so horrified to learn of the atrocities committed by the SS troops in the last war will easily accede to this opinion. For none doubted that those Germans who obeyed the orders of the Führer and slaughtered thousands of innocent Jews were murderers in the truest sense, though they acted "in obedience."

However, when there is only question of a defensive war against an unjust aggressor and the government limits itself to military targets, *e.g.*, destroying airports, factories, bomb-storage plants, then the soldier not only can but should obey.

However, I do appreciate the witness of conscientious objectors who, at the same time, mobilize all their energies of love for peace and social justice among the nations.

This discussion prompts me to repeat the obligation mentioned earlier about creating an atmosphere of respect among people. A country must do its best to broadcast a favorable, peace-loving image to others. Such a public image is impossible if at the same time every effort is directed to the production of weapons. There is also the point of men striving to know the good qualities of other nations and promoting a public opinion conducive to peace among all people.

While I am discussing warfare, I might briefly restate here my opinion regarding the spy who commits suicide. I first treated the question in the *Familia Cristiana*, a periodical in which I regularly contribute answers to readers' questions. However, the opinion I gave has been badly misrepresented by the American press.

The point at issue was: may a spy follow the orders of his government to commit suicide when this is the only means of protecting secret information which, if revealed, would gravely endanger peace? My response was that suicide *in the strict moral sense* is not licit. However, I added that it could be questionable whether or not the action of a spy in such circumstances would be suicide *in the moral sense*. I supported by distinction between taking one's own life and suicide in the moral sense by several examples. There was the case of Socrates who, condemned to death by the government, calmly drank a goblet of poison. In those days, drinking poison was the means used to effect a merciful death. To my knowledge, no moralist has ever called the philosopher's death at his own hand a suicide *in the moral sense*.

In Japan, members of the nobility are not executed by hanging but are ordered to take their own life (harikari) when condemned to death. No one would call this suicide in the moral sense.

Anyone with war experience knows that there are many actions in war in which one fulfills a command though, practically speaking, he knows that by doing so he will sacrifice his life. No one would accuse such a man of suicide in the moral sense.

Finally, after World War II, the name of Father Kolbe became prominent. This priest had been in a concentration camp. Whenever any of the prisoners resisted orders, they were marched into the yards and every tenth man in that camp was condemned to terrible torture and a slow death. It happened that on one such occasion, Father Kolbe saw a man who was the father of several children singled out as a vicitim. He immediately requested to take that man's place, though there could be no doubt in his mind that he was volunteering to die. Yet, who would accuse Father Kolbe of committing suicide?

Having established a distinction, then, between taking one's own life and suicide in the moral sense, I said that the case of the spy is conceivably a moot question. I made no claim to the effect that I had proved that a spy, who deliberately takes his life with the intention of serving the cause of justice and of protecting peace, is not committing suicide in the moral sense.

Let me repeat the line of argument: because the spy has secret information of such importance that betraying it would endanger the peace of his country, his government gives him orders to sacrifice his own life rather than give away the information. It can be discussed whether in obeying this command of the government the spy is committing suicide in the moral sense, because, in disposing of his life, he is dependent on government orders. (Is it not the government who decides in time of war that individuals have to sacrifice their lives to protect peace?) The government executes its decision by giving the order to those who are ready to make a free sacrifice of their lives should that sacrifice be necessary for the fatherland.

The reason I mention this case is to show how carefully we should avoid apodictic teaching in intricate cases. Condemning suicide or abortion as grave sins should not deter us but rather oblige us to take a closer look at some extreme cases in relation to the moral meaning of these acts.

ABORTION

Confessors are often called upon to enlighten or to strengthen the consciences of people with respect to the crime of abortion. Every Catholic should know that this is one of the greatest sins, a direct violation of the most fundamental right of an innocent person. It is a sin against justice and against love, a sin of contempt, of scorn for the gift of fruitfulness which God gave to woman for the responsible fulfillment of her womanly vocation.

In the depths of her being, every woman knows that her consent to the conceptive act entails the moral commitment to its outcome; it is a question of justice in relation to God's gift of her sexuality and feminine nature. As every experienced confessor knows, abortion is the one sin for which many women seem unable to forgive themselves even after it has been forgiven them by God Himself. Physicians and psychiatrists are likewise aware of how deeply women, within their own nature, are committed to motherhood, even if on the conscious level they scarcely realize that commitment. In *Flight from Woman*, the eminent psychiatrist Karl Stern illustrates this point when he refers to the pervasiveness of the "sense of time" reaching into a woman's being:

> We not infrequently see that in those cases in which a woman commits an artificial abortion, let us say in the third month of pregnancy, the act seems to have no psychological consequence. Yet, six months later, just when the baby would have been due, the subject breaks down with a serious depression or even with a psychosis. Now there are two remarkable features about this. First, the woman is not necessarily conscious of the time incidence. The depression occurs without any conscious awareness of "this is the time when my baby would have been due." Moreover, the patient's philosophy is not necessarily such that she would have morally disapproved of the act of interruption of pregnancy. Yet her profound *reaction of loss* (not necessarily even with a conscious preoccupation with the missed birth) coincides with the time of the birth that did not take place. . . . Woman, in her being, is deeply committed to *bios*, to nature itself.

It is considered highly probable that the fertilized ovum, at least once it has become implanted in the womb, is a living being possessed of an immortal soul. Although this is not, strictly speaking, a matter of dogma, the aborting of a fertilized ovum is a sin against human life, just as it is a case of homicide if the hunter pulls the trigger when he is uncertain whether the object he is aiming at is a man or animal. Disregarding the doubt and firing anyway renders him guilty of the sin of homicide.

Every woman should be made to realize that in destroying the fruit of her womb, she is destroying in herself the sense of motherhood and thus depriving the world of one of the highest spiritual values. However, the confessor should avoid arousing a guilt complex, particularly in extreme cases where the termination of a pregnancy was the only way to save the life of the mother.

That the degree of mortal sinfulness is so little realized in the crime of abortion is indicative of the insensitivity in our times to the sacredness of human sexuality through which man is privileged to enjoy a creative partnership with Almighty God. Many girls and women operate on the assumption that at the first indication of amenorrhea they may immediately go to a physician to have menstruation induced even though they suspect that a pregnancy could have interfered with their regular period.

There are some who justify an abortion on grounds of mere inconvenience or material ambitions. For others, however, the temptation or the decision to submit to an abortion may be a painful and difficult one prompted by psychological desperation because of almost unbearable circumstances. The subjective guilt in this sin would vary in degree as for any other sin.

In the counselling of these penitents, a confessor would do well to suggest motives: fidelity to her own womanhood and to the will of God in whose creative power the woman is now required to cooperate. They can be shown how this atrocious crime is a sin against maternal love, and can be encouraged to try to love this unborn child of their flesh and of God. If the child is illegitimate, the priest may be able to help with some suggestions about where the girl may find shelter during her period of waiting; he may offer to talk with her parents in an effort to reconcile them to the fact of her pregnancy and to encourage them in a most charitable attitude toward her. A confessor may also be in a position to provide reassurance to a woman in doubt about a prospective operation, explaining that it is a licit operation and not a true abortion. For cases where it can be doubted whether it is an abortion, "indirect abortion" or a licit operation, refer to my earlier work *The Law of Christ*, Volume III.

For any girl or woman who has become pregnant through actual forcible rape, one must feel and show the greatest compassion. These cases are infrequent but they do exist. Special consideration must be given here, not only because every humane instinct calls out for it, but because of a circumstance not present in any other category of conception except possibly certain cases of incest which could also properly be called rape.

In rape cases there is absolutely no consent by the girl or woman to the conceptive event, but rather utter rejection and revulsion. This is a situation brought on not only by the violation of the law of God as expressed in the commandments but by a violation of nature as indicated even in lower bisexual life forms where the consent of the female is a condition of the act. Because of the dignity of the human person, the personal and parental ordination of the sex act, and the sacred and destinal purpose of human sexuality, this consent—at least to the most minimalistic degree—is a woman's inalienable right. In marriage, of course, she gives a lifetime consent to her husband. In some cases of seduction, for instance, she may give almost no consent but there is always some degree of assent. Man is the only species that violates this rule of nature in the unspeakable crime of rape. At one time, this forcible violation of a woman's body was punishable by death; now punishment has diminished to a point that compares in no way to the heinousness of the crime.

In cases of rape, it is morally allowable to cleanse away

the sperm which is considered to be an extension of the initial act of aggression. Abortion, however, is not allowed if conception has already taken place. It has not been adjudged that the fetus, which would not have formed except for the presence of the "aggressive" sperm, is itself an "aggressor." Nevertheless, we must recognize that although the fetus is innocent, the girl is likewise innocent. We can therefore understand her revulsive feeling that this is not "her" child, not a child that she in justice is required to bear.

We must, nevertheless, try to motivate her to consider the child with love because of its subjective innocence, and to bear it in suffering through the birth, whereupon she may consider her enforced maternal obligation fulfilled and may give over the child to a religious or governmental agency, after which she would try to resume her life with the sanctity that she will undoubtedly have achieved through her great sacrifice and suffering.

If, due to the psychological effects of her traumatic experience, she is utterly unable to accept this counsel, it is possible that we may have to leave her in her "invincible ignorance." Her own salvation may depend on it because of her near despair. If she has already yielded to the violent temptation to rid herself as completely as possible of the effects of her experience, we can leave the judgment of the degree of her sin to a merciful God and try to build up her willingness to integrate both her sufferings and her fault with the sufferings and sins of the world that Christ took upon Himself on the cross.

For those who have committed the crime of abortion, confessors should generally endeavor to explain to them the seriousness of their offense and inform them that the Church excommunicates all who sanction or participate in such a crime. It may happen that their consciences were still in the dark regarding the real nature and gravity of their act. They must be enlightened, nevertheless, because it involves more than a question of the subjective conscience. Consideration must be given the effect upon the environment, on the building up of the "divine milieu" in which love and goodness witness to Christ's presence. And there is, in addition, the duty of the Church to protect those who are unprotected and near to God, the unborn children.

LIFE AND HEALTH OF OUR NEIGHBOR

The "Thou shalt not kill" of the Old Testament becomes, for the Christian, the affirmative "Thou shalt preserve life." It is not enough to avoid killing our neighbor; we must love him and, in the light of that love, look to the things that affect his health and his life.

A formed Christian conscience questions itself on duties relative to the health and life of the family and of the community. The confessor may sharpen his penitent's sense of responsibility in this area through a review of points such as: Do we, as parents, provide the family with adequate medical care, with well-balanced meals, with the cleanliness that promotes effective preventive hygiene? Do we provide special schooling for physically or mentally handicapped children? How do we treat the "old folks"? Do we try to add life to their years or only years to their life? As neighbors, do we help in the emergencies of life within our neighborhood? As citizens, do we work and vote for the type of governmental administration that operates with sincere regard for the safety and health of the whole community? Do we take a civic interest in improved housing, better sanitation, adequate health services, health and fire inspections, especially of slum properties? Are we interested in seeing that the mentally retarded receive needed psychological assistance? Do we initiate steps to procure services from social agencies for families that need special help?

Our greater sophistication in psychology and medicine has resulted in a greater awareness of psychosomatic problems. They call attention to the need for weighing the consequences of our own behavior on the health of those around us, particularly those in our own home. It is well known that to bring joy and hope into someone's life contributes also to the health of that person. It is a great sin, therefore, to injure the health of others by continually aggrieving them.

The plight of lone elderly people should receive special consideration from all age groups. Both their loneliness and their phsyical needs cry out for our gift of love and thoughtful help. We must not only help to preserve life but to bring into it a reflection of the joy and light of Christ's love.

Driving. The death toll on highways in recent years has risen to an all-time high. In the United States alone in 1965, 49,000 people were killed and 1,850,000 injured in automobile accidents. With such grim facts in mind there is no room to doubt that safety rules on the road oblige in conscience. Many moral theologians consider all violations of posted speed limits a venial sin. I personally would not rigidly adhere to this measurement, since often the rate of speed maintained by other drivers is a better measure of prudence than the officially posted limit. The more common opinion is that a margin of five miles per hour is allowable. At any rate, driving that endangers one's own life or others' lives is definitely sinful. This would include driving cars known to be dangerously defective. Repairs necessary for safe driving should never be delayed. It would be contrary to the fifth commandment to drive, for instance, with faulty brakes. The faithful would profit from an occasional reminder of their obligations in this area both from the pulpit and from the confessional.

Obviously, those who are going to drive ought not to drink alcoholic beverages, or at most, only the minimum that would not affect their capacity to drive safely. Some people should give up driving altogether, *e.g.*, anyone subject to blackouts and others with failing reflexes or undependable eyesight. No one should attempt driving when emotionally upset or under severe emotional strain, as would be likely in the death of a close friend or relative.

PERSONAL LIFE AND HEALTH

One aspect of the obligation regarding life and health is the protection of our own. We must so conduct our lives as to be of service to God and our neighbor. Our primary obligation is not to safeguard our own lives, for we have received our lives in order to spend them. Christ's example should be our model here. But, because of the obligation to devote ourselves to the welfare of others, we have no right to kill ourselves or to shorten our lives unreasonably. St. Jerome, a great ascetic, is reported to have said, according to St. Thomas and the *Corpus Iuris Canonici:* "There is little difference between killing one's self at once or killing one's self slowly by unreasonable penances and mortifications." I think that all Christians, even monks and nuns, today would agree with St. Jerome on this point. No one has the right to shorten his life by three or four years by external mortification.

Smoking. I doubt, however, that all monks and Christian laymen would agree with St. Jerome on the question of shortening one's life span by five to ten years through excessive smoking. If we accept the first point, we must accept the second. Excessive smoking causes a person to lose part of his freedom which, psychologically speaking, is the most precious part of one's health. It is possible to guard one's integrity, health and freedom, and practice mortification at the same time by refusing to indulge in unreasonable cigarette smoking.

Many studies, including those by the Royal Commission in England and those reported by the Surgeon-General in the United States, prove that heavy smokers, *i.e.,* those who smoke at least fifteen cigarettes a day throughout their lives, will live about five years less than the average person of their age. A study of seven projects involving observation of 1,123,-000 men carried on since 1951 disclosed that the death rate per thouand from all causes was 68% higher for cigarette smokers than for nonsmokers. Christians, therefore, do well to encourage others to give up a habit of immoderate smoking by their own example of self-renunciation.

From their own habit, priest-smokers might learn a valuable lesson in understanding the difficulties some penitents have in trying to conquer a habit in other moral areas. All priests need at times to make analogies between difficulties or weaknesses in their own lives and those in the lives of their penitents. These tend to broaden a confessor's outlook.

Finally, as spiritual counsellor, a confessor may at times propose to generous penitents who are truly seeking a higher life and who are ready to make sacrifices for it that they deny themselves the pleasure of smoking as penance for and in solidarity with the intemperate smoker or drinker. Their sacrifice would also afford psychological encouragement for weaker Christians.

Drinking. What we have said above in relation to moderation applies also to excessive drinking. Many known alcoholics could have been spared the stigma and humiliating experiences of their weakness if they had been sufficiently influenced by others in their society who voluntarily gave up drinking. In social gatherings, some feel ashamed to stop drinking. Help can become a serious obligation, especially for those closely related to or intimately acquainted with the alcoholic. Those who enjoy full freedom have a greater obligation, of course, than those who are already on the road to alcoholism and have, to a certain extent, lost control of themselves.

Sleep. There are many ways by which one can ruin his health, among others not sleeping enough or sleeping too much. Some people oversleep throughout their lives, thus preserving their health but having little to show in terms of a fulfilled personal experience. Since we are duty-bound to spend our health in a reasonable way in the service of God and neighbor, we do not have the right to waste our health by a lack of temperance in such matters as sleep and food.

CONFESSOR OF THE SICK

It is of utmost importance to convince the sick that their illness is a stage on the road to health in the spiritual sense of the term. They find themselves in a redemptive situation. If they make proper use of the time of their illness, they can grow in the love of God and neighbor. They can offer their ailments as reparation for their own faults and as satisfaction for the sins of others. This is the true meaning of participation in the redemptive death of the Lord. On this point,

Thomas à Kempis in the *Following of Christ* asserted that nobody becomes better through sickness. This is not true. If it were, it could be the fault of confessors and moral theologians.

We must teach the faithful the Christian meaning of suffering. Christians should be aware of the value of sickness. It can be a blessing for some people to have time for reflection, to give up their activism for a time and to devote themselves to thinking about God and their eternal salvation. This is an opportunity often afforded by a serious or prolonged illness.

Precisely because of this redemptive role of illness, nuns engaged in hospital work find in their vocation an important apostolate. Physicians, too, as well as good Christians who work in hospitals would also profit by being reminded of this aspect of illness. All who are privileged to care for the sick seek to heal the body but in so doing contribute to the health of the whole man. Physicians and nurses can do much to help with a confessor's mission in this respect.

About twelve years ago, I tried to be of help to a priest who had fallen away from the faith some forty years earlier. He had been professor of dogmatic theology but had lost his vocation and faith because of a woman. When I visited him, his first words were: "Why, for forty years no priest has ever come to see me!" We spoke for a while but on that occasion he was not ready to renounce publicly his past declarations. Some weeks later, when in the hopsital, he became extremely worried and asked his doctor, a young Catholic physician: "What would people say if an old man like me should return to the Catholic Church and disavow forty years of his life?" The young doctor replied, "In a few weeks or months, professor, you may be more interested in knowing what God will say." These few words made a deep impression on the old man and he told the doctor to call the parish priest immediately. He made his confession and received communion.

We can do a great deal when hearing confessions to make people realize that they can help the sick in this way. The patients in hospitals can also be of great help to one another. Those who have come to a realization of the deep spiritual meaning of their own illness should try to help their neighbors view things in the same light.

Another point to be noted is that we should try to get the sick to look on their situation from an optimistic and accepting point of view. There is great healing power in optimism. Optimism and Christian joy can be strong factors in promoting good health.

The man who likes to work accomplishes perhaps three times as much as the man who does not, and never becomes ill from overwork. Those who worry about their health are almost bound to become sick; they are the victims of their own pessimistic outlook. With prolonged introspection and searching for possible ailments, they evolve into hypochondriacs. The best way for the sick to find health is to entrust themselves entirely to the will of God and accept their sickness as a grace and blessing in disguise.

Another matter affecting the conscience is the obedience one owes to a doctor. The Christian attitude toward sickness should be one of acquiescence in whatever God has in store, even death, if that is His will. But it is not Christian acquiescence in death if one does not do whatever is necessary to care for one's health. One of the greatest psychological dangers for the sick is that of becoming overly preoccupied with their own case. These people would profit from being encouraged to concern themselves about other matters and try to devote themselves to other people. Their constant worry retards their recovery.

Finally, a word about gratitude during an illness. The sick should of course be grateful to everyone who helps them: doctors, nurses and all others, especially relatives. There is a definite danger that the sick may become too self-centered. Therefore, confessors must help them to become aware of their responsibilities toward other people and urge them to do what they can for the welfare of those attending them.

17. CHASTITY AND
THE FORMATION OF CONSCIENCE

A POSITIVE ATTITUDE

In the matter of chastity, a strictly forbidding conscience distorts the human person and obstructs the action of God in him. If we wish to form a conscience that urges the penitent toward integrity, while keeping intact the love and joy essential to the proper understanding and use of human sexuality, we must strive toward a fuller appreciation of its goodness and holiness.

Through human sexuality God channels life and love into the world. He calls man to partnership with Him in the creative formation of His people and the continuing outpouring of His redemptive love on earth. To the degree that a penitent is helped to realize this sacred purpose of his sexuality, he is encouraged to avoid its desecration.

A very wrong attitude, all too prevalent, is to treat sex first as an evil or an occasion of sin, and then as something which marriage excuses from sin. This is tantamount to saying that the administration of the sacraments is sinful but ceases to be so after a priest has been ordained and has received jurisdiction to hear confessions. Obviously, anyone who would dare hear confessions before his ordination would not deserve to become a confessor because he would reveal a pitiful ignorance of the confessor's mission.

Through human sexuality everyone is called, in one way or another, to a fatherhood or motherhood of the children of God. The usual response to God's call is in the vocation of marriage and natural parenthood; but loving concern for neighbor in secular life is also a parental role, and the total giving of self to a spiritual fatherhood or motherhood in consecrated celibacy is an especially blessed form of parental vocation.

All the obligations of Christian chastity flow from these vocations, which witness, each in its own unique way, to the presence of the kingdom of God. Once chastity is understood in this light, one knows why he has to avoid sins against the sixth commandment which contradict or distort the profound meaning of his sexuality and its expression in his own vocation. The formation of the penitent's conscience in this respect means bringing him to the realization and significance of the profound truths involved. One then grasps what it means to sin against God, the highest good in our scale of values and the revealer of this hierarchy of goods.

MARRIAGE AND CELIBACY

What is marriage? It is an enduring and exclusive covenant of love between a man and a woman standing in the presence of God. Through the action of the Holy Spirit and the acceptance of this action by the spouses, their personal love for each other reflects the divine love of Christ for the people of God, His Church. Their joyful collaboration with the Tremendous Lover, God the Creator and Redeemer, deepens their own love until it is transformed into a total giving of each to the other and of both to the children born of their union. Thus they form a community of love, giving praise to the Lord.

What is celibacy? Celibacy is also a covenant of love but a supremely directed love that first gives all of self to God and then reflects His divine love, in act and attitude, in the face of the world. It is one of the highest forms of openness to God and neighbor, an openness that enables man to give himself wholly and joyfully to witnessing the presence of God through his service to the children of God.

OFFENSES AGAINST CHASTITY

Many Christians are told, or think, that all sins against the sixth commandment are *ipso facto* mortal sins. However, this has never been the teaching of the Church. It would be too ridiculous to bracket together a heinous sin like rape or contemptuously loveless fornication with the too intimate caresses of one's fiancée whereby he experiences a degree of selfish pleasure. Nor can it be held that failure to control self in the matter of sexual passion of love is to be judged more harshly than failure to control the destructive passion of anger or hate, as presented in the preceding chapter.

There is no morality especially applicable to the sixth commandment; it is ruled by the same general norms and principles that govern the rest of morality. As in other cases, a mortal sin is committed only after the necessary deliberation and the requisite freedom on the individual's part.

Three elements must always be present to comprise a mortal sin: (1) there must be a deep awareness that the decision is being made on the friendship of God and on salvation, an awareness arising from the felt importance of the decision (or matter of the decision); (2) a correspondingly full deliberation and (3) that degree of freedom congruent with a decision on eternal salvation. However, God alone knows what that exact measure of full deliberation and full freedom is that deserves eternal damnation. The theologians can only propose tentative norms or approximative rules of prudence.

Until the last few years, the more common opinion among moral theologians was that sins in which a person *directly* sought a sexual pleasure contradicting the moral order were all mortal sins, no matter how restricted the degree of this sexual pleasure or sexual disorder. In other words, they taught that every sexual disorder or every disorderly seeking of sexual pleasure was of such importance that the average Christian should realize that it destroyed friendship with God and was worthy of eternal damnation. This was held to be the case even though a person might have the intention to stop before full sexual gratification was reached, *i.e.*, before orgasm. However, well informed moralists always insisted that this applied only if there was a direct, deliberate and fully free will to excite one's sexuality to some degree. But many traditional moralists would have agreed with the following practical rule for discernment: that persons who generally display good will and, on the ground of moral concern, stop before orgasm is reached, can presume not to have committed a mortal sin, at least in cases of doubt about whether they acted with a fully free will, sufficient deliberation and with a *direct* intention to abuse their sexuality or to excite that of another person to some degree.

Today a growing number of theologians challenge this position. They assert that in this field the question must be approached and expressed on the same terms as in other moral categories. By this is meant that if there is a lesser degree of disorder we have very good reasons to think that the average person does not realize that salvation is at stake and does not make a decision arising from the depth of his will; it is an imperfect act of decision, a venial sin. Of course, modern theologians also recognize the seriousness of every sin that expresses an act of a fully free and deliberate decision to transgress directly and intentionally the law of God (the order of love), no matter where one wills to stop in the selfish search for pleasure.

Whatever the theoretical approach may be, the following criterion applies in practice: A person who generally displays good will, and with earnest moral concern tried at least to avoid complete sexual gratification, has not committed a mortal sin. Nevertheless, penitents should be warned that those who decide, with full deliberation and freedom, directly to exploit their sexual urge in all degrees except orgasm cannot, psychologically, intend not to go further; in the end, they will succumb to this innermost and unruly tendency. A warning becomes even more imperative if arousal of another person's sexuality is involved, because of the sin against charity and the mutual implication in a waxing impulse.

The theologians of both schools would agree that a Christian must earnestly be admonished about the danger of toying with his sexuality, especially if this is done with full deliberation or with a stubborn intention. This warning is what the traditional approach in moral theology sought as the essential goal, although the way it was presented often clouded the point and implied that sexual morality was to be treated differently from other moral matters.

However, everyone should know that no well-informed theologian teaches that all sins against the meaning of sexuality are mortal, even disorders which are only indirectly caused or indirectly intended. For instance, not every yielding to curiosity, or failure to avoid an occasion of sin, is necessarily a mortal sin. If, however, one knows that as a consequence of his curiosity or unreasonable actions he will be led to sin, then these "indirect" acts are mortally sinful, provided of course that the person is aware that the situation is a proximate occasion for him, one that he could avoid but does not avoid while acting with deliberation and free will.

It is obvious that many people cannot avoid all occasions that constitute for them some danger of sexual excitement. It would be ridiculous, for example, to maintain that engaged couples may not embrace or caress each other if this provokes some sexual urge and pleasure. If this restriction were imposed and carried out today, no girl following such advice would ever get married. Notwithstanding, a betrothed couple should avoid occasions which they know will constitute proximate dangers of experiencing full sexual pleasure and giving free consent to it.

In the matter of chastity as in other matters of morality, anyone who has good will and strives toward full realization of the virtue of temperance is and remains in a state of grace even if, at times, he feels weak. The important point is that he continue to show good will. By exaggerating the dangers, concentrating too much attention on them and imposing too many restrictions on the manifestations of affection, we tend to discourage people and drive them completely into the arms of vice.

(On the complex problem of homosexuality, see B. Häring, *Law of Christ*, III, pp. 305-306.)

MASTURBATION OR IPSATION

Psychologists have indicated a preference for the word *ipsation* (from *ipse*, oneself) rather than masturbation because it expresses better the self-centered nature of the tendency or act. While this inclination is most common in young people (and I will treat it here mainly from that standpoint), it does not mean that the problem is confined to this age group; many adults are troubled by the habit. Often, it represents a perpetration of youthful habits that were never fully overcome. In other cases, the urge develops under lonely or frustrating conditions which the person either cannot change or is unwilling to change. A single person who finds himself in a strange environment away from family companionship and well-known friends, or married people separated by distance or oppressed by a lack of understanding, may be tempted in this respect. Many psychological factors come into play.

There is a vast difference in the quality of guilt ascribed to deliberate misuse of one's sexuality through willful manipulation and the weak yielding to this impulse under pressures of emotional disturbance. The confessor's effort in all the cases will be directed toward helping the penitent to overcome his difficulty, but his counselling must reflect the differing needs and circumstances. In the first case, the confessor may emphasize the seriousness of the sin, which desecrates a holy power, and point out the need for self-control in all aspects of life. In the second, he may consider it best not to advert directly to the sin at all for fear of adding to the tensions already present. Instead, he may mention in a general way how trust in God, openness to God in prayer and in frequent communion, would help him; he may also speak of the virtue of generosity in works of mercy, such as visiting lonely people. Encouragement is most important. The person must be helped to appreciate his own worth and be urged toward generous involvement in interests outside himself.

Youth is especially vulnerable to this particular difficulty. In today's environment permeated with sexuality, most boys and a large minority of girls engage in more or less extensive masturbatory activities in the process of growing up. But it is not only the environment; other facts oblige us to rethink some of the principles formulated in totally different circumstances.

Sexual maturity today, in Europe and in America, is achieved on an average of two to four years earlier than it was in the last century, while personality generally takes longer to attain maturity. The extended educational requirements force youth into a longer period of dependence on their family, with the consequent delay in the adolescents' assumption of adult responsibilities and decisions. The enforced immaturity becomes an extenuating circumstance in the adolescents' problems. The pervasiveness of the problem of masturbation points up the fact that the earlier biological maturation so far exceeds the psychological that, when faced with the problem, young people have not yet acquired the necessary values and freedom to handle it with sufficient knowledge and deliberation; they are not sufficiently mature to be able to cope with the biological drive.

As a result of the new situation and the importance attributed today to psychological factors, we have found it necessary to adjust our attitude toward this age-old problem. The traditional doctrine of the Church is still valid but care must be taken to express it and interpret it in a way that honestly applies to and that can be understood by the present generation.

In a static society when most young people had nearly reached personal maturity before encountering sexual problems, it was not so wrong to express principles in a static or inflexible way, e.g., by stating flatly that it is a mortal sin to masturbate. Today, however, principles need to be expressed in dynamic terms taking into account the actual tensions and the degree of maturity; otherwise young people will not understand what we are trying to say.

It must be stressed that the habit of masturbation in an adolescent is almost invariably a sign of tension between an early sexual maturation and a postponed maturation of the personality, and the problem can be solved only if the resultant force is one of openness to God and neighbor. This approach assumes particular importance in view of the fact that many youngsters fall into the habit before really understanding what is happening. A temporary difficulty is soon turned into a permanent condition especially when one meets with constant reproach or one's attention is concentrated on it in a negative way.

It would be contrary to tradition, of course, to maintain that masturbation is never a mortal sin or to claim that it is almost never a sin. Pope Pius XII said (AAS 1952, p. 275):

> We reject as erroneous the affirmation of those who regard lapses as inevitable among adolescents and therefore are not worthy of being considered. They accept as a general rule the belief that passions destroy the necessary liberty required to make an act morally imputable.

Although we should first note that the word "adolescent" may have different connotations and that today many who are faced with sexual problems are still children, the Pope's declaration remains the guideline. It is true that we cannot maintain that such "lapses" are inevitable, because moral lapses are never inevitable insofar as they are free decisions. Besides, many boys and girls whose environment and heredity are sound, manage to avoid this condition altogether. Nor can we say that passion alone destroys the moral impunity of sins against the sixth commandment, for, if this were true, it would serve as an adequate excuse for all sins of passion. Then only a diabolic sin would be mortal.

André Gide, the French author whose books were all put on the Index, recounts in one of them how he decided to have a unique experience. He resolved to procreate a child without experiencing any sensation of love or pleasure. He wondered what it would be like if two persons who disliked each other, and did not experience any passion for each other, were to copulate with a view to procreation. He actually went through with his plan. Such an experience is, of course, diabolic and pathological. Abusing the sexual faculty without any passion and love reveals, in a normal person, a stubborn bad will. Disordinate passion is less evil than a coldly calculated abuse.

While passion alone does not excuse, with most boys and girls it is not merely a question of passion or of a tremendous sexual drive. There are many psychological factors involved. They indulge in masturbation because they have not been adequately prepared or instructed in the value of marriage and the dignity of sex. They are ignorant of the forces they are experiencing. In many cases, masturbation becomes a compensatory act whereby adolescents express all their frustrations. They feel lonely or despised and sometimes despise themselves.

Frustrated boys are especially subject to such temptations. They often masturbate after a scolding by their teacher or parents. Their self-abuse convinces them of their worthlessness while at the same time they assert their independence and seek consolation. But even when a boy indulges in self-manipulation, it cannot always be concluded that he is fully free; he may be laboring under some uncontrollable psychological urge. At times, his anxiety or fear of succumbing again may build up to a point where all attempts to resist the urge become impossible. He may have the desire to resist but cannot. That is why a positive approach that removes the focus of attention from the act of masturbation is advocated. When the confessor requests that the masturbating penitent do something in the way of helping others, he is helping him redirect his energies into constructive channels.

Some confessors, in attempting to help, try to solve this problem by providing the boys with motives of fear, and by acting as though such sins were quite extraordinary. As a consequence, they succeed remarkably well in building up a guilt-complex that causes the boys to refrain from confessing these sins or drives them to desperation. We must be perfectly frank with teen-agers and tell them that not all, but a good many of them, generally have difficulty with this problem and that they should not be afraid to mention it or discuss it with their parents or their confessor. Sometimes these difficulties are not a sign of bad will or even a sign of sin.

Proper instruction will convince these penitents that the habit will be more easily overcome as they grow towards fuller maturity as persons. They will achieve maturity sooner if they try to overcome their self-centeredness in view of their future state of life. Marriage and parenthood can be a success only if the partners give themselves fully to each other, but if they remain self-centered, this becomes an impossibility. It could also be God's intention to call the boy or girl to celibacy. Should this be the case, one can only become capable of so high a vocation by rising far above any such self-centered gratification. The vocation to celibacy calls for complete openness to the love of God and the giving of one's life for the service of the Church and other people.

It is helpful when the confessor can show how difficulties in this matter are connected with the whole person. It is the whole person, not just a part, that grows up to maturity and openness to God and neighbor. Anyone who fails to overcome egocentrism is necessarily exposed to many failures, not only against chastity.

How can the confessor best help boys and girls presenting a masturbation problem? The confessor must first have an idea of the kind of person he is dealing with. If one is shy, frustrated, disturbed, the confessor can appraise the problem as mainly psychological. It would be wrong to blame the penitent or insist too much on this aspect. He can be helped by being reminded of the humanity and kindness of Christ. He needs to know more than anything else that his confessor at least is good to him, respects him and understands his problem.

If, on the other hand, the penitent is aggressive and shows a general lack of restraint, the confessor must be more energetic. He will show his penitent why Christian life demands self-control and self-denial. The adolescent will learn to overcome his self-centeredness only if he practices self-denial for the common good, the good of his family or friends, and devotes himself to his duties.

At all costs the confessor should try to integrate this point into the whole of Christian life. Generally speaking, he should not allow the penitent to feel that this weakness is the most important of his failings, but he should try to give a strong impression to the contrary, asking him, for example, what progress he has made in prayer and in the spirit of solidarity with his family and friends. He could be asked if he would like to have as penance the intention of doing some kindnesses for his sister, mother or other person and then examining his conscience each evening about his faithfulness on these points. In the next confession, suggest that he mention whether he has done this or tried to carry out his intention. If the penitent accepts such a penance, the confessor can soon determine whether he is a person of good will.

Furthermore, the confessor must help such boys make the necessary distinctions. Accusations are to be made only when he has masturbated while fully aware of what he was doing; otherwise, he cannot be regarded as fully responsible for his acts. The confessor may help him distinguish voluntary masturbatory practices from involuntary nocturnal emissions ("wet dreams") which often are sources of great anxiety to boys. They also become sources of guilt when accompanied by erotic dreams. If the boy's father has failed to discharge his responsibilities in this area of sex education, the confessor may be the best parent surrogate, the one best qualified to reassure the boy in relation to natural phenomena. The frequency of emissions is also a source of concern for many a young boy. An emission every other week is average for the boy who is not having sexual relations or masturbating, although frequent erotic stimulation through thoughts, conversation or pornography may result in more frequent seminal emissions. Unless the boy is helped in discriminating the voluntary from the involuntary, he will yield to discouragement.

The question is often asked: Should the confessor allow such penitents who have not yet overcome the masturbation problem to go to communion without previous confession? The answer depends on the penitent's moral level, on the

measure of his good will, and on the effect of such a permission. It happens at times that boys and girls want to go
to communion because of the need to conform to the community pattern or family that receives regularly. However,
many adolescents resist conformity on this point and wish to
receive communion because of the meaning it has for them;
the intention is sincere. Then it is only a question of knowing
whether they have the necessary good will. Are they striving
to gain complete control of themselves? If they display good
will by accepting the few remedies prescribed for them by
the confessor, he can presume that they are generally of good
will and he can tell them something like this: "By divine
law and the law of the Church we must go to confession
before communion only if we are morally certain that we have
committed a mortal sin. In your case, however, since you
are so young and show much good will, I would not dare to
presume that you had committed a mortal sin. We can leave
the judgment in this matter to God. Make an act of contrition and an act of confidence whenever you fall, and repeat these acts before going to communion; then tell me about
your progress in fraternal love and on this point in the next
confession."

By placing too much emphasis on this one commandment
and treating the penitent severely, a confessor often tends
to destroy an individual's joy and freedom. If the person
generally displays good will, neither the divine law nor the
Church forbids him to go to communion without previous
confession if there is any doubt in this matter. Whenever
the confessor thinks that it would help the penitent, he
should encourage him to take advantage of it.

If he finds that although the penitent is not making progress in this matter he is progressing with regard to the other
virtues, the confessor should never fail to communicate his
optimism to him. Great harm is done if a confessor con-
siders the case "hopeless." Even if the penitent falls more
often and fails to do what was advised, the confessor should
continue patiently to try to help with that charity which
hopes everything. He should always encourage him to make
a new effort, showing him the great difference between one

who despairs and one who continues to try and to hope. The confessor may explain to him the meaning of the absolution in his perspective: "Now, our Lord Jesus Christ Himself gives you His assurance that He trusts in you. Having good will to make a new effort, you are once more sure to be His friend. He will help you if you keep trying to do what you can, and for the rest, pray for God's help. Have courage."

NECKING AND PETTING

In the life of American youth, petting and necking appear to be so widespread as to be part and parcel of their subculture. Depending on the context, it can mean caresses of a random nature or it can run the gamut of "sex play" short of intercourse. In a number of cases, it is a mode of communication by which immature adolescents seek to establish rapport with one another while having nothing to say. Exploratory touching often starts the first time a boy meets girl. Young people who are exposed to these trends, who feel they must indulge in such activities if they are to be "in" with their peer group, should be taught how harmful the practices can be for their future status as married persons. Their crude fumbling with sex at this stage in their development will obstruct their progress toward maturity, rendering them incapable of distinguishing between the sex play of peers, respectful tenderness between fiancés and the affectionate intimacies of married persons.

It must be clear, however, that not every expression of affection by young people falls under necking and petting. Kisses can often be exchanged without any sexual meaning by youngsters who may have begun this practice early simply because it is a common pattern in their environment; they seldom have a sexual implication. Should there be sexual implication for one partner, it may not have the same meaning for the other; however, it is easy for the sexual implication to be transmitted. Seduction is not an uncommon experience.

Necking and petting lead to sin and are in themselves sinful because the intention is usually exploitation of the body of another for the purpose of sexual gratification. The other person is not truly loved as a person but is merely used or misused for the purposes of self-gratification. Although in necking and petting full sexual pleasure may be intended, intercourse is generally avoided. Such an immature and selfish approach to sex utterly deprives these young people of a proper appreciation of the meaning of their own sexuality and the meaning of love. Such practices indulged in habitually or as a matter of course, can ruin the prospects for a successful and happy marriage or even for real friendships. Sham amities built on exploitation and insensitivity foster attitudes that are bound to be destructive of any meaningful personal relationships.

In dealing with cases of this sort, the confessor must guard against giving the impression that sexual pleasure as such is sinful. As a matter of fact, sexual pleasure is really good when it is part of the mutual cherishing which married couples are expected to display for one another when "two have become one flesh." Pleasure is only wrong when it is sought for itself alone, without respect for the "order of love." The various and most intimate tendernesses in marriage can be an expression of the mutual giving, of the irrevocable belonging to each other, spiritually and corporally. But the gratifying spiritual aspect is lost sight of if intercourse, or near intercourse, is reduced to the crudely physical and external element of mutual sexual excitement. Petting among adolescents is the very opposite of acts of endearment between the married. Marriages between adolescents who have indulged in sinful necking and petting are greatly endangered by their distorted attitudes of exploitation of one another. When this attitude carries over into marriage, mutual respect becomes impossible and the marriage is near failure. Therefore, young people need to be taught the true meaning of tenderness and the pitfalls of modern petting and necking practices.

It is well for a confessor to be aware that underlying the prevalence of these unhealthy practices may be the harsh reality that children did not receive enough affectionate attention in childhood. In the home, a mother expresses her love for her child by various acts of tenderness. The father likewise expresses himself in his own way. The child is quick to realize the difference and needs both kinds of attention. While the child needs attention from his mother he does not appreciate the same kind of attention from a stranger. Nor can the mother take the place of the father. Sisters and brothers, at various ages, also have different ways of expressing their tenderness for each other. But even Freud admitted that there is no sexual meaning in these acts.

It is a curious but undoubted fact that children unconsciously express their need for tenderness and affection by displaying these qualities toward each other. The whole development of the child, the psychological and even moral meaning of tenderness in future life, depends upon the quality of love and tenderness received in its formative years. The genuine affectivity and warmth of a mature person are not independent of the psychological climate that surrounded him in childhood.

FORNICATION

By their very nature, intimacies and intercourse are expressions of the tender love of spouses, of their total and irrevocable mutual giving. It is the legitimate expression of their "being one flesh." It is most evident that the meaning and truth of these acts vary greatly whether they are offered to one another by spouses, by betrothed persons or by people who are in no way committed to one another and do not even know one another as persons. Consequently, those who indulge in sexual experiences while they are unmarried are indulging in a most tragic lie. Their love talk as well as their bodily act expresses something which for them is not true. They become liars in such a deep sense that they even lose the understanding of the most expressive unity "in one body." They do not even wish to be one, irrevocably one, though they do express it.

It is true that intercourse between fiancés who are firmly decided to get married and to be faithful to one another has not the same quality of "lie" as it has in promiscuity. But by anticipating the rights of married persons while yet unmarried they make, to some extent, a mockery of the spiritual meaning of marriage. Though they may experience deep human love and a strong commitment to one another, they overlook the sanctity of marriage, the adoration of God. By yielding to passion, they fail to learn another essential quality of married love, namely, self-control.

Nowadays, through the mass media and other channels of public opinion, the idea is spread that young people should not enter marriage without having gathered all kinds of sexual experiences with different persons. The Protestant depth psychologist and marriage counselor, Theodor Bovet, responds to this popular fable: "It is as ridiculous to indulge in premarital sexual activity in order to be prepared for marriage as to try to find out what death is by a long sleep." From the moral and psychological viewpoint, intercourse and other sexual intimacies within marriage and outside of marriage are two totally different experiences. One is genuine, the other counterfeit. The married couple come together "to give" to each other; the promiscuous partners come "to get" from each other. The uncommitted feel the transient physical pleasure but none of the deep and innocent joy of those who have signed the covenant of their love in marriage. The uncommitted leave the scene only to return to emptiness, whereas the married remain to enjoy the fulfillment of their ever-growing love. The very desire to experiment promiscuously with one's sexuality is itself a sign of such immaturity and insensitivity as to make it doubtful that the person can eventually find real fulfillment in marriage.

Some moralists have taught that people who have intercourse outside of marriage should be asked whether they used contraceptives. They argue that such action adds a new sin "against nature" to that of fornication. It is evident that abortion would be a new sin, a sin against life, but regarding the use of contraceptives, there should be no questioning. The reasons given by the severe moralists are tenuous because fornication in itself is against the nature of the persons and against the meaning of *human* sexuality.

Human sexuality has a definite *purpose*: the mutual giving of two persons in an indissoluble bond of love. It is against this very nature of human sexuality to indulge in intercourse outside marriage even if the couple intend to procreate a child. The full human understanding of sexuality demands that procreation take place within marriage, which alone can provide lasting parental security for the child. The use of contraceptives in an act of promiscuity does not make it moral: on the one hand, it could manifest a deliberate decision to sin; on the other, it could express a certain feeling of responsibility not to procreate life outside marriage. At any rate, it would be most unwise to ask penitents who confess fornication whether they use contraceptives.

It is strange that in a society which seems to condone extramarital sex a condemning attitude prevails when a girl becomes pregnant out of wedlock. There is total disregard if not contempt for the unwed mother and this at a time when the girl's need for understanding and compassion is greatest. The poor girl, and to some extent also the father, are pressed from all sides to get married, even though they realize that the marriage would not be a happy one. It is a case of tragically compounding the first error.

If a couple expect a child outside of marriage, they need special understanding from their families, the community and their confessor; the latter especially should show great kindness and concern. He may explain to the girl that what she has done is not made more sinful because she expects a child; rather, the pregnancy gives her a chance to do penance while preparing to assume her full responsibility. If the confessor has reasons to fear that the girl will be tempted to seek an abortion, he should inform her of the possibility of placing the child for adoption into a good family; the Catholic Charitable Bureaus handle such cases.

The confession of the sin of premarital intercourse can be an occasion for the confessor to give a short instruction on the meaning of marriage and on the motivation; this will help the young people to resist the temptation more decidedly. He may say, for instance: "I know you have good will and your faults are only due to human weakness. A deeper un-

derstanding of the meaning of premarital chastity will surely
help you and your fiancé. . . ." Then could follow the question: "What would you say of a seminarian who went into the
confessional and heard confessions even though he had not
yet been ordained a priest? Would you think such a man
would become a good priest?" An emphatic "no" is the general answer, and the application to their own case becomes
obvious. It is helpful, also, to bring out the fact that in marriage God, the Tremendous Lover, is really the third partner.
He has given them the gift of love and they must not abuse
that gift through premarital intercourse, where the sexual
act has an entirely different meaning.

Another question that can be asked is (timing here is important): "Do you know who administers the sacrament of
marriage to you?" Some know the answer, but many do not
and say, "Father Jones." The couple, of course, administer
the sacrament to themselves. By their union with Christ and
the Church, they are ministers of the sacrament to each other;
this means that they are living instruments of the grace of
God to each other. They fulfill a priestly sacramental function, marking only the beginning of a pastoral concern for
each other which should continue throughout their married
lives; they are called to bring one another to experience the
holy love of God. The time of their engagement is the opportune time to speak to them in this way since their sincere
love could lead them to see God's love in their own. They
must therefore show loving respect for each other and for
God's gifts, which they must hold in trust until the proper
time comes.

The youth of today are extremely desirous of sincerity.
Many of them will understand that premarital intercourse is
not fully sincere because it expresses something that is not
fulfilled. By anticipating sexual experience when there is not
yet full commitment to irrevocable fidelity, they are risking
the possibility that sexual relations in married life will be far
less meaningful; they may even be building up a psychological barrier to healthy relations. The confessor could help
them by explaining that a better understanding of what sexuality is all about will strengthen their will toward chastity.

A positive approach to these cases is always the most effective. The young couple can be told that marriage is the sign of the presence of God who wishes to have sharers in His love and His creation. Holy Scripture constantly pleads for chastity both in marriage and outside of marriage. It emphasizes the cultic side of marriage: to be chaste means to be capable of glorifying God, of giving praise to God in one's body. Sexuality, properly understood, inspires awesome respect and gratitude for the power and love of the Creator and Redeemer who shares that power and love with man.

The choice of penances can help greatly in a proper formation of conscience. Penitents who confess difficulty in maintaining chaste relations during courtship could be asked, "Would you like as penance to explain to your friend what I have told you? You can do it better than I can. Think over what you will say and try to find a suitable occasion. Tell him (or her): "I have confessed this sin and admitted that it is not an expression of true love. There was some love, of course, but much more egotism and lack of self-control." The confessor may add, "Do not put the other person on the spot. Apologize and ask him (her) to forgive you." If they accept this penance, they are really showing sincerity. Very often the penitent has told his friend that his behavior was a true expression of love and therefore what he did could not have been a sin. So if he confesses his part in the guilt and asks the partner for forgiveness, the other party will almost surely reply: "It was not solely your fault; it was mine also. We must try together to do what is right."

If they are well disposed, a confessor can even ask them more: "Would you accept as your penance to try to make an agreement with your partner not to have any more dates if you happen to sin together until you have both been to confession?" If they accept these penances, then it is clear that they already grasp what it means to be an instrument of God's grace in the conversion of someone else.

We must not impose such penances in an authoritarian manner, *transcendentaliter*, but ask the penitents gently if they would like to accept them; they are almost always ready to do so. Sometimes the partner might come later and say,

"I liked what you told my girl-friend. We have talked the matter over and I think we have made a new start. Now we pray for each other." But sometimes they are not yet able to realize the meaning of such advice.

There is nothing artificial about this type of treatment. It is merely the application of sound theological principles. The reasons you give them are not mere abstract concepts but they mean a great deal to them. Consciences cannot be formed abstractly: "you must do this, you must do that." Penitents should feel that they are taking part in a positive program, doing something that is enlightening and attractive. Thus they can be helped to strive together more sincerely.

ADULTERY

Adultery is certainly one of the most heinous sins. In the early Church long penances were imposed on adulterers. In the Middle Ages, adulterers sometimes had to make long pilgrimages from Britain or Germany to St. James of Compostella in Spain or to Rome or Jerusalem.

We must preach the word of God in such a way that adultery is understood by the faithful to be the crime that it is. We accomplish nothing by shouting or haranguing. If penitents confess the sin in humility, they must be treated with respect and kindness. It still behooves the confessor to explain the severity of the wound they have inflicted on themselves and on the other person, and the magnitude of the offense they have committed against God. This will help them to understand how great God's mercy is when we announce: "This terrible sin is forgiven." Once more, it can be useful to find out if the penitents would appreciate any help. The confessor must ground his approach on the motivational: why this sin is so great, why God will condemn those who commit it unless they amend their lives.

The confessor can call attention to the marriage vows made in the presence of God and the People of God, and how the two persons promised to remain faithful to each other. By adultery each penitent has betrayed a partner and broken a vow. This malice exists also when an unmarried person seduces a married one and causes the latter to break his oath.

Adultery is a particularly grave sin against the sacrament of marriage, a kind of sacrilege, because marriage witnesses to the covenant between Christ and His Church, whereas adultery witnesses to the Prince of Darkness. It is a sin against truth, a sign of contempt for God's blessing and His pledge. Spouses become "two in one flesh," but the act of adultery has made one of them one flesh with a prostitute or some other person. The adulterer lives a lie against his state of life and against his partner.

The confessor must be careful about the tone he uses, never implying a lack of love or respect for the penitent. He proclaims in the name of God what it means to have committed adultery but he does it with the love of the Redeemer who forgives. The words of the confessor should help him become more grateful to the God of mercy who tells him, "Your sins are forgiven; go and sin no more." These are the words of the merciful Lord which He Himself spoke to the woman taken in adultery. The woman in the parable realized that she should have been stoned and so she accepted His words with great gratitude. Undoubtedly, she never forgot them and never sinned again.

In Russia while serving in the Medical Corps of the German Army, I had to see that soldiers did not become contaminated by venereal diseases. One soldier, a proud journalist of 25, became infected by a Russian woman. It was my task to find out how he had caught his infection. He indicated the contact, a married woman who had a sixteen-year-old son. All these details had to be written down and sent to the commander of the regiment. I was ordered to have the woman killed since there seemed to be little possibility of having her cured at the front. The commander told me: "Shoot her." A fine order to give a priest! So I went to her and told her: "I have been ordered to shoot you. You have infected a soldier and he has been returned to Germany. But you can be sure that I will not kill you; as a priest I could never become a murderer. God forgives. But don't get me into trouble by infecting any other of my soldiers. If you do, they will order me killed." I then passed on to her information as to the kind of medication to be taken daily for a cure. I regularly made the rounds of my soldiers and whenever she would see me, invariably she would cry, "I will never do it again, never, never!"

She was grateful for my help, but of course, I did not let matters rest there. I spoke to her of divine forgiveness. This experience gave me considerable help in dealing with penitents who had failed against the marriage vow. The great task of the confessor is to help penitents realize how merciful God is when He releases them from so great a sin.

SINS AGAINST CHASTITY WITHIN MARRIAGE

In the formation of conscience of married people nothing is more important than to have them realize the magnificence of their vocation, and this especially from a spiritual standpoint. They should see themselves in the light of their actual, tangible partnership with God in His creative and redemptive work in the world.

In His great wisdom, God has caused the most intense and desired physical expression of love to be centered in the human act through which new life is conceived. In no way could He have shown more clearly His will that children should be born of the mutual love of a man and a woman and should be reared in the atmosphere of that love. Both the love and the life are His creative gifts, channelled to earth through the love of a married couple covenanted to cherish one another throughout their lives. This is what marriage is, and the understanding of its dimensions will give married people great joy in their vocational pursuit.

There is need to improve our teaching and counselling in this area. Too often in the past the subject of marriage and of morality in marriage has been presented with disproportionate emphasis on external laws and too little attention to the conjugal love that is the essence of the vocation. The Second Vatican Council itself set the stage for a change in emphasis in pastoral work having to do with the vocations of marriage and parenthood. Since then, various trends of thought have been developing which may affect counselling in these matters at a future date. I note here two basic questions at the root of the new explorations. The trends, however, are still speculative and varied and have neither final authority nor even definite formulation at this time.

1st question: *Should physiological processes be a determining factor in resolving moral problems having to do with methods of birth regulation?*

There is a growing body of opinion that because the moral problems of harmonizing conjugal love with parental responsibilities are posed by the requirements of man's conjugal and parental vocations, these requirements and not man's biological processes should be the determining factors in judging programs or methods of birth regulation. This question has been approached from many angles. From the standpoint of both anthropogenesis and theology, there is much to be said for some of the tentative arguments. The thinking goes something like this:

Physical processes have no moral responsibility; they are merely a part of man's pre-human physiological inheritance. Of themselves, they are of no absolute concern to moral theology, which deals with man's responsibility to God in his vocation. Man as man did not exist until the faculties of intelligence, free will and spiritual knowledge were added to his physiological structure. These are the faculties that make him human and responsible before God. To assert, therefore, that God can communicate His will to men only, or chiefly, through biological processes is to diminish both God and man and to deny dogmatic teachings regarding the workings of the Holy Spirit through the minds of men. Thus theology approaches man's moral duties through the processes of his higher faculties rather than through physical ones, which have neither consciousness nor responsibility. It is the welfare and dignity of the person, in his relatedness to other persons, that confers meaning on the biological processes.

From this standpoint, theology sees human sexuality as an

instrument of man's parental vocation which includes his conjugal vocation as well. This stance adheres to the line of reasoning with which most moralists approach questions posed by the other commandments.

2nd question: *Should morality within marriage be studied from the viewpoint of the sixth commandment or from Christ's "greatest commandment," that of Charity?*

It must be admitted that there is a certain incongruity in studying moral questions within marriage under the heading of the sixth commandment, whose very meaning is that the act happens outside marriage and is against the meaning of marriage. The moral defects that destroy a marriage from within are almost invariably sins against love rather than against chastity. However, it should be noticed that the final judgment whether something is against chastity or not is to be made in the light of a full understanding of what love and charity are. There is no sin against chastity which is not, in the final analysis, also a sin against well-ordered love of self and of neighbor.

In marriage, spouses have a sexual right to each other's body. The abuse of that right and the manner of the abuse, as well as other types of sin that harm or profane the marriage and incapacitate the spouses for their holy conjugal and parental vocation, are above all sins against the great commandment of Charity. They are sins of selfishness, of self-gratification, of contempt for the person of the spouse or of their children, born or unborn, and thus are sins against chastity.

It can be hoped that there will be an accelerated trend toward the formulation of a theology of marriage that will approach the sins and virtues of the conjugal vocation more from the standpoint of self-giving love, of charity of spouses toward each other and toward their children, and less from mere consideration of sexual self-control or sexual acts not yet fully integrated into their vocation to perpetuate life. Seen in the perspective of the growth of genuine love, their total vocation, both as spouses and parents, will receive better consideration. Values and decisions will be judged in the light of true service to God and mankind through mutual love and consequently through the generous and responsible fulfillment of their parental vocation.

We are all aware of the importance of the newer problematic approaches and will be following their progress with lively interest. However, today's problems still remain to be met with the answers available today. In view of the complexity of the present situation, and especially out of respect for the teaching office of the Church, I offer here chiefly pastoral solutions within the framework of presently accepted teachings. I will outline some principles that need to be emphasized in marriage counselling generally, and especially those points given special emphasis by the Second Vatican Council. Finally full attention will be given to Pope Paul's recent encyclical *Humanae vitae* and to the development of doctrine and pastoral practice resulting from many episcopal conferences relative to that document.

1. Conjugal intercourse can be a full and true expression of mutual love only if the married couple tries to express an unselfish love and respect for each other through the totality of their common life.

The love between a man and a woman is a specific kind of love. Its central and characteristic expression is in sexual union, but it cannot be limited to that. All efforts to educate people to chastity and to the correct communication of conjugal love will fail if married couples do not strive to express the meaning of the sacrament of marriage as a covenant of love in every aspect of their lives together. It must be something that permeates and directs all of their daily joys and sorrows, and all acts and attitudes that concern them and the children born to them. It gives constant proof of their mutual willingness to bear common burdens, to cherish each other.

The documents of the magisterium by no means oblige us to maintain that love is a secondary purpose of marriage, although many of us at one time thought we were bound to that position. This was not the simple case of its not being the doctrine of the Church but it was a mistaken interpretation of many moralists.

Without conjugal love the wellspring of the total vocation of marriage and parenthood runs dry. Marriage is the root of the vocation, parenthood is the tree and the children are the fruit. Only if the root is well nourished with the love that sustains it will there be good fruit to present to the Lord.

Every expression that nourishes conjugal love through true and generous mutual affection is good. Only a very poor moralist would maintain today, for instance, that intimate caresses between married people are permissible only in intercourse. Husbands and wives must never be deterred from expressing conjugal tenderness for one another, and this especially at times when, for one reason or another, they cannot engage in intercourse.

2. The spiritual relationship between the vocation of marriage and the parental vocation should be clearly seen.

Marriage is a convenant of love, but note that it is a love ordained both naturally and supernaturally, toward the service of life: a term I much prefer to the English expression "reproduction." The love of the spouses for each other, merging with the creative love of God, brings to earth new life conceived in their holy union.

Love comes to a man and woman first and then brings them physically together in marriage later. Conjugal love is therefore not simply an element that accompanies the conjugal act nor a backdrop for it. It is the direct cause of the act and therefore the very source of human life, channelled from God who is fountainhead of all love and all life. Not only psychologically and ontologically, but also theologically, it is wrong to play down the importance of conjugal love in order to stress the importance of the service of life. The perspective of theology is man's whole responsibility to God within his total vocation. On this point, the encyclical *Humanae vitae* reveals a remarkable progress compared with Pius XI's *Casti connubii*.

Before St. Alphonsus, many moralists thought that all conjugal intercourse was always sinful, at least venially, if the intention was not to procreate children. God the Creator has made man totally different from animals. With animals, copulation is only procreative. With man, intercourse has a deeply spiritual meaning as an expression of love. As the Bible puts it, married people "know one another" in the most intimate way. Not the individual act but the whole of married life is ordained to the service of life and if married couples exclude the parental vocation as a whole, they do not experience conjugal love in the fullest sense. Their marriage is merely an expression of egotism between the two, the very opposite of what it should be. True conjugal love ardently desires the children of the beloved spouse, children who are part of both of them and made in the image of God.

3. Responsible parenthood and not instinctive procreation should be the ideal of married people.

Parents should know what responsible parenthood means. They must not confuse the term with a negative attitude of "birth control," which often means the artificial limitation of families based on a previous decision about the precise number of children a couple will have. Responsible parenthood means that a married couple, during the varying circumstances of their life, make a prudent and sound judgment in full knowledge of the high vocation of parenthood and the eternal value of each child. It means a positive and grateful response to all the natural and supernatural gifts they receive from God. They regulate pregnancies in accordance with the true Christian perspective, "How can we best render service to God for all He has done for us? How can we present Him with good fruit from the love He has given us?"

Simply to procreate a large number of children is not, in itself, a matter for praise; it can result from lack of a proper sense of responsibility for the immortal souls that are called into being. Large families can and must be praised when the parents have the will and the capacity to educate their children wisely. I was an eleventh child; three years later the twelfth, my younger sister, was born; she is now Superior in a home for 360 abandoned children. No one would accuse our parents of irresponsibility. They were not wealthy. They were simply capable of educating us well, that is all.

A dear Jesuit friend of mine was the first man who died under my eyes on the Russian front on June 21, 1941. He had fifteen brothers and sisters. His father was a simple laborer but they had all received a college education. His mother was a genius at running the household. The children soon learned to help one another and all pitched in with the household chores. His parents were heroically responsible but we cannot impose such heroism on everybody. Some couples with an income of $5,000 a month would still be incapable of educating children, of helping them grow as they should "in wisdom and age and grace."

Responsible parenthood does not look first to the economic aspects but to the gifts of the heart, the power of real love, the power of deep faith and hope that help parents realize what it means to educate a child for this world and for eternal life.

In responsible parenthood parents do not plan from the beginning to have ten or merely one child and no more. An absolute planning reflects a wrong attitude. Responsibility, on the other hand, demands that they maintain an openness in prayer and vigilance with regard to new situations. They try to know the will of God here and now and how best to serve Him in the circumstances of their life. They desire as many children as they can raise, under those circumstances, to the glory of God.

Confessors, of course, do not have the right to tell parents how many children they shall have. The Council texts leave no doubt on this point (cf. Pastoral Constitution on the Church in the Modern World, Art. 50). They have no direct responsibilities with regard to children such as parents have and for the very obvious reason that they can never know all the psychological and other factors that have to be taken into account. However, the confessor may help their penitents to become ever more generous. If the spouses have doubts as to what course of action they should follow, they can seek advice; the confessor may advise them to pray until their next confession that God enlighten them about what they should do to comply with His holy will. The confessor can help them make their own decision without their feeling enslaved by an unhealthy public opinion, but the confessor must always be careful never to overstep the bounds of his competence.

4. In counselling and in the formation of conscience of spouses, emphasis should be given to those points of Catholic doctrine and practical directives reaffirmed in new forms for the world of today by the Second Vatican Council.

No special emphasis can yet be given on points still under discussion, even after the publication of *Humanae vitae.* Prudence is imposed alike on those who hold the more progressive and those who hold the more rigoristic opinions. But in the Pastoral Constitution of the Church in the Modern World, the Council has proposed the crucial marriage problems as:

(a) Responsible parenthood,
(b) with clear acknowledgment of the difficulties and dangers where "the intimacy of married life is broken off" (Art. 51) and
(c) the necessity of "harmonizing conjugal love with respect for human life." . . . "A true contradiction cannot exist between the divine laws pertaining to the responsible transmission of life and those pertaining to the fostering of authentic conjugal love" (*loc. cit.*).

The encyclical *Humanae vitae* again draws attention to the biological aspects of sexuality, the "laws and rhythms of nature." The essential point here seems to be a warning that man does not have an unlimited dominion over his procreative faculties (Art. 13). No doubt man has only a limited stewardship over his organs, and therefore must never act *arbitrarily.* But what does this mean practically? The whole Church is now searching for the significance and limits of this stewardship.

Vatican II did not attempt to offer a complete interpretation of the divine law. The bishops could not claim to know perfectly the divine law with all its implications regarding the difficulties of the spouses of our time. This is especially evident from footnote 14 and from the admonition given to the different professions "to pool their efforts and to labor to explain more thoroughly the various conditions favoring a proper regulation of births" (*loc. cit.*). *Humanae vitae* (Art. 24) makes the same appeal again, but, as numerous scholars have noted, the papal document seems to restrict the meaning. The U.S. bishops give a correct explanation of the intention of the Pope's appeal by stating: "Recourse to the natural rhythms, for example, present problems which the Holy Father has asked medical science to help solve." The Council text clearly said that good intention does not justify all means of birth regulation. "It must be determined by objective standards. These, based on the nature of the person and his acts, preserve the full sense of mutual self-giving and human procreation in the context of true love" (*loc. cit.*). It is highly interesting that this text does not even mention what some conservative moralists thought to be the chief criterion, namely, "the inviolability of the biological processes related to the conjugal act as a procreative act." But it cannot be overlooked that *Humanae vitae* gives great importance to the "natural laws and rhythms," which permit a married couple to avoid rather than to prevent conception. Other forms of birth regulation would seem to include a more direct stewardship over biological functions.

In the Council text, natural law is chiefly seen from the viewpoint of the person and the conjugal act as an act of persons in interpersonal relationship. A means is not bad because it regulates births effectively but it can be immoral if it does not preserve the sense of the conjugal act as mutual giving and destroys the context of true love for procreation. In this perspective, all means of birth regulation, including the severance of "the intimacy of married life," must be examined and adjudged by the same objective standards based on the nature of the person and his acts.

5. All methods of birth regulation—including total or periodic continence—are poisonous and dangerous for

the marriage and married love if the intention and the motives are bad.

The role of the priest is to make clear that no theologian of the Catholic Church can ever approve contraceptive control if the motive is egotistical, springing from selfish considerations. The discussion touches only those who wish sincerely to have the number of children they can properly educate, who wish reasonable spacing of births, and who are properly concerned about those factors essential to raising their children in a truly human and spiritually healthy environment.

6. Priest should be most cautious in appraising the scientific facts regarding periodic continence, leaving it to competent doctors to determine how "safe" the safe period is. It is at least problematic whether this method can be considered absolutely safe regarding the intention to avoid conception and, at the same time, hold that it is open to new life. We must be concerned about the credibility of our language.

Its values and the limits of these values are not yet perfectly known, but all experts agree that it cannot resolve all marriage problems and that the method can even be harmful for certain couples under certain psychological conditions.

7. Whatever may be the method, conjugal chastity imposes an earnest struggle against selfishness. Chastity is based on true love, which respects the other person, brings joy and accepts joy in gratitude and is ready to renounce if the good of the other person demands it.

Love itself imposes a constant self-denial. True conjugal love produces self-control and appeals to it. But self-control must be in the service of a normal married love and must foster it. Total abstinence or a lack of tender and intimate communication of affection can, in most cases, endanger the faithfulness and the harmony so necessary for the upbringing of the children "and the courage to accept new ones" (Art. 51).

The warning of Saint Paul is quite as appropriate in our day as it was in the community of Corinth in his: "Do not deny yourselves to one another except when you agree upon a temporary abstinence in order to devote yourselves to prayer; afterwards you may come together again; otherwise, for lack of self-control, you may be tempted by Satan" (I Cor. 7:5). This temptation by Satan need not be a sexual one. A marriage can be destroyed quite as completely by a lack of communication or by tempers aroused by unrelieved tensions as it can be through sexual infidelity.

8. The cult of conjugal tenderness is dutiful not only in the immediate context of an intercourse but also and especially in times when the spouses do not have the intention of engaging in intercourse.

In the past forty years many discussions of moralists and preachers centered on the fact or danger of "the loss of the seed" from the husband. One of the questions was then, "How great is the sin of *actus impudici* (intimate caresses) among married people if it constitutes a proximate occasion for 'the sin of' the loss of the seed?" (One of the Council Fathers called this *spermatolatria*).

It is wrong to call conjugal caresses *actus impudicos* (shameless acts). These are expressions of love given to one another in the intimacy of married life by two persons who belong to each other in an indissoluble bond. The caresses are part of "knowing" one another and loving one another. As long as the prevailing motif and attitude is conjugal love and not mere sexual exploitation of the other person, the couples should not be disturbed on this score if an orgasm occurs outside the conjugal act while they express their tenderness. Of course, the spouses must strive for a fuller control of strong passions at such times but not by way of anguish and fear. This, in my opinion, is surely a "probable opinion" and can be followed by all spouses who, in their own conscience, consider it right. It is not in contradiction to norms laid down by Pius XI and Pius XII.

9. Consciences of spouses should be formed toward the

obligation of making decisions in the matter of "harmonizing conjugal love with the responsible transmission of life."

The Council made it clear that the decisions regarding birth regulation rest upon the couple themselves. The necessity both of nourishing conjugal love and of educating the children to whom they have transmitted life is their responsibility. All couples must, therefore, be urged toward generosity in the performance of this high vocation and be made to realize that this generosity is a matter of conscience. We must, however, trust the good will of married couples who have already so generously procreated several children, and they should be told, if they are having difficulties, that the choice of limiting their family at that point or of having more children is ultimately theirs.

Regarding methods of birth regulation, *Humanae vitae* approves only of periodic continence (Art. 16). However, it does permit the therapeutic use of means which, according to the principle of double effect, also induce a (temporary) infertility. Thus it is evident that the Pope does not totally deny the stewardship of man over his procreative faculties as far as health is concerned.

In cases where periodic continence cannot resolve problems of marital life and responsible parenthood, several episcopal conferences appeal to the traditional principle of a "conflict of duties." The Canadian bishops, followed by many others, declare: "Counsellors may meet others who, accepting the teaching of the Holy Father, find because of particular circumstances they are involved in what seems to them a clear conflict of duties, e.g. the reconciling of conjugal love and responsible parenthood with the education of children already born, or with the health of the mother. In accord with the accepted principles of moral theology, if these persons have tried sincerely but without success to pursue a line of conduct in keeping with the given directives, they may be safely assured that whoever honestly chooses that course which seems right to him does so in good conscience."

The French bishops declare: "Contraception can never be

a good. It is always a disorder. But this disorder is not always culpable. It can happen, actually, that a married couple consider themselves faced with a true conflict of interests . . . particularly when the observance of natural rhythms does not give them a sufficiently secure basis for the regulation of births. . . . When someone is faced with an alternative of duties, no matter what may be the decision taken, he cannot avoid an evil; traditional wisdom counsels that he should seek before God whichever obligation at the time seems to be the greater. The couple should then reach a decision after common reflection guided with all the care that is required by the greatness of their conjugal vocation. They must never underestimate or forget any of the obligations in conflict."

The U.S. bishops also speak about a possible conflict of values, and declare, along with the Italian and other hierarchies, that the sin involved (if there is a question of sin in the concrete situation) in the use of artificial means is closely related to the degree, or absence, of egotism.

Those who try to find the best way to resolve a conflict of values and duties, provided they remain concerned about preserving the necessary harmony and stability of their marriage, need feel no guilt complex whatsoever.

Vatican II insisted on the necessity of preserving "the full sense of mutual self-giving" in the conjugal act as a chief criterion. This, too, is a matter for conscience formation since only the spouses themselves can know if there is mutual self-giving in their act. In one marriage and set of circumstances a fully completed act may express no love at all, while an incomplete or limited one in another marriage may express the tenderest love of spouse and children. This is not a matter for measurement in the abstract but for assessment by the individual conscience.

10. As to the question of cooperation, I consider the opinion of St. Alphonsus the most reasonable under the conditions of the traditional doctrine.

On the question, "Is it lawful for a wife to render the marriage debt or to ask it of a husband who is willed to seminate outside her body after intercourse has started?", St.

Alphonsus first states the two opinions on the subject. The milder opinion held that the wife could cooperate in the case where she cannot change the mind of her husband; the stricter declared it as always immoral. Alphonsus then firmly expresses his own opinion: *Sed probabilius videtur uxor non solum posse, ut dicit prima sententia, sed etiam teneri.—* "But it seems more probable that the wife not only may, as the first opinion holds, but rather is obliged to act thus, to cooperate. The reason is that, though there is fault on the part of the person who asks for intercourse, he still has a right to it and the other partner cannot refuse it without injustice, if she cannot keep him from committing this fault by admonishing him. Clearly also, the wife in rendering intercourse does not cooperate even materially in his sin for she does not cooperate in his seminating outside her body but only in the intercourse which is begun, which intercourse is of itself quite lawful for both partners" (*Theologia moralis*, liber VI, chap. 11, no. 947).

Still more remarkable is the fact that St. Alphonsus, in the circumstances under consideration, gives the right to the wife to ask for intercourse. He justifies this not only on the ground of a possible danger of incontinence but also on the ground that links up directly with the mutual giving (*mutua traditio*): "Or if she otherwise be deprived of her right of asking intercourse more than one or other time, with a perpetual doubt as to whether on this occasion continence would amount to a sufficiently serious inconvenience for her" (*loc. cit.*).

I cannot see why the same opinion of Saint Alphonsus could not be applied to the husband if he knows that his wife uses a diaphragm. The reasoning of the saint evidently supports this even better. More difficult is the matter of the husband using a condom. But even there the cooperation can, in my opinion, be a more material cooperation and therefore licit if the wife has good motives, as for instance to save the marriage or the harmony in the marriage. This is still said in view of traditional principles.

11. Paul VI has reaffirmed the traditional condemnation

of interrupted intercourse as a means of birth regulation, but in much milder pastoral terms than *Casti connubii*. He refrains from the qualification "gravely sinful." The sinfulness and degrees of sinfulness of this practice depend on the degree of selfishness and arbitrariness involved.

Many theologians behind closed doors and even publicly have expressed doubts on the absolute and irrevocable character of this condemnation. As an interpretation of natural law, where historical changes must be taken into account, the doctrine of Pius XI did oblige the faithful in conscience but was not an infallible doctrine and therefore is not irreformable in cases where good reasons seem to be against it.

The Holy Spirit works in the history of salvation through a development of knowledge in man's earnest search for truth. In this search, the "sin of Onan" in the Old Testament, on which the severe condemnation of this act has largely been based in the past ever since St. Augustine and up to the present, is now being interpreted by almost all biblical scholars not as the act of spilling his seed on the ground but rather his contemptuous breaking of the Law of his time and his offense against charity and justice which his act entailed. The law of his time required that if a man should die without issue, his brother would take his place to raise an heir to him. Because Onan was absolutely selfish, he showed his contempt for his brother and the widow of his brother through this act, and was punished by death for his sin.

Personally, I feel that a systematic and deliberate use of withdrawal, although it need not necessarily destroy the spontaneity of the act of love, tends to make the husband all too attentive to his own pleasure (and to the moment he reaches it) and therefore readily inattentive to his wife. It can represent a male-centered attitude of exploitation of the wife and impair the dignity of the conjugal intercourse as an act of mutual giving. Yet some couples, in their own upright conscience, or in their perplexed conscience, may consider the method of interrupted intercourse as the lesser of two moral evils or simply as the best solution here and now of avoiding danger of incontinence, disharmony or aggressiveness. For couples in poverty-stricken areas where other methods of regulation (except total abstinence) are out of the question but the need for regulation is great if children are to be allowed to escape from sub-human conditions, it appears to them as the only available means for harmonizing conjugal love with responsibility for children born to them.

Different from a systematic use of interruption is the situation of a husband who at first wishes only to be tender and to foster mutual love, but without premeditation, begins intercourse, withdrawing as soon as he realizes what is happening. This weakness does not fall under the severe judgment of *Casti Connubii*. Saint Alphonsus once more has a word in this direction: *Licite interrumpitur actus coniugalis, etsi ex naturae concitatione secutura sit pollutio, dummodo sit iusta causa interrumpendi.*—"It is lawful to interrupt the conjugal act, even though pollution should follow from the excitement of nature, provided there is a just cause for interrupting" (*loc. cit.* no. 954). The causes he cites as examples are dire ones, but whereas other theologians had *ex gravissima cause* (the most urgent cause), Saint Alphonsus says only *iusta ex causa* (a just cause).

Whenever the spouses feel that their motives and actions were not without fault, although fundamentally they tried to preserve a right intention, they must not become discouraged. They should make an act of sorrow and trust as good Christians do after every venial fault; but they still can trust that they are in a state of grace, provided of course that their fundamental attitude is right. They can receive Communion without previous confession. This is also said in accordance with traditional principles.

12. All artificial means of birth regulation are immoral insofar as they are—certainly or with some probability —abortive or insofar as they endanger considerably the health of the mother or of the future children.

This includes all post-conceptive methods or drugs used for birth prevention. In the discussion following publication of *Humanae vitae* it became evident there is no dissension among Catholics on this point. The American hierarchy expresses the firm teaching of the Church as follows: "A human person, nothing more and nothing less, is always at issue once conception has taken place." However, the bishops do not say with certainty that conception immediately gives rise to a human person. Their argument is based on the undoubted fact: "Conception initiates a process whose purpose is the realization of a human personality."

Therefore, if penitents are using means like the intrauterine device which, according to the considered opinion of many scientists, can be an abortifacient (expelling either the fertilized egg or the living being already attached to the womb of the mother), the confessor must explicitly caution them, thus doing his best to protect innocent life. Evidently what is involved here is more than a subjectively good conscience.

13. Regarding the use of artificial means of birth regulation as well as systematic use of the method of interrupted intercourse, the priest must inform the faithful unambiguously about the teaching of Pope Paul VI in *Humanae vitae*.

The American bishops, who, like other hierarchies, explicitly recognize a lawful freedom of inquiry and thought while also indicating the norms of licit dissent, state clearly: "Even responsible dissent does not excuse one from faithful presentation of the authentic doctrine of the Church when one is performing a pastoral ministry in Her name."

Since the encyclical *Humanae vitae* has not only caused dissent and discussions among theologians and laymen, but has also given rise to very carefully prepared pastoral explanations and guidelines on the part of numerous episcopal conferences, no priest can dismiss such guidelines, especially those explicitly or at least implicitly approved by the Holy Father. Therefore he must not impose his own personal understanding of the encyclical on his penitents, especially in cases where a more rigoristic interpretation would do harm to the harmony, peace and stability of the marriage or to the bodily or mental health of one of the spouses. As the various episcopates could not and did not ignore the teaching of the Pope, so the individual priest cannot form and impose his own opinion apart from the context of the interpretations of the various episcopates and, indeed, of the whole people of God. The authoritative teaching of many national hierarchies in response to the declaration of the Pope ranks higher than the opinions of dissenting theologians. It cannot be denied that the teaching of the hierarchies constitutes a probable opinion. While individual bishops as well as some national hierarchies laid down rather severe guidelines, the converging lines of thought and advice contained in the declarations of such episcopates as the American, Austrian, Belgian, Canadian, Dutch, French, German, Italian and Scandinavian, though differing in emphasis and expression, cannot be over-looked. The convergent development seems to be as follows:

(a) Much more important than the decision about the method of birth regulation is a fundamental question of conscience, namely whether the transmission of life is here and now regarded as a responsible or irresponsible act. Therefore the moral evaluation of the use of contraception (including the "methods" of total or periodic continence) is totally different if motivated by an egotistic unwillingness to fulfill the parental vocation, or on the other hand, if decided on as a result of serious difficulties in harmonizing the exigencies of conjugal love and unity with the responsible regulation of birth (that is with the lawful and responsible non-transmission of life).

(b) The "openness" of each individual marital act to the transmission of life, interpreted as meaning that conception may systematically be avoided through the exclusive use of the infertile period but not prevented by any artificial means of birth control, is an *ideal* or an *ideal norm* (abstractly speaking). In difficult situations this norm cannot always be observed, but might or must, in the hard cases of a conflict of duties, yield to more urgent or higher values. A contrary decision, however, should not be made lightly, and without a general striving toward the ideal norm. This striving must be seen in the light of the "law of growth."

(c) Several hierarchies recognize that, at least at the present time, the use of periodic continence presents grave problems and is not infrequently quite impossible. It is noteworthy that neither the Pope nor any major hierarchy teaches that, in such cases, total continence must be an absolute norm whatever might be the consequences for the harmony, peace and stability of a marriage. Attention is thus focused on the degree and urgency of values and duties.

(d) No hierarchy assumes responsibility for approving or recommending any definite method or technique of birth control or specific therapeutic means. The bishops refused to say anything collectively about the pill, but preferred to speak about the responsibility of spouses to choose—in the cases of a conflict of duties—the way that seems best to them after serious reflection, investigation, and prayer. This striking awareness of the limits of their competence with regard to technical questions on the part of the episcopates should induce a similar attitude of prudence on the part of confessors and spiritual counsellors.

(e) The priest has to try his best to illumine the conscience of the faithful by explaining the authentic doctrine of the Church, but in the end he is obliged to respect the decision of a sincere and upright conscience on the part of the faithful.

Confronted with penitents who have formed their consciences after serious consideration of the teaching of *Humanae vitae*, the guidelines laid down by the various episcopal conferences, and the opinions of theologians, the confessor should refrain from calling their convictions "invincible ignorance," if there is good reason to assume that they think and act according to a line of thought espoused by a major group of bishops, theologians, and laymen who are experts in the matter. However, if the confessor is personally convinced that their convictions are not in conformity with the teaching of the Church and therefore are an error or "invincible error," he should act prudently according to the traditional principles for dealing with an "invincibly erroneous conscience." (See St. Alphonsus Liguori, *Praxis Confessarii*, No. 8, where he insists strongly on the obligation of the confessor not to drive into rebellion and "formal" sin penitents whom he can leave in their opinion or invincible ignorance without greater harm for themselves or others.)

THE PILL

Those who expected *Humanae vitae* to deal with the question of the use of the progesterone birth-control pill have misunderstood the general character of the encyclical. Not all those who have difficulties with the teaching of the encyclical (namely, that each individual conjugal act must remain open to procreation even in situations where the transmission of life would be irresponsible) are enthusiastic about use of the progesterone pill. The problem of the widespread use of hormone pills as a means of birth control is discussed critically both by opponents of Pope Paul's encyclical as well as by those who have hailed his decision with relief and gratitude.

From a theological point of view it has to be emphasized that our hope of eternal salvation cannot rest on pills, although we value medical help in difficult situations. Medical science must continue to investigate the problem of birth regulation because it is chiefly on account of the progress of modern medical science that we are faced with the problem of a world-wide population explosion. I think there are good reasons for warning people against placing too many hopes in the eventual discovery of a "Catholic pill," that is, a pill which would artificially regulate the moment of ovulation and thus make possible birth control while observing "the natural rhythms." I am not the only one who cannot see a great deal of difference between a pill that assures punctual ovulation for the purpose of effective birth control and a pill that effectively postpones ovulation until a new conception is responsibly desired. From an anthropological point of view, the medical question to ask is how does this interference with the biological functions in each case affect the well-being and dignity of the person as a responsible being?

The encyclical *Humanae vitae* has destroyed the almost mystical hopes placed by some in the pill—and this can only be a good thing. On the other hand, it has given a new impetus to discussions about the therapeutic use of means which as a matter of fact have a contraceptive effect, although they can be used for other than contraceptive purposes. Henceforth the discussion about means of birth regulation and therapy will no longer be confined to the narrow perspective of the hormone pill.

The reference in *Humanae vitae* (Art. 15) to therapeutic means will probably lead to the same kind of discussion as the allocution of Pius XI in September 1958 (which is referred to in the footnote). Therefore I mention here the different solutions or probable opinions of theologians within the framework of a natural-law concept which gives prime attention to the "laws and rhythms of nature" (namely of the biological nature) and of the traditional doctrine that contraception is always intrinsically evil and sinful.

As in the many other modern questions, there are different opinions among theologians. A great number of respectable moralists explained Pope Pius XII's doctrine within the realm of traditional principles, concluding that it would be allowable to use the pill in most of the problems of menopause. If it is already a clear trend of nature to suppress ovulation at that time and furthermore an irregular cycle provokes troubles or is connected with other difficulties of health, and if competent physicians judge that these pills are a good means of helping the woman, they may be used. This judgment is not wrong and is not changed by the fact that the pill has a secondary effect, namely, the suppression of ovulation.

Secondly, most doctors and theologians agreed that if the pill is capable of normalizing the cycle of the woman, it might be used. But physicians did not encourage this theory because it is not certain at all whether the pill can have a regularizing effect. This is a question for doctors to decide. They must ascertain whether the pill can or cannot normalize the cycle. Regularization is the direct effect intending to restore a perfect function of nature, and that in itself is good. The temporary suppression or inhibition of the ovulation does not matter, because the lack of a regular cycle can be a severe handicap for many women; a temporary suppression of ovulation means the impossibility of conceiving.

The third point in the discussion was: Can the pill be used during the period of lactation? It is probable—not metaphysically certain but probable enough—that nature itself inhibits ovulation when the mother breast-feeds her child. Natural hormones called progesterone, the same as those artificially produced and contained in these pills (enovid, norlutin, anovlar, etc.), inhibit ovulation. Now, if nature inhibits ovulation in most cases during lactation, we can consider this an expression of the wisdom of God who wishes to allow married people full conjugal tenderness without fear of a new pregnancy during the time of breast-feeding. Hence, when "nature" does not perform its function in some cases, owing to inability to nurse, to the circumstances of life or other reasons, medical science is allowed to correct the faults of biological nature.

According to many theologians, such medical treatment is justified morally when there is explicit intention to make possible the expression of conjugal love without fear of a new pregnancy which at the present moment is not desirable either because of some material exigency or because of the health of the mother. This desire is legitimate because it accords with the wisdom of the Creator who, in normal functions of the nature of woman, makes this possible. Similarly, nature makes possible the same conjugal freedom for 24 days of each cycle. When the biological functions of nature are impaired by poor health or by some deviation from the biological norm, it is licit to help nature to restore its perfect function.

Other moralists deny this position, especially when the mother does not nurse because she cannot. But here also, a good many moralists assert that if the mother does not nurse or cannot nurse, she still has a right to desire the effect of normal biological function: the inhibition of ovulation, which allows the couple to express conjugal love without fear of a pregnancy at a time when pregnancy is not desirable, at a time in which the mother normally would breast-feed her child.

These opinions have been discussed for several years and both schools are convinced for their part that they are faithful to the teaching of Pius XII. In my opinion, since this question has been discussed for so long under the eyes of the authority of the Church, everyone can freely follow his own conscience. There are two probable opinions. Whoever is convinced that the rigid opinion is right is obliged to follow it in his own conjugal life. But even if a moralist is convinced that only his position is right, he has to be ecclesial, he has to be loyal to the other part of the Church and therefore cannot impose his opinion as if only his party, his faction, were the Church. He honestly has to inform the married couple that there are disagreements, that a perfect certainty for one or the other opinion has not been achieved, and that the Church until now has allowed a freedom of choice; hence everyone can follow his own conscience. Then he can say, "My personal opinion is that it is not allowable, but I do not have the right to impose my personal opinion when the matter is being discussed by renowned and reputable Catholic theologians."

Although Pope Paul refers to therapeutic means only with reference to the health of the body (*corpus*), the whole development of recent theological thought and above all the guidelines laid down by numerous hierarchies seem to indicate that "bodily health" must not be understood in too narrow or materialistic a sense with reference only to the functioning of single organs and without reference to the concept of a person as a person. "Bodily health" should rather be understood in terms of "anthropological medicine" (as proposed by such Christians doctors and thinkers as Viktor von Weizsäcker, Viktor Frankl and Igor Caruso). We should return to the biblical concept of "body" as the totality of the person and get away from the Hellenistic dichotomy of body and soul. Genuine therapy must be concerned not only with the organs or the organism, but at all times with the total concept of the health of a human being who, both in his bodily and his spiritual life, is always making progress toward better integration and perfection. The therapy or cure that helps a person as a whole to make progress toward this goal is genuine therapy.

18. JUSTICE IN
THE SERVICE OF LOVE

JUSTICE AND LOVE

In the totality of our life it must be evident that love is not mere sentimentality. Man must correspond to the order of love (*ordo amoris*), to the manifestation of God's love revealed in all His work. Therefore to be true, love cannot be restricted to a matter of the heart. True love proves itself when it pervades the total structure of man's life. Love becomes justice when man seeks earnestly the objective *ordo amoris* in the social and economic life, and then does his best to express his love through the exercise of justice in the socio-economic areas of life.

Objectively, all created things, be they of the material, intellectual or psychological order, are gifts of God's love. All of these gifts bear the stamp of the Giver's intent, namely, that of a social orientation in the service of all mankind. We appropriate all these things and truly claim ownership by making them means for fraternal love to the glory of the one Lord and Father. All these God-given gifts are socially mortgaged in the sense that they are given in view of the whole of humanity. This social mortgage is not secondary; material things are, first of all, common property. The need of individual property is a function of the common good. The expressions and meaning of individual property may differ with historical situations, but under all circumstances, the primary purpose of material goods is that they are destined for the benefit of the community; only thus are they also destined for the individual for conversion into a source of happiness. Man finds his true self by using God's gifts in the service of the community, the common good.

If we seek to establish the relationship between justice and love, we find that justice is a mediation of love. Justice takes care of the order of rights in our social relationships; love relates person to person. Justice without love, without the warmth of the heart, is one of the most crying forms of injustice against the person, because the highest right of the person is to be loved and respected as a person. Without love man is blind even to the exigencies of full justice. But love also obliges us to learn to know "how to bring order into our economic, social and cultural life."

INDIVIDUAL AND GROUP EGOTISM

The formation of conscience in this day and age calls for the slaying of the contemporary dragon of group egotism. Many Catholics, while condemning individual injustice in the form of individual egotism harming others, canonize group egotism. The indictment extends to priests and religious as well as laymen. Some priests, exemplary in their generosity as regards their personal property, are fanatics with regard to their parish property. Their concern is limited to the confines of the parish which they want to make rich; somehow, they succeed in being totally oblivious of the diocese, of the Church as a whole. Moneys from the tithing system imposed upon parishioners are sometimes used for rather useless changes in the Church without consultation with parish leaders or representatives. Many pastors nurse their parochial brick-and-mortar mania, giving little or no attention to the upgrading and extension of the high schools and colleges in the diocese.

There is only one name for such behavior: it is group egotism and it is wrong!

When such group egotism is found among religious superiors and administrators, it is even worse. They have responsibilities to their group, but they must also be aware of their group responsibility towards the greater and higher community.

Many persons are scrupulous in the area of commutative justice which rules rights between individuals, but they will vote for a party because it promotes injustice in favor of its own group. Such persons cultivate this particular party or politician because of their vested interests. Trade unions can well illustrate this point. Some can be unjust by failing to do anything to promote the welfare of the working class or by refusing to participate in a just strike. On the other hand, there can be trade unions that promote social injustice toward other segments of the labor force and who thus promote social class hatred. Participation in such activities becomes social injustice.

Workers participating in a strike should examine their conscience: Is this strike just or not? Such an examination should be undertaken by both capital and labor, superordinates and subordinates. Managers and capitalists who convene to resist the demands of trade unions and the workers must seriously examine the basis of the demands in terms of justice. They should further examine their stand in reference to social and racial integration: are they content to maintain an unjust order, or have they initiated steps to promote social justice in the area of integration?

Many instances can also be cited of untenable positions supposedly based on Church doctrine which seek to maintain the *status quo* in favor of privileged classes or races. By spurious explanations and distortions, these men incur guilt for actively promoting injustice. Incumbent on the confessor is the task of calling to the attention of men in high positions their great injustice in so abusing the doctrine of the Church or of the Gospel. Such social injustices are all the more evident today in the light of insights gained through the behavioral sciences providing a deeper knowledge of human equality and solidarity. To so manipulate the social variables in a situation as to maintain a comfortable *status quo* involves blatant sinning against justice. As to persons engaged in social issues of the nature of inter-class or inter-racial problems, let them proceed with love in their hearts. For them to carry out their work with hatred would make it impossible ever to attain the goal for which they are fighting. Vindication of rights must be undertaken in a spirit of mutual understanding and with the greatest patience; this is the meaning of nonviolence (cf. Pastoral Constitution on the Church in the Modern World, Art. 78).

JUSTICE AND LOVE ON ALL LEVELS

The social encyclicals of Pope John XXIII and the Pastoral Constitution on the Church in the Modern World (Art. 63-93) point up the fact not only that justice is a question between capital and labor but that social justice demands a responsibility of love toward all people and all nations. Nations that are blessed with earthly possessions in the form of extensive territories, natural resources and historical advantages have a responsibility to assist poorer nations lacking such natural endowments and skills and who consequently remain underdeveloped. The obligation extends to the promotion of peace and mutual understanding among all peoples. Doing so renders justice and glory to our common heavenly Father who has destined all things for the common good of the human race; to Him all things belong. This obligation of justice becomes an impossibility when privileged peoples and nations concentrate only on maintaining their higher position and power. Peace among men depends upon justice.

Man formally cooperates in grave sins of social injustice when he votes for a man or a party declaring its resistance to racial integration or to giving aid to nations in dire need of help. Social issues of this magnitude claim serious consideration on the part of all Christians. It takes the impact of both pulpit and confessional to underscore the ecclesial dimension of justice and to bring it to the attention of both individual and group consciences. Vatican II was explicit on these points bearing on social problems; however, the conciliar documents will be of no avail unless all priests and faithful try to make it a part of their life. The confessor has a special obligation to form consciences along the actual present-day teachings of the Church, and not according to the manuals of the last century! Professors of moral theology whose convenience is best served by using out-dated lecture notes based on nineteenth-century manuals neglect the proper formation of consciences according to the present and living teaching of the Church *today!* The recent Vatican II documents referring to social justice call for intensive study on the part of all. Closely related to these because of their emphasis on social solidarity would be *Mater et Magistra* and *Pacem in Terris.*

SOCIAL JUSTICE TOWARD THE WORKER

The worker's right to a just wage is an aspect of his primary right to be treated as a human person, with personal and social respect. No man can truly show kindness and gentleness to a worker if he refuses to pay him a just wage. It is quite understandable why the worker rejects the so-called friendliness and charity of his employer, because from his frame of reference they represent the employer's means of efficaciously exploiting him. Justice and kindness go hand-in-hand: justice in the form of equitable wages and kindness in treating workers as persons. Whenever and wherever possible, the system should be initiated or promoted where the worker becomes a sharer in the profits of the enterprise. There are many ways open to the attainment of this goal. Methods could be devised whereby workers would have a voice in determining policies affecting their own work and even their family life. It is not right that a handful of men in the high échelon positions decide all courses and procedures that affect millions of workers and their dependents.

But the worker has correlative obligations toward his employer and these call for an examination of conscience: is he fair and just toward his employer in putting in the time and quality of service expected of him? Is he fair toward his fellow-workers and toward other social groups? Does he, as an individual, fulfill his role as a Christian in the social and economic life? Does he together with his co-workers, as a member of a group, fulfill his role in the same area? These points bear serious responsibilities. There are pious individuals who are very generous toward their parish but who should be exhorted first to pay their employees and only then give donations to the parish. Writers of catechisms on tithing should be informed that they seduce Catholics to injustice and disobedience if they advise people to give the tithe— the 10%—first to the parish, and then to pay their debts with what remains. This is exactly what the Lord forbids, that none cries *corban* who is giving the tithe for the Church but neglecting one's parents. One's duty to support the Church does not supersede one's obligation of justice toward his creditors. It is wrong and unjust for promoters of tithing to use such pressure tactics which propose the principle that the tithing belongs to God and therefore it is to be paid before all other debts and duties are taken care of. The thousands of such catechisms confuse God and the interests of the parish. When they try to prove the obligation of tithing from the Old Testament, they should be consistent and point from the Old Testament to the obligation of fulfilling other laws, *e.g.*, the prescription of circumcision. There are more passages in the Old Testament prescribing circumcision than there are prescribing tithing in a literal sense of paying 10% of the gross income.

It is unjust to impose tithing without making some allowance for the poor people who have to struggle to educate their children and who wish to send them to Catholic schools. To impose tithing indiscriminately on the rich and the poor alike is an injustice. Such an imposition from Church authorities hurts the people's feelings all the more when it is evident that even the State in this modern world refrains from imposing regressive taxes that would bleed the low-income groups. The American income-tax system calls for a much higher percentage of tax from those of high income than from those in the lower income brackets; in every case, the number of dependents is given generous consideration. Therefore, to demand 10% of the gross income no matter how great or small the income or the financial responsibilities of a family is an evident sin against justice.

JUSTICE IN ADVERTISEMENTS

Television viewers are subjected to a daily overdose of lies in the thousands of commercials flashed across the screens. But they no longer seem to be deceptive since everyone understands that they are common exaggerations. Nevertheless, we should educate the public conscience in view of altering public opinion, helping the consumer realize that the ideal criterion in advertising is truth; a good advertisement tells the truth. It becomes a special sin against justice when a company not only extols the values of its own products but denies or deprecates the values of another company's products. Similarly, it is a sin against justice to sell a second-hand car without revealing its latent defects. If farmers, when selling horses, were expected to tell the buyer of any substantial defects in the horses, the same should hold for car dealers. But if it is already the common practice to sell second-hand cars without revealing such defects, then the prospective buyer must carry on his own research in regard to latent flaws. He should pay less to dishonest dealers and place his trust only in dealers who reveal hidden defects. We must not promote by our casuistry this type of injustice: that because it is a common practice to refrain from revealing latent defects, the dealer is not obliged to do so. If they are to be true to their vocations, dealers are required to guarantee the quality of the item they are selling and to reveal hidden defects in that item.

At times, we must remind our penitents that fraudulent maneuvering is sinful. We know how Our Lord responded to the rich man who asked him: "How can I obtain eternal life?" In the Gospel of St. Mark (10:19), Our Lord answered: "Do not commit fraud." To this man who thought he had fulfilled all the commandments, Our Lord posed the question: "How is it with your riches?"

JUSTICE AND HONESTY TOWARD THE STATE

One is obliged in conscience to pay just taxes to the State. Obviously, if payment of taxes spells personal ruin, it is not for the good of the State. Often enough, when one seeks no advice in tax matters, he is likely to pay more than his due. Therefore, it is prudent to seek advice, not to evade taxes, but to fulfill one's duty responsibly. There is always present the temptation to conceal something when one does not know all the laws and thinks that he has committed fraud against the State; in reality, the case could be that he has paid too much in taxes. One must be familiar with the legislation and its interpretation. Laws, because of the technical wording, are very difficult to understand at times. For example, in Germany, a court decision obliged a religious order to pay taxes for the royalties of its members. This meant very high taxation if an individual signed the contract himself; but if the superior signed the contract, there was no taxation. This is an example of a fine legal distinction, but if one knows such things, many worries can be averted. It is a case of the ignorant suffering or feeling tempted to transgress the laws.

Therefore, if people have scruples on these matters and ask our advice, we should tell them to consult an expert. We would do great harm to people if we did not so inform them. Often, they have a bad conscience and yet they have not committed any objective fault. Others might have dishonest lawyers to help them; in these cases, caution must be exercised in the confessional. They have to pay just taxes as the law is to be understood, as it is in the common understanding of State decisions.

Another method of defrauding the State is to obtain State support in a surreptitious manner, such as lying or by misrepresentation of facts. We should alert the consciences of our penitents that such practices are against justice.

RESTITUTION

Caution is the guideline when people ask: "Do I have to make restitution?" It is a decision that could mean for this person thousands and thousands of dollars. Unless you are expert in this area, give an honest answer: "I do not know. You should consult someone knowledgeable in the matters of economic justice."

It may be that occult compensation is not advisable, for the person would expose himself to dangers and diminish his claim to the confidence of others. It is possible that the person did not sin against justice because his employer was not paying him a just wage. On the one hand, in most of the cases the confessor must tell him to discontinue these actions of clandestine compensation out of love for his family, for the sake of his peace of mind and good name, and for love of the common good. However, we cannot oblige him to make restitution when he did not sin against commutative justice.

We must generally form the consciences of penitents so that they realize that a sincere conversion is not possible if they desire to keep unjust mammon. If one has had recourse to unjust methods to become a millionaire, he cannot quietly use his millions for his private benefit and still seek conversion. Somehow he must give away what was evidently acquired by injustice. Great millionaires should subject themselves to a serious examination of conscience: "Were my actions towards my employees just?" And if they were unjust: "How can I make restitution to them or restoration for the common good?" Obviously, it is often difficult if not impossible to make restitution directly to these workers. A possible solution would be to make the employees sharers in the profits. Many wealthy individuals make generous donations towards cultural and social goals. This is one form of real restitution. But if they have justly acquired their riches, such donations are of the order of generosity.

It is not impossible for a rich man to be able to assert: "My methods were as honest as those of most honest men." But he was able to acquire such wealth only because of the common structures of the economy, which did not correspond to justice. What is he doing for the building up of better structures and better convictions?

Injustice committed against the State must also be countered by restitution. Some moralists wrongly state that injustice against commutative justice alone obliges to restitution. Such a statement is an incorrect interpretation of a text of St. Thomas and is not commonly accepted today. If one has definitely committed injustice, he must make restitution. However, when dealing with the State, this is often very difficult if not impossible without going to jail. In this case, one could make restitution by donations to hospitals and other public institutions in the U.S.A. and other countries, even to Catholic schools since the State itself most probably commits injustice by double taxation of Catholics who wish to send their children to Catholic schools. We must be very prudent when treating of this matter in the confessional. One should never attempt to obtain restitution for one's own institution, for one's own parish. This could make a very bad impression and lead to serious misinterpretations. If the penitent wishes to make restitution to you, advise him instead to make it to another institute for another social goal.

19. TRUTH IN CHARITY
AND CHARITY IN TRUTH

TRUTH, THE EXPRESSION OF LOVE

With an infinite love, the heavenly Father expresses His own glory and love and majesty in His Son. And the Son in turn breathes and reveals love Itself, the Holy Spirit. St. Thomas stated the same truth in the following words: *Filius Dei non est verbum qualecumque sed Verbum spirans Amorem.* He is not any word; He is the word which essentially breathes the Spirit, a Person; He is the Word which expresses this self-giving Love. Genuine truth must always be an image of the One who is the Truth. Therefore, one's misuse of fact or information against his neighbor cannot be an assertion of truth. And if he claims to be a devotee of truth, he should not use the information he has against his neighbor by sowing hatred for him. If anyone knows what truth is—and a Christian has to know it in Christ Jesus—he will always be sure to express truth in a way that fosters the dialogue in a truly personal community, in a way which builds up the Mystical Body.

This expression of love holds especially for the truths of salvation. A priest or a theologian using revealed truth as a wedge against opposing schools of thought, or as a means to enhance his own glory, misuses these truths. He is not in truth, because the truth of salvation is essentially and totally the expression of the love of God. Truth can be expressed and rightfully understood only if we love God and those to whom the truth of salvation is destined. The same applies for every expression of truth since in reality all truth is an image of the eternal truth, the Son of God.

Sometimes it is good for a confessor to give a penitent a polite jolt when he notices that the penitent is using truth for his own advantage only, or diplomatically. It makes a great deal of difference whether a person accepts truth forthrightly or if he sees it only in the light of personal gain. For example, there are theologians who first ask: "Will I make a good impression if I assert this; will it cause me trouble or give me sleepless nights?" Theology does not lend itself to this approach. Faith demands total openness, even if truth hurts and exposes us. The whole of our life demands this approach to truth. In our expression of truth we need always to be considerate of the hearer. The final question becomes: "Is my way of expressing truth building up the community of charity and truth?"

TRUTH IN THOUGHT, WORD AND DEED

The strong negative formulation of the Eighth Commandment: "Thou shalt not bear false witness against thy neighbor" readily makes one aware of the obligation not to give false testimony and not to lie in speech. But in the light of New Testament law, since we are obligated to the One who is Truth, the New Covenant also obliges us to cultivate the essential truth in our heart and mind. We are not to indulge in gossip, to waste our time on newspapers or before TV sets unless they merit our attention. We are obliged in our whole person to grasp the essential truth, namely, the truth of salvation, and those sciences which help us in our task, in the development of our total personality. We also have to think truthfully concerning our neighbor, ever conscious of him as an image of God, redeemed by Him. All his faults must be viewed in the perspective of his redemption for together with us, he has been called to eternal beatitude, to the communion of saints and to the Triune God. When we communicate with our neighbor, let us make it worthwhile. Of course, we are not always capable of profound discussions but we should at least try to have our conversations enrich our neighbor and bring him to a deeper understanding of truth. This requires that we do some listening—unfortunately, a lost art.

Finally, we must be honest in our deeds. One of the outstanding traits of modern youth is honesty; their strong dislike for phoniness in adults accounts for their being viewed by them as iconoclasts. In the formation of the consciences of youth, we should appeal to this honesty and show young people that sincerity of purpose must result in sincerity of behavior. Their deeds must express what they are; they must also express their noble ambitions. Youth must be a witness to the truth.

THE MALICE OF LYING

We can easily see the malice of lying if we consider Christ, and this we must always do since He is the Truth and the faithful Witness to the truth. As Christians, we are called to be apostles; this means that we are to be witnesses to the truth of salvation. But if those witnesses intersperse their testimony with small lies, they make themselves incredible. This is true for the priest as well as for every Christian. Everyone must periodically repeat his credo in relation to his life conditions. His whole life must be a testimony to the Faith. The whole Catholic Church in every member has to keep that testimony credible and make it grow in credibility. When we make ourselves incredible we destroy our highest vocation. On the other hand, by truly living our Christian commitment, we remove the credibility gap.

KINDS OF LIES

Some lies are against the unity of the Church. It was sad to hear these lies when the Council was in session. If one asserts, as one monsignor did, that he knows of a Dutch parish priest who married civilly before his two assistants and that the bishop, knowing this, still allowed him to function in his office, he sins against the unity of the Church. If, moreover, he is a man who hears stories of this kind and then repeats them for his own pleasure he not only transgresses the Eighth Commandment, but he sins against the unity of the whole Catholic Church. He provokes for his part a kind of schism in the Church. Again, without knowing the facts, if one defames different schools of thought or other Christian Churches by asserting that they are teaching this or that, he does great harm to the unity of the Church. He sins against faith, that faith which creates unity.

If men criticize books which they have never read, if they point an accusing finger at men they have never known or studied, they make themselves the laughing stock of the Church. They sin against truth in essential questions. If one asserts that this or that bishop or this theologian is a heretic, without knowing the language of that area, without having contact with the bishop or having made serious study of the problems involved, then he commits a grievous sin against truth. Before one makes such accusations or utters such specious statements, he must seek to verify his position.

By lying, one can also sin against the unity of the Christian churches, as for example, imputing to Protestants certain beliefs without knowing that they hold those beliefs. One cannot afford to generalize from the error of one man to the assertion that all Protestants are guilty of this error. He sins against the unity of the Christian Churches, and this is a serious wrong.

In general, there is a need to awaken the conscience of Catholics in this area. So many make statements without sufficient grounding in knowledge and without having made the necessary efforts to learn. Too often, we limit our concept of injustice to violations of justice in economic matters. There is, however, injustice in the violation of truth. For forgiveness in these matters restitution is necessary, both in the economic sphere and in the realm of truth.

LYING THROUGH HUMAN WEAKNESS

Full deliberation does not always mark our human acts. That is why it can easily happen that a word escapes us before we fully realize it. If we recognize our mistake, we should simply admit, "What I said was not deliberate," especially if the matter was of importance. It will help us be more careful in the future even in minor matters.

There is a special problem for those who are reared in an atmosphere where respect for the truth is not cherished. It is practically impossible for them to be truthful for any length of time. But under these conditions, they do not greatly harm the salvation of men or the unity of Christians. Generally speaking, these are lies of frailty and venial sins. If no deliberation is present, they are lies of weakness.

We Catholics should not act as if lies were unimportant, as though they were only slight aberrations. Research studies carried out in different countries seem to suggest that some Catholic environments show a greater propensity to lying than do Protestant environments. Could it be that the "saving face" attitude fostered in the Catholic schools has led to deviousness? Perhaps the moralists have misled us by teaching that all too generally, lies are only venial sins. There was considerable incongruity involved in asserting that under the laws of abstinence, two and one-half ounces of meat on Friday is a mortal sin but a hundred and fifty lies from one confession to another is only a slight matter. This is indeed warped thinking! There is something wrong, also, if in our rigidity we claim that a person who has eaten fifty-eight minutes before communion cannot receive the sacrament, whereas one who lies continuously can go to the sacrament as long as he did not commit a mortal sin. It is a different story if a person deliberately breaks his fast within the hour before his communion because he lacks good will or shows contempt for self-denial and law. He who continually lies needs a serious effort to convert from this bad habit. He causes great damage to himself and to the community. Generally speaking, it is at least as important to overcome the habit of lying as it is to overcome the habit of masturbation. This does not mean that a single act of lying is a mortal sin, but the careless attitude toward truth is highly dangerous.

LIES OF CHILDREN

Many children lie because it is the accepted thing to do in the family; it is a family sport. They have been contaminated by their environment. Even if children believe fairy tales as, for example, the story of the stork, they are hurt later on when they learn the stories are not true; their faith and trust in adults may be seriously undermined. The whole family atmosphere bears a strong influence on the child. If lies are commonplace, if honesty is an unknown quantity, lies will come naturally to children. They might even fear to tell the truth when caught in a misdemeanor.

Parents should be taught not to punish a child for honestly admitting his mischief. Furthermore, it must be realized that for a young child, it is very difficult, at times impossible, to discriminate between fact and fancy, between fantasy life and reality. Parents and teachers should not reprimand the children as "liars." Nor should a confessor tell children of five or six or eight that they lied . . . He should tell them, rather: "You are an intelligent boy, you have to learn the difference between what is truth and what is fancy. You will soon be a man. What do you think of a man who lies all the time, who mixes up truth and fancy?"

We must help children in this important matter of overcoming a habit of lying. We can tell them that this is a disease of childhood, a sign that they need to "grow up." Children have good will and as a rule readily accept advice. They should be encouraged to admit their lying to their mother; the mother should then indicate how pleased she is with the child's honesty.

HARMFUL AND INNOCENT STORIES

When telling stories or fables to children, adults should explain to the children that what they are being told is fantasy. The children should be helped to understand the story, not in its literal sense, but as a method of explaining some aspect of life. One must, however, avoid confusion when dealing with events in the history of salvation. Children should not confuse fairy tales with the great events of the Gospel; parents have a responsibility in this area.

Are jokes lies? No; they are not harmful since they are merely designed to tease, and some people like to be teased. Jokes are usually based on a peculiar use of language, a play on words or a twist of intent. They have a way of expressing wisdom and in the end no one is deceived or disappointed.

Half-truths are very different and are often malicious. A certain part of the whole truth is taken out of context, with the result that the total truth is distorted. This is a common form of slander as well as a common form of propaganda. In moral theology, it is of the greatest importance that we do not take parts of a whole action and express the morality of the part alone. The whole is the only way to perceive the true meaning, and justice requires that the whole picture be presented.

TRUTH AND FRATERNAL CORRECTION

Fraternal correction is one of the important expressions of fraternal charity. But one cannot correct his fellowman at any moment nor is anyone qualified to do so. Some are especially adept at fraternal correction; they are properly guided in their thought and have a natural psychological approach. Since they have special gifts, they also have corresponding responsibilities.

If, however, fraternal correction makes one scrupulous, he has no obligation in the matter. Also, if one knows that he is unfit and that the person corrected will react violently, then the obligation to correct him ceases; someone else should do it.

MENTAL RESERVATION

First of all, let us be aware of the complexity of the matter. In the first edition of my book, *The Law of Christ*, I naively presented several examples of mental reservations taken from older moralists. They evoked strong reactions from the reviewers, especially Protestants. Mental reservations can at times appear as lies. Nothwithstanding, they have their place. A mental reservation must be made in the spirit of charity.

By way of example, let me cite the case of a commander of Hitler who came to a German hospital. He asked the sisters in charge if they had any mentally defective children there. The sisters replied that they had some. This meant death for eighty children. If the sisters had said, "We have no mentally defective children here," they would have been telling the truth because they had no children to be murdered. The situation makes the meaning of mental reservations clear. A mental reservation here would have prevented the execution of a bad intention, protected the children, and preserved the "truth." The fact that the children were mentally deficient was true, but it has meaning only if it is expressed in the total reality of charity. It is imperative that we look at the total situation. The words alone give the semblance of lies, but the whole situation gives them a totally different meaning.

It happens frequently enough that people in difficult situations cannot find the proper words to elude indiscreet queries; they only know that they cannot reveal the truth without doing great harm. They know that they must hide the truth, but at the moment, they do not know how to do it.

Therefore, they objectively tell what looks like a lie. Their good will preserves them from a subjective lie.

Occasionally, it happens that we hit upon very apt solutions without fully realizing it. At the end of World War II, I served as pastor at a Polish church. At the time, I had only a German passport, although I needed a Polish passport. The Russian soldiers had received orders to put all men to work, and in order to keep them at work, the men had to surrender their passports. The elderly mother of the sacristan suggested that I hide under the bed when the soldiers came in. Instead, I asked them what they wanted. I knew that they would request my passport, so I boldly said, "I won't go to work; don't you know that I am the pastor of this parish?" And then, I as boldly asked them, not knowing it to be the truth, "Don't you know that Marshal Stalin gave strict orders to respect priests?" They apologized and went their way. Nine years later I learned that Marshal Stalin had indeed given such an order!

20. THE SACRAMENT OF PENANCE AND THE DIVINE MILIEU

The Sacrament of Penance purifies the Church in her members, and so makes her more efficaciously the divine milieu in the world. The Church herself is the divine milieu as a community of love and as a community of worship. She is a sacrament, an efficacious, visible sign of the present kingdom of God, a sign that urges us to expect the full manifestation of His kingdom.

As a sacrament of the kingdom of God, the Church is similar to a fishing net with good and bad fish, or a field in which one finds good seed, weeds and poisonous plants. The pilgrim Church, says the Second Vatican Council, is aware that she is always in need of purification. It is in a very special sense that the Sacrament of Penance keeps the members of the whole Church aware of this need for continual purification, aware of the necessary struggle in the eschatological time of separation.

PROCLAMATION OF THE KAIROS

The Sacrament of Penance may be likened to a Manifesto of the *kairos*, of the present opportunity. Where God's word is proclaimed, there is an opportunity of grace, purification, growth, an opportunity for continuous conversion. The Sacrament of Penance proclaims not only a hidden opportunity of an invisible reality; it proclaims the present opportunity for this man living in this society, in this environment, representing the whole Church living in the positive realities of culture and society and confronting the dangerous forces of this world. The priest-confessor who celebrates the sacrament and proclaims the present opportunity of conversion should know the history of salvation and the present challenging opportunity within it. He has to realize that the history of salvation is not outside human history but is very much a part of it.

The confessor has to know, at least sketchily, the sociological conditions in which the penitent finds himself. What are the opportunities, the positive forces in his surroundings? What are they in the parish, ideally a representation of the whole Church as the divine environment but which often, unfortunately, incorporates too much of the selfish world? What are the conditions of life: the factory, recreational facilities, media of communication (television, newspaper, movies) that affect him? For a Christian, the present opportunities for a life conversion cannot be conceived in abstract terms as a mere internal reformation of a good intention. He has to implant this good intention in the real world, which is a part of man. With all his thoughts and desires, he is related to its possibilities—the good and the bad. He is part of this environment and he brings it to the priest. The Church must then proclaim the time of salvation, the favorable time the great possibility, but in a realistic way, knowing that if one does not use the present opportunity to the fullest, he might succumb to the evils of his day (cf. Eph. 5:16, Col. 4:5-6).

IN THIS TIME OF SEPARATION

The summary of the preaching of the Lord presented in the Gospel of St. Mark (1:14 ff.) reveals that Our Lord began to proclaim the good news: "The favorable time has come, the kingdom of God is upon you." What does He mean by the kingdom of God? Simply that a man lets himself be led by the gracious love of God. God Himself is the ruler, not through intimidation but through His compassionate love made visible in His only begotten Son made man, through the open heart of the Redeemer, through the Church as a community of love. One accepts the kingdom of God when instead of asking, "How far can I go without sinning mortally?" he inquires, "How can I render to God all that He has given me?" Thus we must know the great gifts of God.

The confessor proclaims the present gifts of God, gifts of conversion, in the Sacrament of Penance. Here I recommend to you the solemn rite of penance as you find it in the *Pontificale Romanum*. In this solemn liturgy of reconciliation, the Church exposes the social aspects of sin to the penitent. Our sins pollute the environment, diminish the power and the witness of the divine milieu of the Church and thus strengthen the forces of the prince of darkness. All sins harm the social achievement of salvation. The kingdom of God is the great commonwealth under the one rule of love. It is a gathering, a rallying call. The bishop, in the first part of the rite (expulsion of the sinner from the community of the altar) shows the penitents that they are not worthy to stay around the altar and receive the great sign of the Mystical Body, the sign of the Eucharist. Through their sins, they have done great harm to the unity of Christians, to the divine milieu, to the altar. Therefore, they have to stay away during a time of penance so as to better realize that their sins have been harmful to the community. They must be converted and then contribute to the building up of the Mystical Body. In all the prayers, hymns and the public reconciliation, this rite shows the joy in heaven and in the whole Church over these members who are reconciled and who are no longer harmful, dangerous, or contaminating. They have returned, have been reunited to the altar, the great sign of unity. They are now purified and worthy to build up, to atone by penance and by a new life.

SINS CONTAMINATING THE ENVIRONMENT

Christ says that where two or three are gathered in His name, there He is in the midst of them. Christian brotherhood conveys the rallying call of the love of Christ. Where men answer this call, are together in love, they feel the presence of Christ. They make Christ visible through their mutual love. There are sins that expel Christ, so that in this community there is no longer a witness of Christ's presence, of His love. It can no longer be said of this community: "Look how they love one another, how they show that they are disciples of Christ, how Christ is among them."

St. Paul speaks of the sins of the flesh, *i.e., sarx,* an egocentric self-centered existence. It is interesting that most of the sins which he mentions are sins which directly destroy the divine milieu, the environment of charity which makes Christ present. "Now the works of the flesh are manifest, which are immorality, uncleanness, licentiousness, idolatry, witchcrafts, enmities, contentions, jealousies, anger, quarrels, factions, parties, envies, murders, drunkenness, carousings and suchlike" (Gal. 5:19).

The sin of *sarx* is direct self-centeredness where the sinner seeks himself unreservedly. In fornication, one seeks his selfish interests and abuses another person, destroying the likeness of Christ in himself and his partner, and building together a milieu of darkness. He may declare "I love you," but, indeed, he only wishes to exploit the other for his pleasure; so there is no community of love, no presence of Christ. They become, as it were, one flesh in self-centeredness. All the sins of inpurity, indecency and lewd talk detract from glorification of God by these people.

In the midst of this catalogue of self-centeredness, you see the attitudes which are ruining the divine milieu, directly destroying the witness to Christ who is in their midst. Christians do this by an unhealthy criticism of their superiors, confrères and their fellowman, by evidencing a contentious spirit among those with whom they should live and bear witness to the presence of Christ. It is well known with what energy Pope Paul admonished Church institutions and colleges in his talk at the Lateran University in 1963. He strongly urged them never again to engage in the jealous competition and spirited contentiousness they had evidenced in the past.

St. Paul speaks of this when he says: "Some of them preach Christ by envy, with a contentious temper" (Phil. 1:15), and so they do not manifest the divine milieu, the unity of the Body of Christ. By envy one does not seek the good of another or of the community, but only his own egotistical understanding of life.

SELFISH AMBITIONS

There are great sins committed by the clergy who consider the sacrament of the *diakonia*, the ministry, as a means of ascending to a higher social class, of increasing their prestige and powers. In seeking these advantages for themselves, they occasionally resort to dissensions, party intrigue and the like. Take a monastery: it should be a veritable witness to Christ, a very visible sign of unity and charity, promoting the holiness of everyone. But if there are factions, dissensions and party intrigues, the common effort to strive toward sanctity will be overshadowed by a desire to win over the other party. Whoever views this spectacle would not feel Christ is among them. They are expelling Christ from their community, refusing to experience His nearness through community, the communion of minds that builds up a sense of community. They do not manifest His gracious presence.

The same is true of the lay apostolate in the parish. It is in the factories, the township, the state, the trade union, that Christians, by jealous ambitions and a contentious spirit, work against one another. It would be different if their dissensions were just different approaches to arrive at a higher and better solution, a real and fruitful dialogue or compromise; rather, everyone wishes to affirm his own power. Such laymen fail to testify to the divine milieu, to the presence of Christ.

Drinking bouts and cocktail parties where self-control and mutual respect are lacking certainly do not contribute to an environment that testifies to the presence of the crucified Lord. The attitude of a priest who has renounced marriage and then tries to get as much as he can out of life is out of order. The excessive smoking and drinking, self-indulgence in food and sleep, enjoying life in the self-styled golf-course ministry—these activities do not constitute nor contribute to a divine environment; they do not build up Christ's body; they do not testify to the Paschal mystery. Absent is the redeeming and uniting power of unselfishness leading to real Christian joy.

The divine environment presents itself positively in the same epistle of St. Paul when he says: "We must not be conceited, challenging one another to rivalry, jealousy of one another. If a man should do something wrong, my brothers, on a sudden impulse, you who are endowed with a spirit must set him right again very gently" (Gal. 5:26, 6:1). There is a sacrificial element to fraternal correction. I feel that it is a great temptation to the indolent to say "let well-enough alone." Christ is among us if we very gently and courageously correct one another. It is conceded that this must not be done "in fits of rage" (Gal. 5:20) but very gently with the collected energy of love.

And St. Paul continues, "look to yourself, each one of you. Help one another to carry these heavy loads and to bear one another, and in this way you will fulfill the law of Christ" (Gal. 6:2). This is the law of Christ: a solidarity, a common effort to purify our environment. It calls for a common effort in full solidarity to build up an environment testifying to all that Christ is among us, Christ is in our hearts and that we are gathered in His name and sustain one another patiently.

There are sins that destroy in a very direct way the environment of divine truth and charity. St. Paul shows the root and source of sin: "Knowing God, they refused to honor Him as God or to render Him thanks. Hence all their thinking has ended in futility and their misguided minds are plunged in darkness" (Rom. 1:21). The sinner is seeking his own glory. He then lists those sins that destroy the unity and dignity of mankind, and adds: "not only do they do these things but they applaud others doing them" (Rom. 1:32). The situation is aggravated if a man, not content to testify against the law of God by his sinful acts, also applauds such practices.

We need knowledge of the social milieu we are serving if we are to become sensitive to situations and circumstances applauding sinful practices. Several empirical sociological studies have been conducted covering certain aspects of our Christian morality. It has been found that in Europe and in this country, even among those who frequently and regularly come to Mass, petting and full sexual experiences before marriage are considered by some to be licit and necessary human experiences. And not only do they assert it for themselves but they preach this in the crowd.

It may happen that such opinions are voiced for the sake of being accepted by others; they are not necessarily deep personal convictions. An example may help clarify the point: In a small town there was a branch of a national lay organization which sought to promote better practices throughout the whole country and spoke on the importance of good practices among unmarried youth, stressing the necessity and the possibility of purity before marriage. One officer of the organization addressed two hundred people, mostly young people. After the speaker's message, a young man, the son of the most prominent farmer and innkeeper in the town, got up and said, "All this talk is pure nonsense. Everyone here has had affairs with at least ten different girls and this is needed before he can choose his mate." No one stood up to oppose his views; nobody witnessed. There were many boys and girls who did not share the same conviction, but he was considered a leader. They did not wish to make a bad impression. Five months later the same young man got married in the Catholic Church with full solemn liturgy, without having made any public penance for a sin that had directly poisoned the environment. On the night of his wedding he slept with another woman. And yet there were no courageous responses made on the part of the community. It should have been made clear, however, that this young man and his like are not Christians.

ENVIRONMENTAL POLLUTION

To take any part in building a wrong public opinion on racial justice and racial integration is a sin that poisons the environment. If a parish priest advised his faithful not to sell a house to colored people because the arrival of a colored family would depreciate parish property or lower the standards of the parish, we would have a case in point. Any person who thinks this way or persuades others in this manner promotes a mad psychological racial illness. The faithful so instructed would most likely look unfavorably on the prospect of living with colored families in the neighborhood, and so, once a colored family arrives, they would leave in panic. This is one way of polluting the environment. Such a priest would certainly have sinned against the mission of the Church as a divine milieu. The truly Christian approach would have been this: "If colored people come into our parish, it is our obligation to welcome them into our midst and to show them that we are one community of love, receiving them as we would receive Christ Himself. We will be happy to testify for the one heavenly Father, the one Lord Jesus Christ who redeemed all."

Those who defend social injustice or bad commercial practices, and perhaps even applaud these practices, are poisoning the whole environment of our social and economic life. The same is true of those who promote ideas of selfish birth control—one or two children and no more; those who say, "In Indonesia and in Japan there is overpopulation, therefore in North America nobody should have a large family"; of those who say it does not matter how one limits family size; the end justifies every means, etc. Remarks like these all poison the environment and do direct harm to the divine milieu of the Church that everywhere should testify to the eternal value of the child and every person, to the covenant of love and marriage.

THE PURIFICATION OF THE ENVIRONMENT

The visible sign and the visible goal of the Sacrament of Penance is the unity of God's people. (*Res et sacramentum Penitentiae est unitas populi fidelium*. This is a scholastic expression that testifies to a whole tradition.) The Sacrament of Penance manifests and has as its primary appealing grace the unity of the people of God. Its aim is to build up a community that makes visible the presence of Christ. Therefore all acts of the penitent and the confessor must be directed toward their environment. The examination of conscience and the confession of the sins have to be explicitly directed toward their environment, toward those things that destroy and pollute the environment of the Church, poison and contaminate the human environment in the social, cultural and economic life.

This is the case if the faithful have been taught to see all acts, desires, and words in the light of the great commandment of fraternal love. Not only love of one man for another, but fraternal love as a factor in building up the community of true love. Brochures that help people to make their examination of conscience, our preaching on the Sacrament of Penance, the direct admonition and help within the sacrament itself: all serve to strengthen the conscience as to the responsibility for the environment.

A Christian conscience today must be fully aware that we are living in a pluralistic society, a society often devoid of Christian values; thus one cannot simply avoid the poisoned environment of the world. In other words, he cannot be liberated from the solidarity with the self-centeredness of the first Adam unless he chooses explicitly the divine environment of love, the solidarity with Christ, and with all in Christ.

This great pastoral principle could then reveal why many sins, especially when a man slavishly follows the pattern of his poisoned environment, often are not without guilt. He seemed not to be free, and wished not to become free because he had not made his total commitment to testify to his

solidarity with Christ, to enlighten his environment. Our
social elite should see in their examination of conscience their
great responsibility. There are the weak members. The man
who has received only one talent will not be held as highly
responsible for the environment as the man with five talents.
The less fortunate are to a great extent excused. We understand their confession and even their blindness if we understand their environment. But this must not lead to fatalism.
We know then that we must form a clear consciousness of
social responsibility in those who are sociologically, culturally,
and religiously the elite. All Christians should be included in
this latter category. But among the Christians, there are those
who have received "five talents." If these people wish to be
pious only to save themselves, their own soul, and do not
directly care for building up a divine environment of justice,
purity, truth and charity, then they must know that they are
guilty, guilty of the failures of those they should have sustained through their gifts.

I repeat once more what I mentioned in another context.
The sin of priests and faithful destroying the divine milieu
of the Eucharist is most harmful. The celebration should
give the most visible, tender, and strong experience of a
fraternal community, the presence of Christ among those who
are gathered in His name. Those who do not obey the Second
Vatican Council in this great time of the Church, and do not
renew the liturgy, especially the Eucharist as the expression
of a community of love, hope and faith, as a community of
praise of God, who destroy it in an individualistic, egocentric
sense—they are responsible for the consequences. They are
responsible for various multiple sins in the whole environment, the economic and social environment, in the neighborhood, the factory, etc. Our recalcitrant priests and faithful
must be taught this in the sacrament of the divine milieu.
They must be made aware of the harm done if the very center
of the divine milieu of the Church is spoiled by individual-
ism, self-centeredness and formalism.

If the examination of conscience and the confession itself
must be related to the environment, so also must the act of
sorrow and contrition look directly to the harm done to the

environment. This corresponds perfectly to the oldest traditions of the Church. Irené Hausherr, famous professor of the Oriental Institute in Rome, showed in a book called *Le penthos* that the Eastern Fathers acknowledged as the chief motive for their tears, their conpunction, this point: that through infidelity to the special graces of God they were responsible for the lack of light and warmth in the Mystical Body and in their environment. The act of sorrow must express our conviction that through our sins we are hurting Christ, causing Him to suffer on the Mount of Olives and on the cross, and we are always hurting and affecting His Mystical Body. "If one member glories, all the members glory, if one member on his part wastes grace, he is wasting, as far as it is affected by him, the whole body." The act of sorrow should then especially bear on those sins which in a more evident experience wasted the body of Christ, wasted a member and a whole environment that should belong to the divine milieu. Every infidelity to the rallying call of God—and every grace is a rallying call—is a sin against the Mystical Body. Therefore a deep act of sorrow by one who is aware of the social implications of his sins builds up a social consciousness with the corresponding responsibility.

The purpose of amendment must not be formulated as: "I will save my soul and leave the world to the devil." A real purpose of amendment accepts the kingdom of God over all the dimensions of life and promotes as far as it is within our power all things in our life and our whole environment which proclaim that God rules us through His love. A special intention should be avoidance of all these sins that poison public opinion and, in a more positive vein, building up with all our strength, with all our might, with all our skill, an environment that testifies to love through justice and purity, sincerity and honesty.

THE PENITENT LEARNS TO SEE

It is evidently the work of the priest as teacher, preacher and confessor to help the penitent to this clear examination of his conscience, to the manner of confession and to this social achievement of salvation. This must be his endeavor in the dialogue with the penitent. He has to show, to some extent, his deep understanding of the extenuating circumstances of environmental influences.

An example may explain the point better. A woman confesses that she hates her husband. The confessor asks, "Will you allow me to ask why you hate him? Perhaps I can help you." She answers, "He made me pregnant; I have already had four children." The priest who knows the environment would reply: "I know that you are a good mother and that you would like to have children. You would see the greatness of your vocation even better if it were not for the people in your environment who accuse you of being imprudent, who accuse your husband of no self-control." The woman reples: "This is the case. It is especially my mother and my mother-in-law who cause so much trouble for us." This gives the priest an opportunity to explain in a positive way this mission of the divine milieu: "If you are a woman of deep faith, who still knows all that you can give your children—faith and eternal life—if you are suffering under the darkness of the environment in such a dangerous way that you sometimes have difficulty in loving your husband, then you can understand why other women have still greater troubles. In a situation like yours, they could even be tempted to commit an abortion. You can see how important it is that you not quarrel with your husband or complain about him to other people; design, deepen your faith, accept the trial, and tell other people that you like to be a mother. Do not make yourself ridiculous by complaining and do not submit your whole family to ridicule. Tell other people, 'We have a roof over our heads; we have bread for the family. My husband gave up smoking and he has renounced so many other things. We can educate our children and do not need other people's help.' And so, by being prudent, you can help to build up a better environment."

Another similar case: A good Catholic family expected a third child in the fifth year of marriage. The woman was active in Catholic associations. After the child's birth, she told everyone about the great expense of this child, how greatly restricted they were financially as a result of this new addition to the family. The people's reaction, as expected, was: "This stupid wife. Why do you have children if you don't like them?" The husband acted in another way. His co-workers teased him several times and his reply was: "Do you wish to be the godfather for my fourth child? We are already looking forward to another." In a humorous way he showed that he was proud to be a father. He built up an environment of light, and his wife, who seemed more active than ever in Catholic life, was building up the environment of darkness. We have to instruct people about the meaning of their words and actions for life in the world around them.

A RALLYING CALL AND SEPARATION

The Sacrament of Penance has to proclaim with urgency the kingdom of God that gathers us and makes us a community of love; this sacrament must make visible the presence of the Church where there is a community of love and give us a special experience of the presence of Christ among us. The sacrament should proclaim the kingdom of God obliging us and urging us to live as adult sons and daughters of the Church, to live from the rallying call of Christ and to communicate the call to others. The "favorable time" of the celebration of the Sacrament of Penance brings the penitent in touch with the first coming of Christ and places his life in the perspective of the second coming of the Lord, thus filling him with alertness, hope and energy. He will long for this second coming if he is shown how to recognize and to use the present possibilities of his life in the light of the first and second comings of the Lord.

The Sacrament of Penance is the sacrament of solidarity in conversion. In sin, man has put himself into solidarity with the first Adam and his followers. He has struggled for the prince of darkness, isolating himself from the divine milieu of the Church, integrating himself into the polluted milieu of this world ('world' here is taken in the typical Johannine sense: the world that has taken position against the Lord and against the divine milieu of charity).

The Sacrament of Penance is the renewal of the baptismal vows for integration into the divine milieu in order to become a living member of the Mystical Body, and to witness to the presence of the divine milieu in his environment. It is a sacrament of eschatological separation; the firm resolution is not only a purpose of amendment made by an individual; it is a firm purpose of separating oneself from darkness and from the prince of darkness of this world; it means separation from the attitude of those who are living the self-centered existence of Adam and thus are implanting the collectivism of Satan. It is a positive commitment to testify for Christ and for the community of salvation wherever man stands and works: in his family, in his office, in the factory, or in his neighborhood.

RENEWAL OF THE CHURCH

The Sacrament of Penance promotes renewal of a part of the divine milieu. The Church herself is "the people of God in pilgrimage" and as such is always aware of the continuous need of purification. The Church is most aware of this in the Sacrament of Penance where the priest and the penitent, as well as the whole people of God, confess their need of purification. The Church herself, in her members and communities, renews herself, renews her spirit; but this renewal would not be sincere if it were not joined with the firm purpose of renewing the structures of our Christian life: renewal of the Christian family, making God's kingdom more visible; greater collaboration in the parish, in the liturgy, in matters of shaping sound public opinion, in all forms of the lay apostolate, thus implanting the kingdom of God. It should be evident that the Church is making an effort not only to renew her members in their hearts but also to renew the communities so that they become a witness, a visible sign, of the renewed people of God, and a sign of redemption for every environment. One's social responsibility is underscored in the celebration of this sacrament. The visible sign of renewal must be expressed in all acts of the penitent and above all in the proclamation of the messianic peace.

We have already seen how this must be expressed in the examination of conscience and in confession, by confessing especially and explicitly those sins that have poisoned the environment of the Church herself, the parish, or which are opposed to unity in the lay apostolate or which poisoned the environment of the family, friends, the neighborhood and all other cultural, economic or social structures. The communal celebration of the Sacrament (with an appropriate examination of conscience) brings us to an ever greater awareness of this need for renewal.

SORROW AND PURPOSE IN VIEW OF THE MILIEU

The act of sorrow must look not only to the wounds inflicted on our own soul by our sins. A deep act of sorrow of a man converted to the kingdom of God must include the understanding that his sins (sins of thought, of desire, and more still of word and act) have hurt and have affected the earthly environment and the divine milieu, the Church. They have diminished the splendor and the fruitfulness of the Church. Therefore a man with a truly renewed heart is not only sorry about his personal loss but is even more sorry for the loss suffered by the whole Mystical Body, the whole of mankind. All God's people should represent the divine milieu of redemption. The priest has to help the penitent to come to this viewpoint of penitence and sorrow.

Our purpose of amendment has to be related to the environment. If we are confessing in the darkness of the confessional and are not ready openly to declare the same convictions on the roof tops and in the market places, then our confession is not sincere. One's confession in the sacrament has to be continued in the profession of faith; an essential part of the profession of faith is to confess and to profess that God's law is holy and good and just, and to make it known through the witness of our life. Therefore, the purpose of amendment has to be directed toward the social and cultural environment, and especially towards the ecclesial milieu of the communities of the Church, family, parish, diocese, the whole Catholic Church. This purpose of amendment has to be incorporated into the earthly milieu where we have to testify to the presence of the Church as the sacrament of redemption for the whole world.

The priest in his explanation of the message of peace—and that includes the communal celebration or the whole dialogue which the priest conducts with the penitent—has to make him aware of the great injustice of his sin against Christ and His Mystical Body as well as against the whole of mankind, against the whole world yearning for redemption. And then the penitent can understand how great God's mercy is; He delivers him from these sins and gives him a new mission of witnessing the divine milieu in the places where he lives and works.

The priest can help much more if he knows the actual situation in the history of salvation, the situation of the ecclesial as well as the secular environment of the penitent. Therefore the priest of today needs firm grounding in psychology and religious sociology.

ROLE OF THE PENANCE

The priest can direct the penitent's attention to Penance as a sacrament of renewal by the kind of penance he gives. Through the penance assigned him, the penitent should begin to realize the injustice he has done to the world of God, to his environment, to the whole Mystical Body. He should now try, with a transformed heart, to renew his environment, to collaborate better with all men of good will, to give witness of charity and unity, justice and gentleness, prudence and fortitude.

We should free ourselves from the routine of the last centuries that made prayer essentially a penance. It is true that for most priests, the breviary had become a penance, and many were frustrated in reciting the office. It now becomes a great joy for many priests since they understand the message in their living, native language. Likewise, it is one of the most essential changes brought about by the Council, to make our people newly aware of the great privilege of prayer, of the Spirit Himself crying in our hearts: "Abba, Father!"

We falsify the concept of prayer if we give only prayers as penances in the confessional. Prayer is not essentially a penance. It is a penance for those who are lazy; they should overcome their indolence and idleness. It may be that the confessor has to admonish such people not to neglect prayer and to set aside certain times during the day for prayer: reading, for instance, three minutes from Holy Scriptures and praying a short prayer every evening until the next confession. But all should realize that prayer and reading of Holy Scriptures *per se* are not to be a penance but a joy. It is a penance for him only who is neglecting it and is yielding to his sloth.

A boy tells you in the confessional that he generally forgets his morning and evening prayers. You may use the following argument: he is surely respectful to his parents, greeting them every morning and evening; but he is less respectful to God because of his forgetfulness. You know he has a brother. You will not then give him as penance to kneel down every evening and say his prayers because he would be ashamed to be such a pious boy in the eyes of his brother. But you can propose to have him ask his brother to pray with him, telling him that if both of them pray together, they won't be so apt to forget their prayers. This penance, if he accepts it—and I know from so many confessions that often they accept it gladly—this penance builds up the divine milieu between these two brothers. They are now more aware of their togetherness in Christ.

It is a penance for engaged couples who are sinning with one another that after telling the one present why such behavior is not right, to ask him kindly and gently to explain the same reasons to his friend and ask him to promise to help. "He will show his redeemed love by helping you and you will promise to help him. And if you fail in spite of your good will, then why not stop seeing each other until you renew your redeeming love through the Sacrament of Penance?" This would create a divine milieu between those who have to build up the divine milieu of a Christian family.

Take the case of a husband who is rude and unkind toward his wife. Why give him the rosary as penance? He may not know how to say it; he may dislike it. It may result only in an added accusation at his next confession that he did not fulfill the penance or that he was distracted in his prayers. Try to convince him that the most natural penance is for him to apologize whenever he has offended his wife. At least once in his life he would be made to recognize that he could be nicer toward his wife. I remember once a good lady telling me, "I am not so much affected by the unkindness and harsh words of my husband; I would not be hurt so much by these things if he would just once tell me that he is sorry." It would help her psychologically if the husband were to be given this penance. It is not asking too much of him to acknowledge at least once that he was wrong. And until the next confession he will make it a rule to apologize as soon as possible for his outbursts and unkind treatment of his wife or his children. It will help create the divine milieu of kindness and gentleness in the family and set good example. Also, if there are other sins which disturb the divine milieu of the family, let the penitent accept a penance in which he begins to build up anew.

He should also apologize to his children if he has punished them only because of material damage or impatience instead of doing so out of zeal to educate them. If he holds himself to this rule, he will gain in loving authority instead of inducing fear of violence in the children. He will help the children distinguish between the divine milieu and that of its counterfeits. If we know the present situation of our penitents, where and how they are living, it is not difficult to enlist their cooperation in finding adequate penances. Seek to find a penance that builds up the milieu of gentleness and kindness.

In some rural areas, farmers have an unhealthy attitude that a woman should do more work; she should milk the cows on Sunday while the sons and husband lounge about the house. It would be a good penance to suggest to these young penitents that on Sunday they do not allow their mothers, wives and sisters to work on the farm alone. Even if they hold a job elsewhere, the men can contribute to the family chores. But if more young boys would do this as penance until the next confession, they would find it difficult to tell their mother afterwards that they will stop being nice to her. We can change the milieu but we owe it to our penitents to know which aspect of their life differs from the Christian witness of gentleness, kindness, humility, solidarity.

These penances work well if the confessor does not impose them in an authoritarian manner. Do not assign them in a way that would make the penitent feel that he must accept the edict. But if you celebrate the sacrament with him, if you analyze the motives with him, then he likes it and becomes most cooperative. Truly, I never had difficulties in finding penances.

Better results will be achieved if the confessors of a whole diocese or of a whole area agree on the way of giving penances. If one begins imprudently, he does great harm to renewal; but if all have reflected together and have explained in the sermons on the Sacrament of Penance what are the reason, the motive and the goal of the penance and then try it together, then it will be much more effective. We have had a great deal of success with this in our mission work. We assembled all the missionaries of the same area together to agree as to this type of penance in view of building up the environment. For instance, for those who are away from the sacraments for many years, we would not give prayers as penances. Of course, we exhort them to pray since this is a necessary means to conversion. But we *celebrate* with them the sacrament of reconciliation and then ask them if they would like to express their gratitude to God by trying to win another friend or colleague to go to confession or to come to the sermons. But the reasons must be explained. This must be done because until now the penitent has exercised a negative influence on others and failed to build up the Christian community. It looked as if he felt happy to be far from the Lord and from his invitation; now he gives witness in his environment. Thus he commits himself to the building up of a better milieu.

Finally, the priest has the highest function of proclaiming "Shalom"—the peace of the Lord is with you. He is a courier of peace and a peacemaker. Our task of hearing confessions is blessed by the Lord and we become peacemakers in the fullest sense in that we let the penitent feel that he receives the peace of God; we oblige him, urge him to bring the peace of God to his environment, to be a witness for the reconciliation with God, and of the reconciliation among men. He must feel that it is not a penance imposed arbitrarily but that it follows from the peace message of the Lord, from the reconciliation with the Church and his God.

He has to bring joy to others, like the apostles on Easter evening when the Lord came and they received the pledge from Christ, "Peace be with you"; and then He breathed upon them, "receive the Holy Spirit." And he repeated the "Peace be with you" and made them messengers of peace. Everyone who is reconciled with God, if he wishes to preserve himself in continuous conversion, has to be a witness in his environment of the messianic peace. It is not only a peace of the soul with God, with "the sweet Jesus of my soul." That is not how the Gospels and the prophets preach the messianic peace. You have intimate friendship with Christ if you are working for His kingdom, if you are building up the order of love and justice. So we must feel that it is the very message of the sacrament, that it is the active word of peace that urges the one who receives it and makes him capable of being a conveyor of the messianic peace, of bringing the experience of the divine milieu, of the Church, into the environment of his family, of his neighborhood, and into the whole of the cultural, economic and social environment.

THE LITURGY OF THE DIVINE MILIEU

The actual renewal of the liturgy—a hopeful beginning—makes the liturgy a witness for the living God, whereas prior to Vatican II, in many parishes and religious communities, the liturgy was almost a sermon of the "God is dead" theology.

The liturgy of the Sacrament of Penance needs great improvement. The dark confessional box presents a problem in itself. It does not foster the warmth of a real "con-celebration" of God's merciful love by confessor and penitent. The communal aspect of the sacrament is not manifest enough. The sacramental absolution in its present form does not fully convey the joyous message of a renewed and deepened unity and charity. The one "ecclesial" element which is now expressed directly is the absolution from excommunication and interdict. However, these words are a shocking formalism, when proclaimed in a living language and expressed to little children, holy married people, pious nuns and zealous priests. When the absolution was still said in Latin I did not feel hurt when my confrère gave me the absolution from excommunication and suspension. Were he to do so now in a living language—and many still do—I wonder what he is thinking. Does he really think that his penitent was excommunicated?

The present renewal in the Church allows us to develop new communal forms of the Sacrament of Penance. We can hope that soon the Church will give us a renewed liturgy, maybe different forms or rites for different occasions. For the Lenten season at least, differently structured rites are needed. New experiments within the present structure of the liturgy should be inspired by the wonderful liturgy of the Sacrament of Penance which is still a part of the *Pontificale Romanum*. There two phases are clearly distinguished: (1) *publica expulsio peccatorum feria quarta cinerum*—a liturgical celebration of the word of God, prayers and admonitions which all together awaken a great awareness of the social aspect of all personal sins; (2) the conclusive part is entitled *publica reconciliatio feria quinta, in coena Domini*. Absolution is given in the form of a sung preface. The motif is joy in heaven and in the whole Church. As mentioned earlier, the penitents "are given back to the holy altar" in a most impressive rite by the bishop, who leads them hand in hand.

In the communal celebration of the Sacrament,[1] the rite can conclude with the solemn absolution: at the present mo-

---

[1] See concluding section of Chapter 2.

ment given with the official formula, but without mentioning "excommunication." If a penitent is excommunicated he is to be absolved individually. The whole of this liturgy should integrate hymns and songs of sorrow, trust, gratitude. A more fully developed form of "absolution" can at any time be added as a "paraliturgical" catechetical explanation.

Such a communal celebration in the parishes, when repeated for the different groups, is a unique pastoral means for building up a renewed ecclesial milieu and contributes greatly to making the people of God more effectively into a Divine Milieu for the world around them. It also helps toward a deeper realization of the communal dimensions in the following celebration of the individual confession.

DIFFICULT SITUATIONS IN VIEW OF THE ENVIRONMENT

1. *Divorced persons.* Have we not been using the wrong approach? In some dioceses, they are still discriminated against. In some, they need special permission to be allowed to receive the Sacrament of Penance. In many parishes, the pastor does not allow the assistant to visit divorced people. The divorced are discriminated against. It may be that many are innocent. We should not perpetrate the greatest suffering of injustice. It may be that they are sinners on this point, but the peace of the Lord can restore them to the full living community even if they are not capable of returning to their husband or wife. Divorced persons can give highly important witness to the indissolubility of marriage if they live in charity and help to form the public opinion on the same issue.

2. *Divorced people who have remarried.* People living in so-called "bad marriages" should make an effort to understand the social implications of their act, and should realize that the way they talk about their married status or justify it before others may have an effect on their environment. While their legal status remains the same, namely that of a canonically invalid marriage, the impact they make on others can be very different depending on the circumstances. Some

may have caused great scandal by selfishly and irresponsibly destroying their first or even second marriage and then attempting remarriage without the least sign of repentance. Such people usually try to justify their action by pooh-poohing the indissolubility of marriage.

Others may have had an originally valid marriage fail through no fault of their own. They may even have made heroic efforts to save their marriage, and only remarried when they realized that their first marriage was hopelessly dead. In order to avoid scandal they contract a new civil marriage in a place where the fact that they are divorced is not known. In other cases, the divorced person has tried desperately to obtain an annulment from an ecclesiastical tribunal. Since all the practical evidence seems to indicate that the first marriage was not made in heaven, the persons involved, and most likely also people who know them, feel that the Church should allow them to contract a new marriage. Did they really cause great scandal when they remarried? If these people are firmly convinced that their present marriage is a true marriage blessed by God because they have achieved peace and harmony in mutual love and as responsible and generous parents, the confessor should realize that a harsh refusal of absolution may possibly destroy a sincere attempt to live within the confines of divine grace and within the Church despite what appears to be an impossible canonical situation. It might also be more harmful to the environment, especially public attitudes toward the Church, than the clear exercise of respect for a sincere conscience and a generous good will.

Of course, there are cases where divorced and remarried people have contaminated the environment, especially by advocating easy divorce or by denying the right of the Church to insist on an absolute commitment and lifelong fidelity in marriage. Such people may have learned later on from experience that stability in marriage cannot be achieved without great sacrifice, particularly without a readiness to forgive. How should such penitents be dealt with by the confessor?

In the past rigoristic pastoral practice simply kept all such people away from the sacrament of peace. As long as they were living in a canonically invalid marriage they were just "written off," at least as far as this visible sign of God's graciousness was concerned. But does the Church really have no word of divine mercy and forgiveness for such people if they are doing what they can, here and now, while praying for what they cannot yet do? All Christians should be made aware that the minister of the sacrament of peace has a message of hope for all men of good will, no matter what their past mistakes or present difficulties are.

If these people actually "confess" before their neighbors in their own way, namely by warning against the indulgences and evils that can destroy a marriage and by encouraging the idea of reconciliation, they are indeed visibly on the way to a sacramental confession. Of course, by acting thus they cannot "earn" the grace of God; but they can, with God's grace, truly open themselves to the reconciliating action of Christ. They have already become instruments of peace in their own environment. What are the conditions of absolution?

It is a matter of prudence whether the confessor should try to exhort couples who are aware that their marriage cannot be considered valid to live "as brother and sister." Some people can be convinced or persuaded that they have to make an effort in this direction. The confessor should encourage those who make such an effort not to lose heart if they do not succeed fully. Those penitents who sincerely try to make progress along these lines should be given absolution. The sacrament is not a reward for complete success, but a remedy to be applied in life's difficulties and struggles.

Nowadays other couples may be convinced that God does not wish to impose total continence on them although they realize that their marriage was and is not all right. I think that even in such cases absolution must not be denied without exception. For example, if they are living a generous family life, giving their children a good Catholic education, are kind and helpful toward those who need them, and at the same time are actively engaged in an apostolate on behalf of the stability of marriage in the manner explained above,

I cannot imagine that Christ would have sent them away without a kind word of peace.

However, in all situations of this kind, even in cases involving excellent dispositions and heroic efforts, great attention must above all be given to betterment of the environment and particularly to the avoidance of scandal to others. If the confessor is convinced that he can or must give absolution, he still has to find a way to explain his decision so that it will not be misunderstood as an approval of divorce and remarriage. Especially with regard to the reception of Holy Communion, clear instruction must be given where to receive it and how to explain such action to others, for example the members of their own families who might wonder what was going on. Such couples should not receive communion in a parish where their married status is known, and where some people might be tempted to draw wrong conclusions.

3. *Mixed marriages.* We can also show the divine milieu with reference to mixed marriages. This holds true both for valid and invalid mixed marriages. People in these marriages still have the greatest need for pastoral help; we should bring to them the experience of the divine milieu, the fact that the Church loves them. We must show that we care for them; even in cases where the couples have not fully lived up to their responsibility to raise their children Catholic, we can still help them. In fact, if they show good will, they have a right to be absolved from excommunication and sin. This is a general principle, that if one is not contumacious, he has a right to be absolved. And if these people do what they can, they can be absolved even if you cannot allow them immediately to go to Holy Communion in the parish where their case is publicly known. They should feel that our procedure is not a punishment, but only a point of great pastoral concern not to bring a negative influence to bear on the environment. They could be advised to receive the Eucharist in another parish so that they see that the Church is indeed their loving Mother, and they themselves act in love for their brethren.

By acting in this way, we can bring joy into the hearts of these people. And only if they are joyful Christians will they be qualified to be witnesses of the Catholic faith to their non-Catholic spouse and to their children. We must help them to understand this message of peace. And to make sure that they receive the urgent call in this particular mixed marriage, they should feel the great love and the understanding of the Church.

21. SACRAMENT OF CONVERSION AND GROWTH

Baptism is the great sacrament of conversion. Through faith and Baptism we are converted by God Himself from the darkness of unbelief to the light of the chosen ones, the People of God. In Baptism, the person makes the great transition from death to life, from an existence without divine life to grace, to life in Jesus Christ.

We should think that normally the baptized person remains in the life of Christ. It should be considered as abnormal and unusual for a baptized Christian, sealed with the blood of the Redeemer, to return to the life of darkness. But after Baptism, the Christian still needs the full transfusion of the new life. He must make a continual effort to eradicate all the consequences of the old, selfish approach and to counteract by proper antidote the noxious effects of the Satanic environment and collectivism. Anyone who returns to the death of mortal sin after Baptism can still have "a second baptism" (a term used by the Council of Trent for the Sacrament of Penance), not a Baptism like the first, but a Baptism full of challenge for penance and satisfaction. It is to serve as a reminder that it is horrifying for a man who has tasted the goodness of the Lord and the true meaning of life in Christ to return to the darkness of pre-baptismal days.

In the normal Christian life, the Sacrament of Penance is not a sacrament of conversion from death to life or a repeated first conversion. The whole tradition of the East and West calls Baptism the first conversion. Justin called it the "bath of conversion." For those who have sinned mortally, the Sacrament of Penance is the sacrament of repeated first conversion. For the Christian who lives in grace, the Sacrament of Penance is the sacrament of second conversion, meaning a continual conversion, a sign of growth in the life of the love of God; a sign of a more decisive stand against self-centeredness and sin. In this case, when it is a sacrament of continual conversion, we call it a sacrament of *devotion*. Devotional confession is not an adequate expression; I prefer sacrament of continual conversion. There is a difference and the latter has deeper roots in tradition, going back to the early days of the Church.

NECESSITY OF GROWTH

Where there is life there must be growth. When one starts resisting the law of growth or refuses to grow further, he condemns himself to death. The present time, partially spanning the period between the first and second coming of Christ, is a time of hope and growth. Hope means longing for the coming of Christ, for His victory in the decisive battle against Satan who is fighting "aware that his time is limited" (Apocalypse 12:12). Therefore, the Christian operates on the conviction that only a firm stand in this battle against the wickedness of Satan himself, against the darkness of the environment and the very heart of self-centeredness will keep him alive and make him grow.

We must grow in this continual conversion (1) in the examination of conscience. Our eyes must be cleared through sorrow and a deeper knowledge of Christ, a deeper understanding of the underpinnings of a true Christian life. The penitent should not only examine his conscience against the decalogue, but he should look first of all to the urging reality of grace to the law proclaimed in the Sermon on the Mount. In comparing his present life with this law of faith, not only does he examine his deeds, but he scrutinizes his deepest desires and motives for action. No one knows himself perfectly; were one to think so, he would be a Pharisee, one in great need of conversion. Those who make progress usually initiate their course by taking an objective look at themselves, by seeking the deeper knowledge of their own heart. It takes humility to indulge in self-criticism, but it has to be done under the compassionate eyes of the Lord.

(2) A second aspect of this continual growth and conversion is *growth in sincerity before God and men*. The Apostle St. James exhorts Christians, "confess your sins to one another and pray for one another" (5:16). "My brothers, do not blame your troubles on one another, or you will fall at the judgment" (James 5:9). A man who does not confess sincerely in the eyes of God, "I am a sinner," is still blind and in darkness. And St. John adds, "If we claim to be sinless, we are self-deceived and strangers to the truth" (I John 1:8). The same apostle asserts that one who is reborn in Christ does not sin, "A child of God does not commit sin, because the divine seed remains in him" (I John 3:9), namely, he does not fall back into the death of mortal sin. But everyone who grows up in divine life, in the love of God, becomes ever more aware of his deeply-rooted egocentrism and painfully contends with the base pursuits of the unruly lower nature. So he confesses before God not only that he has done this or that, but also "I *am* a sinner. It is because my heart is not yet purified enough that I committed these faults without being aware of what I was doing." But if one confesses before God, he must confess also before his neighbor whom he sees. This means especially that we must confess our faults to those whom we have wronged; we must admit to them, "I was wrong."

Going to confession every week is a kind of pharisaism if we do not "confess" to those whom we have hurt by our misdeeds, if we still pretend that our contentious spirit is naked zeal for the kingdom of God. We must admit how fundamentally sinful we still are. We have to change something. We confess to Almighty God in the presence of the saints and angels and the Church. We confess to the Church. The willingness to go to confession and the attempts to confess more humbly before God and before our neighbor are signs of the continual conversion, signs of growth.

The general law that can be urged by the confessor as obliging everybody is only to confess mortal sins. There may be special reasons to depart from this norm, *e.g.*, a scrupulous person may sometimes be restrained from enumerating too much if not actually forbidden to go to confession frequently. But if there is no special reason, the normal process is that loving Christ urges us to a deeper, more humble and acceptable confession.

Not only before God but also before the People of God will we make this confession. This is the law of growth in penance. Those who are emerging from great darkness are subject to the optical laws of "light adaptation"; they are not so totally open that grace could fully wash their blindness away. They are not yet ready for a full penance, a full reparation and satisfaction. It is a sign of growth, a sign that continual conversion is going on if a person recognizes the need to do more penance, the need for a more profound conversion in thought, word and deed.

THE SECOND CONVERSION

It would be an error to assert that the Sacrament of Penance is the only means of promoting and testifying to continual conversion. The Council of Trent says clearly that several means are available to us and are to be chosen in freedom. Venial sins can be remitted in many ways, even without sacramental confession and absolution. Remission may be best achieved by frequent and humble reception of communion by which we are freed from our daily faults. Through loving conversation with the Lord in the Eucharist there is driven from the soul that laxity which is the source of most of our venial sins. The Eucharist has been instituted above all, instructs the Council of Trent, as a spiritual nourishment for the loving union with Christ and the members of His body. But because this unity is brought about through love, whose ardor brings to us not only the remission of guilt and punishment but also the internal transformation, we receive as a consequence the remission of sin and the deepening conversion in the measure of the fervor of our piety.

A growing fervor of piety demands growth in the spirit of penance. If the spirit of penance is lacking, if piety is wanting in that striving toward an ever deeper purification, and if one is careless regarding his venial sins, not only is the effectiveness of the Eucharist in blotting out venial sins lessened, but the fruitfulness of all the sacraments of the living is diminished and practically all means of salvation lose somewhat in efficacy.

It cannot be asserted that the reception of the Sacrament of Penance for those who have not sinned mortally would be absolutely necessary. However, it would be understood that the confession of mortal sin is only the minimum of the law, obliging all under the sanction of forfeiture of eternal life. Confession of one's known mortal sins stakes one's eternal life. He has to confess at least by the following Easter; however, he cannot defer his conversion until the next Easter. One must be immediately converted. One must do everything necessary to be converted because there is no greater evil in life than to remain one hour in the darkness of mortal sin.

If one contemptuously refuses the most efficacious means being offered by the Lord, he fails to arrive at a real conversion. But nobody is under absolute obligation to confess as soon as possible after having sinned mortally. Notwithstanding, he must do his very best to regain God's friendship through a perfect act of contrition, and this, as soon as possible. It is not uncommon to find persons who will not regain their peace of heart until after the reception of the Sacrament of Penance.

For any Christian under the law of grace, it is essential that he view Christian life in its totality. It becomes evident that in this time when both doctrine and practice are more clearly developed, one cannot easily refuse the reception of the Sacrament without diminishing his possibilities of continual growth and continual conversion.

According to the *Constitution on the Sacred Liturgy*, it is through Eucharistic piety especially that one gains a growing awareness of the sanctity of God and acquires the holy fear of God. The Christian can only experience the joy of Easter if he encounters the all-holy God. If he feels the need for purification as the Prophet Isaiah who was not in mortal sin when he saw the mystery of God's holiness and cried, "I am a lost man. . . . I must die because I saw the God of the universe, I being a man with impure lips and living among sinners" (Is. 6:1-5). He was then purified by the fire that came from the altar of the Most High. So if a Catholic wishes to grow in true Eucharistic piety, he will also feel the need for conversion which comes from the very fire of the love of the altar, from the cross of the Lord. So he gratefully accepts the Sacrament of Penance as a sign of continual conversion.

The confession as a sign of the continual conversion has the blessing of the first beatitude: "How blessed are those who know that they are poor, because on them is the kingdom of God." To "know that we are poor sinners," and the other words, "blessed are the sorrowful because they receive consolation," aptly apply to the free reception of the Sacrament of Penance. The Council of Trent has rightly stated that sometimes those who receive the Sacrament with fervor experience a tremendous joy and consolation. God Himself extends the comfort of the beatitudes to draw us to the altar with a more childlike fear of God, with the experience of God's bliss.

SPIRITUAL DIRECTION

The sacrament of continual conversion is a service, and the confessor, as incumbent in that office of the Church, should consider his correlative role of spiritual director or spiritual guide to the penitent. He should not act as though it were just a matter of giving absolution. If people receive the sacrament as a sign of continual conversion, then they wish the special help of the Church for their growth. The confessor must help the penitent to a greater and better knowledge of his conscience so as to bring about a more maturely integrated Christian life in the love of God and fellowman.

Spiritual direction should not be viewed as an accessory service for a few; the spiritual tradition recommends it very much as a special purpose of confession, not as something artificial or arbitrary. It should bear on the heart of the difficulties, dealing with the real life problems; that is the task of the spiritual director.

FREQUENT RECEPTION OF THE SACRAMENT OF PENANCE

Practices which essentially are left to the freedom of the individual should never be promoted by way of correction and discrimination; only a necessary minimum can be urged by human authority. If one is aware of having sinned mortally, then it can be pointed out to him to what dangers he exposes himself if he refuses to go to confession. But a pastor should never try to obtain frequent reception of Penance and the Eucharist by shouting and casting blame on the penitent. There is only one way open: to celebrate the mystery of the Sacrament of Penance with joy and thus let all be invited to come. We should preach the good tidings, the values, the invitation of the Lord through this sacrament. We should make the faithful feel that they are urged not by an external law but by the compelling love of Christ, by the hope that one wishes to grow in sanctity.

The confessor himself may exhort the penitent, as he would a friend, to respond to the invitation of Christ more frequently. However, he must do it without blaming the penitent if he fails to come often. We wish to have mature Christians who act in liberty and not under pressure.

FREQUENCY OF COMMUNION

Most of the practicing faithful receive the sacrament of continual conversion at least every Paschal season. By a law of the universal Church, we are not obliged to go to confession during Easter time; we are only obliged to go to communion. The obligation arises for confession at Easter time only when one has sinned mortally, but I feel that good Christians have no difficulty in coming to confession at this time without being strictly obliged.

Some may be deceiving themselves by thinking that not having committed any mortal sin, they have no need whatsoever of annual confession. It is possible to go through life in a state of grace, but one should look closely to the need for greater effort and the need of the purifying action of the Lord. In its pastoral directory relating to the administration of the Sacrament of Penance (No. 45), the French episcopate has this to say: "Even though confession of venial sins is not required before every real reception of Holy Communion, yet the frequent reception of Holy Communion suggests and invites us to a correspondingly frequent reception of the Sacrament of Penance which is of particular value in the attainment of true purity of conscience."

The pretext that the present practice of devotional confession in the Western Church is contrary to the practice of the early Church, as shown by studies regarding the history of penance is, in my opinion, utterly absurd. The early Church did far more than we are doing today to maintain the lofty ideal and a living spirit of penance among all the faithful. If one claims that the early Church did not do this, then he should join the early Church in his penances.

It should be borne in mind that there is a developmental aspect of the Sacrament of Penance that is frequently overlooked; it pertains to the development of the rich treasure of faith not merely on the level of doctrine but also in discipline and practice.

Priests should receive this sacrament frequently in view

of their celebrating daily the mystery of God's holiness, the Eucharist. In the codification of Canon Law, there is no exact definition provided for "frequently"; there is no law about weekly confession. It has been my experience in many countries that good priests generally go to confession once or twice a month or every week. When living at great distances, they go once a month, but then, they take it more seriously. Religious are generally obliged by the present legislation to confess every week; this comes as a directive of Canon Law and as a rule of their respective congregation or order; but in my opinion, it is not a law that obliges under sin. It is an ideal towards which they should strive if there are no special reasons precluding doing so. The confessor can—and sometimes must—exhort religious who are scrupulous that it is better for them to come on a once-a-month basis or even more seldom. He may also advise them to confess only one or two sins and only those sins which they really wish to correct and amend.

By far the more important question is not how often we should go to confession but *how* we should go. If after every sin we bring ourselves to an act of sorrow and humble trust in God in view of the signs of His great mercy, then the hour of the Sacrament of Penance will find us better prepared. It is more beneficial to go twice a month and make a really serious confession with thorough preparation, with a good purpose of amendment, than to go every day or every week with less earnestness. In itself, frequent reception is no danger, but we tend to make it a routine if we do so superficially. The effort must be to celebrate it as a real encounter with the Risen Lord, an encounter with the suffering Lord, an encounter with the Christ who will come to be our judge.

On general confession, you can find a more thorough treatment in *The Law of Christ* (Vol. I, pp. 466-467). It is unfortunate that many priests, especially those preaching missions, have sometimes given the impression that most confessions are unworthy and that therefore most of the faithful ought to make a general confession. It should be made absolutely clear that God has given this sacrament of mercy in a way that everyone who has some good will truly receives it worthily, even if he is not skilled in these matters or has not confessed according to the scientific terminology in vogue among theologians. Cases of really unworthy confessions, of a truly sacrilegious reception of the sacrament may exist; but they should be considered exceptional. In such cases, the penitent is obliged to confess all the mortal sins which he committed since his last valid confession. However, if he returns to the same confessor, it is sufficient for that priest to be able to remember in a general way what the penitent confessed in the past, and he can tell him that all these sins are included, and then add those sins that he has not yet confessed.

Sometimes the confession of sins already submitted to the Keys of the Church can be wholesome, especially if there is a prudent doubt about the previous confession, but this only if the penitent is not scrupulous. If a scrupulous person doubts, he must never be allowed to confess his sins again. If he cannot swear without fear of hell that he has made an unworthy confession, never allow him to re-confess his past sins. It is a grave danger to keep looking back and never forward. Therefore, for these people who are always living in retrospect, constantly re-examining their past, they should be helped to rechannel their energies in more productive ways.

If those who are obliged to make general confessions are anxious to be complete, the confessor should explain to them the meaning of integrity, good will, and the avoidance of scrupulosity. If one wishes to make a general confession without having doubts about the validity of early confessions, it can be wholesome provided he is not a scrupulous person. St. Thomas says that through frequent sacramental confession there is effected a greater remission of the penalty due to sin both because of the humiliation in the self-accusation which is considered a penitential act, and because of the power of the Keys of the Church. It is good to make a general confession in great moments of life, for instance when embarking on a religious life, before receiving Holy Orders, for lay people before marriage, on retreats, etc. The theological reason is that if one, by the grace of God, has a deeper understanding of what sin is and what his own sins are, and confesses these with greater humility and deeper sorrow and purpose of amendment, he opens himself to greater sacramental awareness. He shows in this way that he has a clearer perception of the state of his past life and the grace of God, and that the purification and grace of perseverance are nothing less than a gift of God.

But a priest should never promote general confessions by asserting that most past confessions were probably invalid. The priest's keen sense of discrimination should make clear that evidently, at the beginning of a conversion, after a long time away from the sacraments, the first confessions are likely to be imperfect. They could not be as perfect as they will become later as the result of time spent in faithful service to the Lord.

If one freely makes a general confession, then he should be told that there is no obligation to make a complete confession of all mortal sins previously absolved, especially sins regarding the sixth commandment. As St. Alphonsus used to tell people who were making a general confession with some scrupulosity, they should make better use of their time: *potius piis meditationibus tempus impendant.*

22. DIFFERENT STATES
OF LIFE

The proclamation of peace which also urges the necessary commitment of a future striving toward a fuller life in Christ must be related to the actuality of this person's life, innervating his whole situation, respectful always of his sex, age and environment. It is of importance then, that the confessor know with whom he is dealing. If he does not know his penitent, then he should bring the penitent to declare: I am a butcher, an innkeeper, a married man with ten children, a good Catholic wife, and the like. Such statements help the confessor treat his penitents accordingly.

THE CONFESSIONS OF CHILDREN

Should children be obliged to go to confession before their first communion? We cannot forbid the practice. If the confessor is prudent and knows how to deal with children, it can benefit the children to go to confession before their first communion. But there is no obligation in this sense. Several dioceses recommend that children first go to communion. Normally, a child should be prepared by his parents to receive his first Holy Communion by the age of five or six; the rationale is simple: they have more time than any other adult to talk informally to the children. Enlisting the cooperation of the parents in this noble task contributes to a stronger family life by making sacramental life an important element of it. In addition, children internalize more readily the religious values exemplified and taught by their parents, their first identification figures, than from any other source. When parents tend to neglect their children, it may be that the children are not ready even at eight years of age. However children are taught, when it comes to the Sacrament of Penance, they should never learn stereotyped phrases and formulas. In a way that they can understand, the parents should explain to them how they have offended the Lord. They should confess rather few concrete examples, such as: "When my mother asked me if I had hit my sister, I replied no—but I had. I knew I was lying." "I have a nice little sister but I am jealous of her because she is liked more than I am. I am not so good to the others; but I try not to be jealous." These are examples in terms of a child's level of comprehension.

The confessor should never pursue his questioning with, "What else did you do wrong?" Rather, he would help the child by an explanation of how, on the points he has mentioned, a greater effort would please the Lord, and then the Lord would be pleased to help him. The confessor then explains what the Lord is doing now: He purifies hearts, prepares them so that they can go to communion with greater confidence. "He has prepared you through His word: your sins are forgiven."

Is our present practice of having children go to confession at a specified time every month a good one? In cases where they are closely supervised and accounted for, they may feel compelled to go to confession even when they are not ready for it; they may feel that they are discriminated against when they are told, during general confession sessions for adults, that they should go at the time assigned for school children. Evidently, the practice is not a good one, since there is no divine law obliging them. How then, can we oblige them and discriminate against them if they do not come? The pastor can invite the children to come to confession on a certain day at a certain time, but the children must always feel that they are free children of God. They should not feel that the confessor or the pastor is imposing laws that are not made by God or by the universal Church. We should rather attract children to confession through proper celebration of the Sacrament of Penance, such that they gain true appreciation of the greatness of God's grace. Let it be clear to them that it is not only the penitent's own effort to become better but it is the acting word of the Lord that makes him sure of the friendship of the Lord and that makes him grow up to fuller friendship with Him. It is the action of Christ that gives full value to our own effort. It would be helpful to have the children know that they are not obliged to any material integrity as long as they are not capable of committing a mortal sin.

The most rigid opinion would maintain that after ten years, children are capable of mortal sin. As I said before, I doubt if the average child of eleven, twelve or thirteen can commit a mortal sin. They must first know what a mortal sin is which the merciful and just God punishes with a terrible sentence for all eternity. However, we must drive home to them the importance of their effort towards the good life in view of their future development. It is not in a moment that a child or a man decides his destiny; it is through the whole of his life.

Every exaggeration is harmful to the sacrament of mercy. Therefore, it is clear doctrine that children are not obliged to confess unless they are conscious of having committed a mortal sin; and for a mortal sin, clear deliberation and sufficient freedom are necessary. The priest's efforts cannot be limited to leading the child to proper differentiation of right and wrong in terms of the Ten Commandments; the focal learning centers on the understanding of the New Law, the law of grace, and how they can express their gratitude to the Lord for such a great sacrament, especially through a compassionate and forbearing love for others. On the one hand, children should never be encouraged to make a scrupulous enumeration of all their sins and shortcomings; on the other, they should learn to attend to their motives. Since motives are most decisive in the process of continuous conversion, children should make them an object of their examination of conscience and humble confession. Thus the priest will be in a position to help them more effectively on the road toward Christian maturity. They will also understand better the message of peace which brings order into man's mind and heart.

How often should children confess? Here one cannot lay down any general rule; it depends very much on circumstances. If the parish is small and the pastor has enough time for adults and children alike, it is good that the children go to confession often, say once a month if they are going to Mass and communion occasionally during the week. But if the size of the parish imposes heavy and urgent obligations on the pastor, it would be inadvisable to urge children to confess every month. It would only result in "getting confession in" superficially and hurriedly on the part of both, the pastor and the child. This would encourage routine and external sacramentalism. If there is to be change along the lines of children's confessions, I would suggest provision for some continuity. My own preference is not to have the compulsory school-time confessions. The ideal would be for the confessors to give the children an opportunity for some kind of communal celebration of the penitential rite or to arrange for regular confession sessions at the days of their own choice. Children should be invited to come to confession with their parents. All should know that they can come anytime for confession.

But if until now the class type of confession was urged, then we should not make an abrupt change during this time of transition. One could consider the possibility of reducing "class confessions" to three or four times a year in a big parish, telling the children that they can come to confession any time. They should be taught at an early age to make their own decisions, for only then do they witness to the freedom of the children of God and show a real spirit of gratitude and spontaneity. The use of various pressure techniques in

DIFFERENT STATES OF LIFE

imposing monthly confession for every child will only lead to dislike for the sacrament and avoidance of it once they leave school. One cannot gauge success by having *all* the children go to confession; it would be a success only if they come freely and learn to make their own decision. They should realize that confession is not a matter for school only but their right and privilege as children of God when they are freely responding to the invitation of the Lord.

THE CONFESSIONS OF SEMINARIANS

Seminarians should have a great appreciation of frequent confession, for the reception of this sacrament indicates a desire on their part to place themselves more serviceably within the pale of the Kingdom of God, professing their strong allegiance to the Law of Grace. Frequent confession will rally the initiatives dulled by venial sin and alert the seminarian to his promise of a fervent response to the call of God and to His every grace. Seminarians have a special right to the help of a spiritual director who can encourage them on the road to sanctity. But here again there should be no legal compulsion, no rule that one has to confess every week or month or at a certain time. Give them opportunities for confession during the daytime, but place them under no compulsion; they must learn to be witnesses to the freedom of the sons of God. Help them learn to appreciate the liturgy of the sacraments, especially the liturgy of penance as a great gift of God. The communal celebration of the Sacrament is most fitting for seminarians, but should not lead to a depreciation of individual confession. We have a special obligation not to block their gratitude, the great Easter joy of the sacrament, by misguided legalism. Scrupulous seminarians are usually advised not to confess too frequently. Since seminarians are encouraged to have a regular confessor, the scrupulous can generally be restricted to monthly confession or less. Many boys have transitory periods of scrupulosity from which they can be liberated much more easily if they are told not to confess too often. The confessor can even advise them to wait eight weeks until their next confession, but they could be advised to make an act of contrition and deep confidence in God every evening.

The celebration of the Sacrament of Penance in the case of seminarians usually is guided by two aspects of the kingdom of God: (1) that one is to be led by the Spirit, by the law of grace, the law of the Spirit in gratitude; (2) the rallying call of the kingdom of God: that their whole life is to be penetrated by the spirit of response to God, generosity toward the call of God, towards every grace, and they should see every grace as given in view of the building up of the Mystical Body through the spirit of responsibility in generosity and solidarity. Besides, from the very significance of the sacrament, this should be pointed out so that they learn to consider the whole of their life in the perspective of a social achievement of salvation, in a spirit of freedom, generosity, and at the same time, in a spirit of responsibility towards God and the community.

THE PROBLEM OF CHASTITY FOR SEMINARIANS

What is true for all adolescents and for all people applies in a very urgent way for seminarians, namely the necessity of integration of one's life: the problems of chastity are not to be isolated from the whole of Christian life. They must learn to see the values of chastity in view of celibacy and marriage. They should be brought to realize that they are still potential candidates for either vocation; they cannot yet be sure of their call. Therefore both celibacy and marriage must be presented to them and they must learn to respect their own sexuality and the bodies of others, *i.e.*, the person of the other.

The sixth commandment and its usual negative overtones should be approached differently, stressing the great beauty and values of chastity in the light of celibacy for the kingdom of God and in the light of marriage. For instance, marriage is to be presented as in the fifth chapter of Ephesians or the seventh chapter of First Corinthians: that those who are married should have freedom to work for the kingdom of God in a way similar to the freedom of the unmarried. It must be shown first of all that the maturity of the personality is the condition of chastity in all states of life. Masturbation is frequently (but not always) a sign of a retarded or arrested development of the personality. Maturity in relation to personality development precludes self-centeredness. Masturbation is often an expression of self-centeredness: victims are not yet open enough to their neighbor and to God. If they wish to overcome their difficulties—many have difficulties in this respect without their being "bad boys"—they must strive toward maturity, the full maturity of the personality, to a very personal way of prayer life, to a very vigilant watchfulness in the ways they can do good for their fellowman; how they can be good comrades, how they can show the spirit of sportsmanship and solidarity in athletics, and their social responsibility in school and in their daily lives.

Judgment of their worthiness for the priesthood should not be made on the basis of this one item, especially in the minor seminary; no judgment can be made against their vocation when boys of 15-17 years have difficulties with masturbation. A judgment as to their fitness for the priesthood can be made only in the light of the total personality: their prayer life, their reverence and love of God, their attraction to the liturgy, their active membership in the family life of the seminary, and their initiative.

It is not uncommon to overrate passive obedience to superiors. Very often masturbation difficulties and great passivity, seemingly great docility in obedience, go hand in hand. One is obedient because he possesses no will of his own. In most masturbation cases, since childhood their will was broken and so they are externally obedient—they always avoid difficulties with superiors and others—and in yielding to the stronger, they also yield to their sexual desires. Therefore, confessors need to be alerted to this kind of obedience. Boys who sometimes manifest willfulness, who indicate their inability to understand all the commands of their superiors, these give us greater hope that they will be able to overcome this problem. If the confessor and all the other personnel of the seminary work together to break the will of the students just to make them obedient and to have them conform to a pattern, it becomes hopeless to educate them to maturity and to attempt to break a habit of masturbation.

At times, difficulties of this kind cannot be resolved satisfactorily in the confessional alone. Professors and instructors must be gentle in helping the boys, allowing them freedom, educating them towards initiative, and so on. There are cases, of course, where boys of 16-18 are frequently masturbating and not cooperating with their spiritual directors in overcoming this habit; then it is a sign that they are not called to the priesthood. But if they are cooperating and striving to be of service to others, taking the initiative of building up a better spirit in the seminary, trying to find ways of doing good without being commanded to do so, then we can have confidence that they will also overcome their difficulties in this one matter. Non-cooperation must not be seen solely in the light of their actual difficulties. If by the time one enters the major seminary he shows no signs of overcoming masturbation and at the same time does not show a good character in other things, the confessor should advise him to choose another vocation or profession. When he becomes a man and a good Christian, he can once more examine the question of whether he has a vocation to the priesthood.

The confessor's first obligation is not to educate seminarians to be monks or priests but to be good Christians. This is also the primary condition for a real vocation.

THE CHOICE OF A VOCATION OR PROFESSION

Confessors have a duty to help penitents in the right choice of a vocation since it involves one of the most decisive judgments which a Christian has to make, both for his personal salvation and for the Church on the whole. The confessor needs to bear in mind, therefore, the individual's own salvation, his personality, and the common good. Individual salvation always has to be achieved within the social environment. The more a Christian is directed in his whole approach toward the social achievement of salvation, the more his individual salvation will be assured.

In the Sacrament of Penance, the confessor represents the Church. As a spiritual director, he can make known to penitents that what best fits their personal capabilities is also best for the Church, for everyone has to find the individual name by which God has called him. The Christian gives his individual contribution in order to build up the Mystical Body in its unity and variety.

A confessor is rightly mindful of the recruitment of vocations to the priesthood, to the brotherhood, sisterhood or religious orders in general. What would American Catholicism be without its Sisters? The whole system of Catholic schools would be impossible. Not only would the schools be lacking, but also a witness to the real freedom of the children of God, generosity, total dedication to the service of God and man. Therefore a confessor must do his best to foster vocations which God may be preparing, always, of course, in the spirit of freedom.

Vatican Council II teaches that all Christians are sharers in the vocation of the whole Church to an ever greater sanctity. Everyone is called to sanctity; at the same moment, it asserts that everyone is to fulfill a specific role within the whole Church.

How can we promote vocations? The first effort should never be to awaken vocations for one's own congregation or order: either for the priesthood or religious life. The first effort must be to educate Christians who live "not under law, but under grace" (Rom. 6:14). Those living under the law, i.e., legalists who only ask what they must do to avoid mortal or venial sin, are not prepared for the choice of a vocation. They will never understand the loftiness and dignity of a priestly or religious vocation nor will they truly understand the vocation to the married state.

Young Christians who early in their life ask first what they can do to return to God whatever he gave them, how they can please God and express spontaneously their gratitude to him for all the gifts he has given them, these are the generous people ready to respond to the Lord's beckoning.

A man who is urged only by the question of what he should do to avoid mortal sin is not capable of heeding the call of God. God's invitation to the priesthood and especially the religious vocation is a call to liberty. But the real liberty of the sons and daughters of God begins when one surrenders oneself totally to God and lets himself be led by the Spirit of God (Gal. 5:25). Since the Spirit is our life, let us be led by the Spirit. This is the great principle of St. Paul, and it must be the basic motive of the Christian, *i.e.*, to live under the law of grace, to live according to the beatitudes, to come ever nearer to the great commandment, "Love one another as I have loved you."

It is of great importance, when speaking of vocations, to emphasize the freedom of the sons of God. What does this complete freedom mean? It means, for instance, that no human authority, either of parents or the confessor, can compel the person concerned to follow this or that vocation. Complete freedom means that a person has no other motive or intention than to please the Lord. He accepts the gifts of God, the action of the Holy Spirit, the needs of his neighbors, as the rule and measure of his life.

When referring to vocations, marriage, of course, is included. The great Protestant theologian, Karl Barth, wrote in one of the volumes of his *Church Dogmatics*[1] that the Catholic Church is, without doubt, faithful to Holy Scripture in her teaching with regard to virginity, but he makes an application which many priests forget. Marriage can become a vocation only for those who know that they are not condemned to marriage, for those who make their choice only after they have reflected on whether it is in marriage that they can better fulfill their role for the kingdom of God or in a state of celibacy. Only after having reflected with the one intention of doing whatever God wills can marriage become a vocation to them.

The preaching of virginity in the Church is a condition for a good vocation to the married state, so that marriage does not become only an earthly thing, but a vocation, a role in

---

[1] German edition, III-4, p. 164.

the Church. A final consideration is that not only religious life but the priesthood and marriage must be considered and subsumed under "vocation."

Also, a Christian will be more relevant to his milieu if he chooses an occupation or profession in civil life with a view to charity. Where can he do the most for the common good, and where can he best fulfill his apostolic task? If all Christians would look upon occupations and professions in the social and economic spheres as a service for the common good, then our whole society would be much healthier. Then we would also have enough religious vocations. Everyone must be led to understand the importance of priests, brothers and religious in the life of the Church.

THE CONFESSIONS OF PRIESTS AND RELIGIOUS

In view of the importance of priests and religious in the life of the Church, the confessors and spiritual directors must be aware of their special role in relation to them. They have to be generous with their time for spiritual counselling and the hearing of confessions. As these men and women are devoting their whole lives to the welfare of the Church, they deserve to have the Church take the best possible care of them by providing not only good preachers, but also good confessors. Everyone who is responsible for hearing the confessions of priests and religious must prepare himself by study and reflection, and ask himself how he can best fulfill his assignment.

Religious and priests must be witnesses to the freedom of the sons and daughters of God, and therefore, they must be aware that they have been called to sanctity in such an outstanding way that they are witnesses to Christians in general of each individual's call to sanctity.

In the formation of the consciences of religious and priests, the importance of obedience to the bishop or religious superior calls for consideration. Thoughtless and uncharitable criticism of superiors is to be presented to them as directly spoiling the divine milieu, the environment of charity that must prevail. Generally, confessors can help them not only through exhortations but also through penances. It is a good penance for those who like to criticize the bishop or superior of a community to say one "Our Father" for the man before criticizing him, and to pray to God that he is being criticized through love for Him. If they criticize before they pray, then they should pray much more for him and for themselves; they may eventually come to realize that they themselves need to be converted first.

But the right of discernment belongs to Christians as well as to those who witness to the Christian life, namely, priests and religious. They are entitled to ask the question, "Does our Superior act clearly in accordance with the Gospel, or do we not have the obligation to speak, to score his not doing so?" Perhaps he is opposed to the spirit of the New Law as expressed in the Sermon on the Mount which contains the whole spirit of the Gospel, the spirit of the evangelical counsels.

The *Corpus Iuris Canonici* in use before 1918 had a special chapter *de peccato taciturnitatis*, inculcating a proper fraternal correction toward prelates. It admonished Christians under pain of sin to have the courage to give fraternal correction to superiors. For instance, if a bishop in our difficult times displays an attitude of hesitancy toward the decrees of the Council, Christians of the whole diocese and other bishops, by appropriate means, should make him aware of the great scandal he is causing. These are exceptional cases, but there are also a number of priests and bishops who do manifest this spirit of resistance to the renewal of the Church and are thereby doing great harm to the Church which they intend to serve. If people would speak out on proper occasions and admonish them about this unwholesome and harmful attitude, they would be less likely to fall into this error. But we are obligated also to warn ourselves and our dear confrères that they are not to consider themselves infallible in all things as if the bishop and chancery were always wrong. It is in the Sacrament of Penance especially that we incur the obligation to form the consciences of our penitents on this point. It would help to remind them that they must reflect before they make a judgment in all those difficulties where they believe themselves to be right and the superiors wrong. We must help them to criticize themselves first.

The formation of conscience goes beyond the question of obedience to superiors and the Holy Rule. There is a more important aspect to be considered. First of all, let us try to form good Christians. This means viewing all things in the light of the fullness of time, under the law of grace, using the present opportunity (*kairos*) to the fullest, the opportunities to do good provided by God, being vigilant and watchful. By these virtues which are ranked so highly and granted so much dignity in the Gospel, priests and religious become witnesses to the time of grace, to the law of grace. Priests and religious who are our penitents would profit by guidance in the examination of conscience in the light of: "Was I mindful and vigilant for the present opportunity in the pursuit of perfect charity?" In the consideration of such matters, the first questions could be: "How can I express my gratitude to God? How can I love my neighbor as myself?" Or, one can stay by the New Testament, saying that we should love one another as Christ loves us.

Then could follow the duties of their state of life: the priesthood and the special tasks of the priest, brother or sister, which they have to fulfill. It is not uncommon for priests, religious men and women to forget to make an examination of conscience with regard to their specific duties, because they do not find this explicitly stated in the general *speculum conscientiae*. St. Alphonsus drew up a *Speculum Conscientiae* for bishops and sent it gratis to all the neighboring bishops. A chief rule for the confessor is: be more positive than negative. Perhaps remembering our many obligations to follow our vocation and the tasks we have to fulfill in the Mystical Body would be most pertinent. I recommend as helpful for this purpose Lebret and Suavet's work, *An Examination of Conscience for Modern Catholics*.

HEARING THE CONFESSIONS OF THE SICK

We have already treated some of these questions when we
dealt with the formation of conscience in relation to responsibility for our health. Everyone should devote his health to
the service of his fellowman and everyone is obliged to protect the health of others. Those who are assigned to hear the
confessions of the sick must realize that sickness is a special
means of salvation. One can explain gently to the sick person
how near their situation is to the mystery of the Lord's death,
the mystery of salvation. If they accept this explanation
generously, then they are close to the mystery of the resurrection. The confessor can help them utter a wholehearted
"yes" to their present situation.

This holds even if they are to some extent responsible for
their bad health or have exposed themselves to danger. It is
a matter of accepting the situation as a challenging call for
the following of Christ in his suffering: to do penance for
oneself, and penance and satisfaction for others; to use to the
fullest the present opportunity. The same applies for those
who are suffering from scrupulosity or some neurosis.

Not only bodily illness but mental sickness or neurosis need
be accepted. This kind of illness cannot be overcome, one
will not return to better health in the fullest sense if he does
not first accept his suffering, the limitation and the trouble.
Acceptance in love of his present condition will help one find
more easily his real possibilities to do good, to use construc-
tively whatever psychological strength remains.

In dealing with the sick, one cannot overlook the role of
Christian hope; in confession, the sick must continually return to this motive: nothing is lost for one who loves God.
All things turn to one's advantage and even to the best if
one surrenders himself to God and puts his trust in Him. We
should preach a real optimism about sickness, one stemming
from Christian hope, not an artificial one. This optimism
concerns eternal life and the full use here and now of the
'present opportunity.' This supernatural optimism embraces

all the natural faculties and is one of the great healing powers. He is convinced that "things are all right" if he accepts them from God. And of course, a man of Christian hope is not a pessimist as to the possibility of his regaining health.

For the seriously ill, the confessor would do well to inform them that they are not obliged to make a great effort as to the integrity of the confession. This effort is rendered impossible because of our hospital system where several persons share the same room in close proximity to one another. But even if they are alone, their illness may not allow them to go into matters with much detail. It may be that they expect to be asked by the confessor. But only if they express this desire to be questioned do we have to do so; even then, we should not get lost in details. After a while, it is better to tell them not to search for what they may have forgotten. If in better health later on, they can return to points they may not have confessed.

If a patient is seriously ill, a detailed inquisition would do them much harm. It is quite a disheartening experience for a person who has been seriously sick to have to confess and be questioned, point by point, making an examination of conscience according to the whole of Noldin or Tanquerey.

If the sick penitent has mentioned some essential points of Christian life the confessor may tell him that he has made a humble and sufficient effort. Sometimes they are in such poor condition that we have to explain: "It is sufficient for you to make an act of contrition which shows that you are sorry, that as a humble sinner before God, you wish forgiveness for your sins." Even if they cannot speak, they should hear that this suffices. Then they are sure that the words of the Lord, "Your sins are forgiven" are true for them and that it is not necessary to do more than they can. It will be a consolation for them to hear this stated explicitly.

Are we obliged to alert penitents if they are in danger of death? I have treated the question more explicitly in the *Law of Christ*, Volume III. If the penitents are in fairly good shape spiritually and have lived as good Christians receiving the sacraments etc., it is not up to the priest to warn them directly as to their imminent situation. Such duty belongs to the parents, the spouse, the children or closest of kin, who should explain the situation to the patient with the greatest charity. At times, the confessor does well to seek their help. But even the doctor's diagnosis that there is no hope for recovery leaves one open to hope that there still may be, because doctors are not omniscient.

If the sick are already prepared to accept their illness, they are indirectly prepared to accept death. Nevertheless, it is one of the greatest tasks of Christians to embrace consciously and directly the last call of God, the call to the highest priestly function of the People of God: to unite their death to the death of Christ.

A confessor bears some responsibilty for bringing the sick person to the realization that this hour may have come. At least generally in his talks, he may inspire the thought, "Whenever God calls me, I am ready." It is one of the greatest comforts of Christian life to be able to say this. The question becomes more difficult if the sick person does not realize his danger and refuses to make his confession. The confessor's task is then a difficult one and he must pray to find the right expression. Very kindly, he can approach the patient with, "Even if there is only some possibility that the sickness could become dangerous, that is reason enough now to receive the sacraments." If they have made their confession, and if we are kind and gentle, and make clear to them what it means to be sure, then we can compensate for the initial shock that may be injurious to health.

At all times we must do this with the greatest gentleness; nevertheless, the moment may come when we can be more insistent. But if we have found another person who can do it, if the close members of the family are available, it is better for them to perform this task. But sometimes we have to do it. We are then performing one of the greatest services of charity if we do it with kindness and gentleness, making the sick person aware that now is the time to prepare himself for his final response, "Lord, here I am."

23. THE CONFESSIONS OF
SCRUPULOUS PEOPLE[1]

Modern psychology helps us distinguish various phenomena, different anxieties or difficulties, and pathological situations which previously were labelled "scrupulosity." It is imperative that the confessor distinguish at least the principal forms of so-called scrupulosity.

There can be a time of awakened conscience when men, who until now lived on a superficial level in a false certainty or security, are shocked by a deep experience—a fear of God, love of God—so that for a period of time they lose all certitude and firmness of conscience which they previously had on a superficial level. Instead of viewing the situation as pathological, it should be viewed as a symptom of growth, a time when such a man needs to be guided to a deeper understanding of the call of God, moving away from superficial certitude or an unhealthy fear.

There is also scrupulosity due to a neurotic fixation and this can take different forms: one of these is the anxiety neurosis. This can be a general anxiety, not limited to one area, just a fearful attitude in general; it differs from fear in that the

[1] See B. Häring, *The Law of Christ*, vol. I, the long chapter on this topic, pp. 157-169.

object of fear is not focalized, is not known. To some extent, this is an outgrowth of childhood experiences; for example, if a father was cruel and tyrannical, if he punished his children too much and too often, or if the mother was anxious and fearful toward the father. A family climate such as this often gives rise to a psychological experience ascribing such characteristics to God himself: a God who is out to catch man in every misdeed and find him worthy of hell. This image of God, deeply impressed on the scrupulous person by a terrifying experience in regard to the father, is continued by the catechist, the priest, and then by a confessor who says, "You are the best food for the devil." After an anxious, excited confession in which the scrupulous penitent always exaggerates his situation, nothing can help more than the presentation of the image of Christ as the good shepherd, the image of the heavenly Father. The confessor should indeed represent the understanding and kindness of God; the whole celebration of the Sacrament of Penance is the proclamation of the goodness of God. But the confessor must also help these persons to a deeper understanding of the origin of their trouble and to a resolution to accept the suffering while doing what they can to change it.

Anxiety often goes together with a fixation in one area; psychologically, the problem becomes very difficult and very different from the above. There is also a great difference if the anxiety is fixed to an essential commandment, for example, charity, fraternal correction, chastity or truthfulness. Here you have a soul that desires the essential, but the education became fixated at one point, and resulted in lopsidedness. Excessive emphasis placed on one duty or on one virtue has an obliquely morbid effect on the emotions, produces anxious forebodings regarding the future and disturbs the whole emotional life. To a great extent, one can see it as a problem of integration, one of helping such persons find their freedom, their joy in other areas. Help them to fulfill the good they can do in other things and tell them clearly that they should not give so much attention to this point for a certain time. The greater the attention given to this one point, the more will they be blocked and the whole of their life stunted. If their concern is the sixth commandment, this together with anxiety can produce continual temptation and trouble. Help them accept the suffering while, at the same time, learning to develop their energies and realize their potential in other areas, especially in the area of fraternal charity. They could focus on bringing joy to others.

Very different from this anxiety neurosis is the compulsive-neurotic scrupulosity. Very often the concern here is anxiety over legalistic quibbling. In the depths of their soul, they sometimes wish to appear as very conscientious people and so they are very, very conscientious regarding the eucharistic fast, for instance, refusing to receive communion if they have broken the fast by one minute less than what was prescribed by the law. Once Father Cappello gave a lecture in which he said that one was to interpret the law of fasting in a human way, and that not everyone has to keep an eye on the clock to make sure it has been the exact amount of time before receiving communion. After this, Father Hürth insisted in his lecture that an hour has 60 minutes and every minute has 60 seconds and if one second is lacking, then you simply do not have one hour. There must be the full readiness to bring a sacrifice, but not the fixation which some have on seconds.

The compulsive neurotic can make his life miserable on a number of other counts. He would rather die than eat meat on a Lenten Friday even if he is invited to the home of a dear Protestant friend who did not remember or did not know Catholic legislation for Lent. The scrupulous person of this kind would refuse to eat the meat in spite of the fact that he would be extremely upset about offending his friends. He keeps the laws very punctiliously. He is blind to fundamental moral issues if they are not clearly proposed in legal form. If he seems oblivious to the essential moral values and commandments, this is due to this nearsightedness causing him to focus only on the clear-cut rules and precepts. In many instances, the individual has progressively built up this psychological structure through the repeated reinforcements provided by a legalistic training.

Another form of neurotic compulsion is a tendency toward .

self-assurance; the obsessive-compulsive individuals, the one-hundred percenters, the perfectionists. Such a person is continually excited and remembers the 100% in one area and forgets the 99% in all others. He is not striving toward Christian perfection and growth; he just wants to be exact in small things, especially if the religious and moral formation overemphasized these things. The whole of his nature is directed toward these things and the psychological conditions favor it. It then becomes a very legalistic form of scrupulosity. This is very different from other forms of scrupulosity of noble souls regarding the duties and responsibilities which they may share with others. The legalistically-restrained scrupulous person does not even think that the great virtue of the Christian is to be vigilant, to see the present opportunities and to use them to the fullest. He is arrested in his thinking. It takes education and much patience to lead him to the first steps, to see the examination of conscience in this way: was I vigilant, did I use the great opportunities, was I understanding toward the feeling for my neighbor? Did I try to help him for his own good?

There can also be a scrupulosity of compensation, or as modern psychology labels it, cases of reaction formation. Such a scrupulous person feels the need to strive toward the fulfillment of the great commandment of love of God and neighbor, but when faced with a real Christian life situation, he is unfaithful. Lacking the humility to appear a sinner before his own eyes and those of his fellowmen, he goes to extremes, into the very small details of canon law; he becomes obsessed with a few questions of law or the Holy Rule. More or less unconsciously, he can hide his lack of conscience behind this "scrupulous personality."

All these forms have deep roots in the experiences of one's early childhood, in the helpless psychological dispositions or the wrong moral instruction of a legal-minded teacher or confessor. It is important that we distinguish the various forms of scrupulosity. If we are inept in this area, unable to make the discriminations called for, it would be advisable to refer such a penitent to a confessor especially adept in the handling of such cases. In very complex cases, the penitent may need the help of a depth psychologist or a psychiatrist.

A right *praxis confessarii* where the confessor sees the proper hierarchy of values, where he first of all proclaims the peace of God, where he directs the whole attention of the penitent toward God and helps him to free himself from self-centeredness, has in itself a great healing power. One of the great Protestant spiritual writers, Tersteegen, was convinced that constant concern with self merely made men ill, and that health was restored through the contemplation of God and concern for one's neighbor. At any rate, he was certainly on a safer path than those confessors and directors of souls who have their penitents occupied with themselves all the time. The formation of conscience through the great commandment of love of God and man helps men to accept their suffering, to realize their limitations, to find, step by step, their real possibilities of freedom. If the confessor, in addition to his assimilation of the Gospel of the Good Shepherd, has deep psychological insight, he can do more good. Therefore, he must try to acquire a good psychological formation.

CONCLUSION

Theology and the modern sciences provide us with various and precious insights. However, knowledge helps us to convey the message of peace only if we are men of faith, and love the persons to whom we speak. We are not sent to analyze "cases" but to witness to God's compassionate love. Therefore, it is faith and love that enable and oblige the confessor to perceive and to fulfill his role and to "know" those to whom he is sent.

As messenger of peace, the confessor does not occupy the chief place; he is to be, rather, like John the Baptist, pointing with his whole existence to Christ and manifesting His love. It is Christ Himself who through the ministers of the Church proclaims peace and makes known the heavenly Father's compassionate love. It is He who brings with His peace the order of love and justice. Only His life-giving law can liberate man from the slavery of sin.

The highest function of the confessor is to hide himself behind the person of Christ and to testify through his own person to the presence of Christ, to lead the penitent to the deep experience that it is Christ Himself whom he encounters, who asks him, "Are you my friend?" and who gives his peace. And with his peace comes the invitation, "Come, follow me." Then will the penitent understand better what it means to be invited by the Lord to be His disciple and friend, and thus fulfill the test of a Christ-like life by completion of the great commandment in all things, in all those situations calling for love of one's neighbor as the Lord has loved us.

The love of the Lord experienced in the Sacrament of Penance is a redeeming love. The confessor who is permeated with the redeeming love of Christ, in deep gratitude, in great humility, can communicate this redeeming love. Redeemed love can lead to the experience of the redeeming love of Christ. All other things must be seen in the essential light of Christ, His wonderful presence, His powerful word, and the new way He paves for us, the new life He opens to us.

APPENDIX

COMMUNAL CELEBRATION OF PENANCE AND PEACE

---

1. *Entrance Procession.*
   Entrance Hymn.
   Celebrants and assistants proceed to the altar; reverence at the altar; they then proceed to their respective chairs in the sanctuary.

   President: "To Him who loves us and has redeemed us from our sins through His blood, who has called us to penance and peace to become a kingdom of priests before God and Father, to Him be glory and power now and forever."

   All: "Amen."

   First Assistant: "Please, Father, your blessing."

   President: "May the Lord be in your heart and on your lips that you may properly confess all your sins together with us. In the name of the Father and of the Son, and of the Holy Spirit."

   All: "Amen."

2. *1st Reading:* Book of Daniel, 9:3-19.

   Appropriate examination of conscience according to the special needs of the community. After every question, all repeat:

"Have mercy, Lord, for we have sinned."

Schola sings Psalm 50. After every verse, all repeat:

"Have mercy, Lord, for we have sinned."

3. *2nd Reading:* John 21:15-23 (or another Gospel on Christ's power to forgive sins). Homily.

4. *Service of Repentance*

All: "O Lord, open my mouth to praise you in humble confession; fuse into my heart a new spirit."

President: "We are not only guilty, brothers and sisters, toward God, our Father, and our Lord Jesus Christ by taking the grace of the Holy Spirit for nothing, but we are also guilty toward the community of the Church. Through our sins, love grew cold within the body of Christ which is the Church. Hence, we confess our sins before God and before one another."

All: "I confess to Almighty God. . . ."

(After the words, "through my most grievous fault," a pause for individual examination of conscience)

"Therefore I beseech . . ."

5. Individual confessions. All those who want to confess go to the priest of their choice. No introductory form is used. According to the liturgical legislation of the country or diocese, the priest gives the individual absolution or (giving the absolution more solemnly afterwards) says: "The Peace of the Lord be with you."

During this time the community is singing psalms.

6. Solemn proclamation of God's forgiveness and mission.

One of the celebrants may sing the preface from the Liturgy of reconciliation in the *Pontificale Romanum* (Publica reconciliatio peccatorum feria quinta in coena Domini).

All confessors pray together: "May Almighty God have mercy on you . . ."

"May the Almighty and merciful Lord grant you . . ."

"May the Passion of our Lord . . ."

All priests who have heard confessions give (if allowed by the diocesan rules) together the absolution with the usual form.

3rd Reading: Gospel according to Luke 5:11-33 (*or*: Mt. 9:2-8; Mt. 18:22-35). Short homily to the praise of God.

7. All sing: "Our Father. . . ."

President: "Your sins are forgiven; your faith has saved you; go in peace."

Recessional.

INDEX

OTHER IMAGE BOOKS

THE IMITATION OF CHRIST – Thomas à Kempis. Edited with an Introduction by Harold C. Gardiner, S.J. (D17) – $1.25

SAINT THOMAS AQUINAS – G. K. Chesterton (D36) – $1.45

ST. FRANCIS OF ASSISI – G. K. Chesterton (D50) – $1.25

VIPER'S TANGLE – François Mauriac. A novel of evil and redemption (D51) – 95¢

THE CITY OF GOD – St. Augustine. Edited by Vernon J. Bourke. Introduction by Étienne Gilson. Specially abridged (D59) – $2.45

RELIGION AND THE RISE OF WESTERN CULTURE – Christopher Dawson (D64) – $1.95

THE LITTLE FLOWERS OF ST. FRANCIS – Translated by Raphael Brown (D69) – $1.75

DARK NIGHT OF THE SOUL – St. John of the Cross. Edited and translated by E. Allison Peers (D78) – $1.25

THE CONFESSIONS OF ST. AUGUSTINE – Translated with an Introduction by John K. Ryan (D101) – $1.75

A HISTORY OF PHILOSOPHY: VOLUME 1 – GREECE AND ROME (2 Parts) – Frederick Copleston, S.J. (D134a, D134b) – $1.75 ea.

A HISTORY OF PHILOSOPHY: VOLUME 2 – MEDIAEVAL PHILOSOPHY (2 Parts) – Frederick Copleston, S.J. Part I – Augustine to Bonaventure. Part II – Albert the Great to Duns Scotus (D135a, D135b) – $1.75 ea.

A HISTORY OF PHILOSOPHY: VOLUME 3 – LATE MEDIAEVAL AND RENAISSANCE PHILOSOPHY (2 Parts) – Frederick Copleston, S.J. Part I – Ockham to the Speculative Mystics. Part II – The Revival of Platonism to Suárez (D136a, D136b) – $1.45 ea.

A HISTORY OF PHILOSOPHY: VOLUME 4 – MODERN PHILOSOPHY: Descartes to Leibniz – Frederick Copleston, S.J. (D137) – $1.75

A HISTORY OF PHILOSOPHY: VOLUME 5 – MODERN PHILOSOPHY: The British Philosophers, Hobbes to Hume (2 Parts) – Frederick Copleston, S.J. Part I – Hobbes to Paley (D138a) – $1.45. Part II – Berkeley to Hume (D138b) – $1.75

A HISTORY OF PHILOSOPHY: VOLUME 6 – MODERN PHILOSOPHY (2 Parts) – Frederick Copleston, S.J. Part I – The French Enlightenment to Kant (D139a) – $1.45; (D139b) – $1.75

A HISTORY OF PHILOSOPHY: VOLUME 7 – MODERN PHILOSOPHY (2 Parts) – Frederick Copleston, S.J. Part I – Fichte to Hegel. Part II – Schopenhauer to Nietzsche (D140a, D140b) – $1.75 ea.

These prices subject to change without notice

OTHER IMAGE BOOKS

These prices subject to change without notice

OTHER IMAGE BOOKS

OTHER IMAGE BOOKS

These prices subject to change without notice